Catholic Social Teaching and Economic Theory

Catholic
Social Teaching
AND *Economic*
Theory PARADIGMS IN CONFLICT

MARY E. HOBGOOD

Foreword by Larry L. Rasmussen

TEMPLE UNIVERSITY PRESS
Philadelphia

TEMPLE UNIVERSITY PRESS, PHILADELPHIA 19122
COPYRIGHT © 1991 BY MARY E. HOBGOOD. ALL RIGHTS RESERVED
Published 1991
Printed in the United States of America

*The paper used in this publication meets the minimum
requirements of American National Standard for Information
Sciences—Permanence of Paper for Printed Library Materials,
ANSI Z39.48-1984* ∞

Library of Congress Cataloging-in-Publication Data
Hobgood, Mary E., 1946–
Catholic social teaching and economic theory : paradigms in
conflict / by Mary E. Hobgood : foreword by Larry L. Rasmussen.
p.   cm.
ISBN 0-87722-754-3 (alk. paper)
1. Sociology, Christian (Catholic)   2. Economics—Religious
aspects—Catholic Church.   3. Catholic Church—Doctrines.
I. Title.
BX1753.H575   1991
261.8'5'08822—dc20   90-34082
                                                          CIP

*To my parents whose struggles in a sexist
and classist society have impelled my work;
to the women who have nurtured and challenged me,
especially the members of
the Religious of the Sacred Heart of Mary,
Eastern American Province, and the
Northeast Consultation on Feminist Social Ethics;
and to the men who support me daily,
my beloved friend and partner Thomas Chittick
and our children, Nathan and Luke Hobgood-Chittick.*

Contents

Foreword

MODERN ECONOMICS HAS BEEN the most secular of the sciences. Economists have gone about their work with little or no reference to either God or morality. They have assumed an understanding of human nature and behavior but have drawn meager, if any, connection to religious life and faith.

Of late all this has changed, though not at the initiative of the academy of economists. Religious bodies, among others, have doubted that economics is as secular as most economists contend. In fact, economic theory is value-laden and its practice has many of the marks of a faith and a way of life. No doubt Roman Catholics have given the current leadership here. The landmark work in what is now given considerable attention by many religious communions was the 1986 pastoral of the National Conference of Catholic Bishops, *Economic Justice for All: Catholic Social Teaching and the U.S. Economy*. It brought economic issues into the public eye and made clear that there are moral and, indeed, theological dimensions of economic life that must be addressed. The pastoral letter provoked widespread response to its analysis and proposals and stimulated the work of several other faith communities in their own efforts to assess our pressing national and international economic reality and to provide guidance for response.

Granted, some of the reponses to the Catholic pastoral were as shortlived as the conferences organized to address it, or the op-ed pieces and the innumerable letters to the editor. Other responses, however, led to deep analysis that ranged far beyond the letter itself. They reached back into the traditions of Catholic social thought on economic life and into secular economic theory itself. It is the latter—deep analysis—that Mary Hobgood undertakes in this volume. She asks what

Catholic teaching itself has assumed about the way the economy works, and she brings to the fore hidden assumptions that are fundamental to the policy prescriptions in Catholic teaching.

This book is thus far more than a critique of the bishops' pastoral. It uses the current Catholic interest in economics to make a different and very important move. Dr. Hobgood has studied the whole tradition from 1891 to 1987 and uncovered the social paradigms that are critically important in Catholic teaching but not sufficiently recognized in other critiques of that teaching. She finds that in the traditions of Catholic teachings on the economy—which are rich, considerable, and a surprise to many—there are conflicting social models. She calls these different social models the organic (feudal) model, the neoclassical (capitalist) model, and the radical (liberationist) model. It is utterly fascinating to see how these wildly different but interacting models function to shape Catholic teaching on economic life in the period since the Industrial Revolution first caught Catholic attention. The result is a clear picture of the divided mind and practice of Catholicism when confronting twentieth-century economic realities. If Catholic teaching did us all the service of finding a strong moral and theological voice for a critique of secular economics, Dr. Hobgood points the way to make that voice a clearer one, more aware of its limitations and of its potential.

Hobgood does not stop with criticism. That would be cruel. She goes on to mount the argument that better use of the Catholic radical perspective can overcome the self-contradictory policy proposals for economic change. The hierarchy is equivocal in its interpretation of capitalist political economy and its proposals flounder on the equivocation. Structural analysis of the economy is somehow followed by nonstructural policy proposals! Hobgood shows what has happened to create this anomaly *and* she shows the way ahead. The sum total is thus more than illuminating the place of competing social theories in Catholic teaching; it is a proposal itself. The outcome, if attended to, might be not only more but notably better leadership from those who have already helped make the troubled economic life of the modern world a deeply religious matter. Dr. Hobgood has done her part, and not only for Catholic response. This book is simultaneously a valuable resource for other communions and communities working for economic justice.

Larry L. Rasmussen
Reinhold Niebuhr Professor of Social Ethics
Union Theological Seminary, New York

Preface

THIS BOOK WAS WRITTEN by the granddaughter of two Mississippi sharecroppers. As a small child I traveled back and forth between my struggling poor grandparents in rural Mississippi and my relatively affluent ones in New Orleans, and fundamental questions were raised for me about the social, political, and economic arrangements of our world. This book has been a way I have come to grips with some of these questions, which remain vital in my adult life. I believe my work illustrates that how we see the world, including how we do scholarship, is deeply shaped by our social location, even our earliest formative experiences.

I have set out to do three things in this book. The first is to emphasize the importance to religious ethics of a lively debate occurring within the field of social theory. This debate concerns conflicting assessments of capitalist political economy from two well-established and influential "streams" of social theory—the orthodox/neoclassical paradigm and the radical economic paradigm. I describe the main contours of this debate in order to demonstrate that there is more than one interpretation of why such great differences are manifest in people's social, political, and economic lives in late twentieth-century capitalist societies.

My second purpose is to illustrate how the paradigm conflict within the field of social theory is also reflected in Catholic documents that have addressed the issue of economic justice for the past one hundred years. I believe that there are ideological tensions and conflicts within the Catholic social justice tradition that are explicable only in terms of this clash of fundamentally opposing perspectives about the nature of capitalist political economy. It is important to see how the normative values of the Catholic tradition, such as universal dignified social participation, economic democracy, and a preferential option for the poor, operate out of assumptions that are tied to these social models. When assumptions shift from the neoclassical to the radical paradigm, the concrete actions mandated by these justice norms change significantly. I believe that Catholic ethics, as well as religious ethics in general, needs a deepened understanding of how social theory shapes the very meaning of moral values.

My third purpose is to argue that those who issue official Catholic social teaching need to clarify the social models that inform normative moral claims. Perhaps even more importantly, there is a need for the Church to assess these models for their compatibility with actual capitalist dynamics and with the Church's traditional ethical concerns. I argue that the moral values that inform radical theory are ones that it shares with the Catholic social justice tradition.

Finally, a word about the function of the Catholic documents themselves is in order. According to Church teaching, papal encyclicals are more weighty than the pastoral letters of national hierarchies because they are not regional and are clearly intended to instruct the entire Church. Yet pastoral letters often interpret the meaning of papal encyclicals to local and regional congregations. Although informed Catholics are not in agreement as to the status and authority of these documents, many would hold that although social teaching is not infallible, it is binding on the consciences of sincere Catholics.

Beyond the official authority questions, the actual role of papal encyclicals and pastoral letters in people's lives is hard to define. In intellectual circles these documents have often received enormous amounts of attention and debate, at the theoretical if not the practical level. Yet they are often thought to be the Church's "best-kept secret" among rank and file Catholics worldwide.

The Catholic social justice tradition is important to me as a

Catholic scholar because I believe it documents a transformation of self-awareness that has been emerging in sectors of the Catholic hierarchy as popes and bishops, in conjunction with other clergy and laity, try to make not only intellectual but concrete pastoral responses to the escalating economic suffering of poor and formerly middle-income people throughout the world. As greater numbers of us travel between struggling poor and affluent family members and other friends, neighbors, and parishioners, fundamental questions of economic justice press upon us with increasing urgency. I hope this book helps to extend the questioning and evaluation initiated by this tradition.

Acknowledgments

THE MISTAKES CONTAINED in this book are my own. What is of value is the result of my collaboration with others and their gifts to me of scholarly insight and support. In addition, the readability of this book is greatly enhanced because of the editorial skills of Lesley Ann Beneke and her astute perceptions about the overall manuscript.

I wish to thank Leonard Swidler and David Watt of Temple University. David offered important suggestions on the very first draft, and Len's disagreement with the thesis helped me sharpen my argument.

I am also grateful to three colleagues in Maine. Douglas M. Allen of the Philosophy Department and Melvin Burke of the Economics Department at the University of Maine gave me generous portions of their time. Each read sections of the manuscript and met with me on several occasions to offer direction and suggestions. My friend Marvin M. Ellison of Bangor Theological Seminary offered inspiration and ongoing encouragement during a long and lonely period of research and writing.

I especially wish to thank my mentor, Beverly W. Harrison of Union Theological Seminary. I consider this book an extension of Beverly's work. My thesis was inspired by her call to religious social ethicists to identify their normative assumptions in social theory, a mandate found in one of her important essays in *Making the Connections: Essays in Feminist Social Ethics*. Without the generous gifts of her time and critical insights, this project would not have been undertaken or completed.

Finally, I thank John C. Raines of Temple University. John taught me the central importance of human work, and I was led to radical theory through his conviction that capitalist ideology is a "justification of sorrows." His support and direction in the writing of this project, over many years and across many miles, finds some fruition in these pages.

Catholic Social Teaching and Economic Theory

Abbreviations

ECPC	*Ethical Choices and Political Challenges,* Canadian bishops, 1983
EJA	*Economic Justice for All,* U.S. bishops, 1986
EREC	*Ethical Reflections on the Economic Crisis,* Canadian bishops, 1983
GS	*Gaudium et spes,* Vatican II, 1965
JW	*Justice in the World,* World Synod of Bishops, 1971
LE	*Laborem exercens,* Pope John Paul II, 1981
Med-Justice	Medellin Documents, Latin American bishops, 1968
Med-Peace	Medellin Documents, Latin American bishops, 1968
MM	*Mater et magistra,* Pope John XXIII, 1961
OA	*Octogesima adveniens,* Pope Paul VI, 1971
OSC	*On Social Concern,* Pope John Paul II, 1987
P	Puebla Document, Latin American bishops, 1979
PP	*Populorum progressio,* Pope Paul VI, 1967
PT	*Pacem in terris,* Pope John XXIII, 1963
QA	*Quadragesimo anno,* Pius XI, 1931
RN	*Rerum novarum,* Pope Leo XIII, 1891

Chapter One. Economic Theory: A Necessary Tool for Catholic Social Analysis

FOR ALMOST A CENTURY the popes and bishops of the Roman Catholic Church have issued economic teaching that has exhibited concern for those marginalized in societies dominated by modern capitalism. This body of thought has analyzed the capitalist system and has proposed various strategies for social change. It has become part of the social justice tradition of the Catholic Church and it obliges all persons "to aid in the creation of patterns of societal organization and activity which are essential for the protection of minimal human rights, and for the creation of mutuality and participation by all in social life."[1] Catholic social teaching endorses a world in which the joys and the hopes of people, especially the poor, are nurtured and celebrated in community and their griefs and anxieties are addressed and borne in solidarity.[2]

To this end Catholic social teaching first responded in the late nineteenth century and the early twentieth century to those suffering economic marginalization in the industrializing nations of the West.[3] By the mid-twentieth century it was addressing the plight of the poor in the so-called Third World nations. Most recently it has responded to marginalization caused by the creation of Third World conditions—unemployment, underemployment, and economic insecurity—in First World countries.

Catholic social teaching proceeds from the conviction that the Church has the right and the duty to teach about the moral implications of economics. The Church believes that its own traditions, as well as Scripture, offer a critique of the values inherent in some, if not all, of the economic policies of western capitalism. One tradition that undergirds Catholic social teaching is based on a philosophy the Church adopted from Stoicism. Known as the natural-law tradition, this philosophy claims that people have access through reason to what is a universal and eternally applicable natural law. The natural-law tradition is presumed to provide sufficient ethical guidance for all people, even apart from Scripture.[4]

The Church draws upon another tradition when it issues social teaching—organic social theory. It is a model of society and a social theory that has been adopted largely from feudal social relations (see Chapter Two). This social theory has been called organic because of its tendency to see society as continuous with nature. The organic social model assumed by the Church values a society that is hierarchically organized and stresses the values of paternal benevolence, social cooperation, and commitment to the common good.[5] Social relationships are restricted by the requirements of organic harmony in a hierarchical society.

The first purpose of this book is to point out the presence of different social models in Catholic social teaching on economic issues. This is important because the moral implications of the Church's teachings about economic ethics are contingent on the social models that the Church assumes. As economics is never a value-free science but is always based on a particular social theory or model of society,[6] so also is economic ethics. In its teachings on economic justice, the Roman Catholic Church reflects perspectives not only from the organic model but from two other social models as well. They are the neoclassical, or liberal, social model and what I call the radical social model.

Because the organic model the Church inherited from feudal society is inherently different from the neoclassical model of capitalist society, the Church has developed an ongoing

critique of capitalist economics since the late nineteenth century. Imbued with communitarian and cooperative values, the
Church's social model is in many respects in conflict with
modern liberal social theory.[7] In the economic sphere, liberal
or neoclassical theory promotes the free agency of autonomous individuals who seek their financial self-interest in a
world presumed, if left to its own devices, to function in a
rational and harmonious way.[8] Liberal theory also assumes
that social, economic, and political structures function autonomously and that social and political structures can discipline economic power. This liberal theory has become the
orthodox social theory on which western capitalism is based.

True to the assumptions of the organic social model, Catholic papal and episcopal teaching opposes some of the central
tenets of economic liberalism that today inform much of U.S.
and European academic perspectives. The Church has spoken out against the beliefs that individuals should always be
free to pursue their own self-interest in the marketplace, and
that markets should always be free from state interference,
and that the role of the market is to be the unguided agency
for the production and distribution of goods. The Church has
also spoken out against the orthodox assumption that economic, political, and other social structures are autonomous
entities. This critique of economic liberalism emanates in part
from organic social theory, which mandates the right of every
person to the conditions necessary to live a dignified human
life, and the responsibility of all persons to the common good
of the community that nurtures and sustains them. A recent demonstration of the Church's continuing concern for
the common good, beyond the dictates of the marketplace, is
found in the U.S. bishops' pastoral letter *Economic Justice for
All*.[9] This letter offers "constructive guidance" for building a
society in which everyone participates in its formation as a
basic human right (*EJA* 23).

Nevertheless, despite its rejection of some of the tenets of orthodox social theory, Catholic teaching on economic matters often has affirmed the moral acceptability of the capitalist system and the assumptions of economic liberalism. This may be due, at least in part, to the fact that capitalism generates socioeconomic hierarchies in both the economy and the family, and thus is congenial to the organic social model assumed by the Church.

The Church's attraction to aspects of economic liberalism, however, did not prevent Leo XIII and Pius XI from sometimes drawing on a structural analysis of political economy. Contrary to neoclassical theory, structural analysis assumes that social, economic, and political institutions form a single, interlocking system in the service of private capital accumulation. This is a central feature of a third social model that I call the "radical" social model. Neither the Church's inherited social model nor its concessions to the neoclassical model prevented John XXIII and Paul VI from questioning some of the basic assumptions of both organic and orthodox views. Both John XXIII and Paul VI sometimes engaged in a social analysis and proposed policies that may be aligned with radical social theory.

Radical theory can be understood as both affirming and extending, but also critiquing, various aspects of organic theory. Like organic social theory, radical theory affirms that there are specific shared goods that make concrete the notion of the common good.[10] But radical theory extends organic theory's critique of economic liberalism by applying democracy to the arena of the social production of wealth. Radical theory also applies the principles of democratic participation and accountability to all spheres of social power and critiques the hierarchical social arrangements of organic theory, especially with regard to such spheres as Church and family.

These three very different social models—organic, orthodox, and radical—are found in Catholic teaching on modern capitalism from 1891 to 1987.[11] These models are not perfectly reflected in any given economic analysis, nor are they contradictory in every last detail. They are models or explanatory devices that help to establish a perspective of interpretation on complex historical and social processes. They are conceptual constructions that set up essentially different explanations as to how socioeconomic processes actually work. Hence, they illumine tensions and contradictions that otherwise might remain unnoticed. I contend that the hierarchy's inherited organic social theory, as well as the Church's ongoing legacy of grassroots struggle with poor people, has predisposed various popes and bodies of bishops toward appropriating, consciously or not, perspectives that may be aligned with elements in both orthodox and radical streams of socioeconomic theory.

The central focus of this book, however, is to explore the radical critique of the orthodox paradigm in order to argue for the presence of radical perspectives in the Roman Catholic social justice tradition. In particular, I am interested in how the less well-known radical model relates to a self-contradiction that persists throughout the hierarchy's analysis of the socioeconomic arena. I argue that the hierarchy sometimes analyzes the socioeconomic arena in a structural way so as to preclude the workability of its own nonstructural, orthodox policy prescriptions. That is, the Catholic social justice tradition contains an analysis of capitalist political economy that points to the interstructuring of political and economic power while at the same time proposes remedies to economic crises that assume the nonstructural or autonomous relationship of government and economic systems.

Thus the Catholic hierarchy exhibits a divided mind when addressing twentieth-century economic realities. Competing assumptions from the organic social model, as well as conflicts between its institutional needs and pastoral obligations, have split the hierarchy's loyalties between orthodox and radical perspectives and their contradictory interpretations of capitalist political economy. By using a structural analysis, the hierarchy has at times demonstrated that the interlocking processes of capitalist political, social, and economic institutions preclude the nurturing of the common good, a major organic value. But the hierarchy has also clung to a value emanating from organic theory that supports the orthodox model, namely, that capitalist social hierarchies are necessary and potentially benevolent. Additionally the hierarchy often has accepted the nonstructural analysis of orthodox theory that assumes the autonomy of political and economic systems. The result is a social ethics that contains a less-than-coherent mix of structural analysis of the political economy followed by nonstructural policy prescriptions. It is only by an explicit unveiling of the radical social model present in Catholic ethics that one can untangle what remains self-contradictory in the Church's teachings about economic justice.

To accomplish this task, I discuss economic theory in this chapter. I root both orthodox and radical streams in the classical period of the eighteenth and nineteenth centuries. Economic theory, once a unified body of discourse on political economy in the classical period, split into two major streams at the end of the nineteenth century and the beginning of the twentieth century. These streams are understood to be broad ideological trajectories, not tightly woven traditions. They analyze economic processes for purposes of comparison and contrast. Since economic theories are complex bodies of analysis with divergent positions within them and among them, the delineation of characteristics that follows must remain introductory.

Competing Social Theories

The orthodox and radical economic paradigms are called social theories because they claim to offer explanations of how capitalist society functions. They offer different analyses of the interrelationships of the primary social structures within late twentieth-century capitalism. These two perspectives suggest different explanations about the way that production, government policy and spending, and social institutions (schools, welfare and unemployment programs, and labor market structures) are related. Orthodox and radical paradigms both claim to offer the best analysis of the origins, manifestations, and potential solutions to problems generated by the political economy of capitalism.[12] Both paradigms claim to give the most accurate explanation of capitalist socioeconomic reality.

In capitalist societies orthodox theory predominates. It addresses both the nature of economic activity and the nature and functioning of the capitalist system. Orthodox theory, which views market exchange as the primary economic activity, emerges from the classical, neoclassical, and Keynesian economic traditions. Although some of its proponents operate with explicit theories of politics and culture, this social theory separates economic activity from political, social, and cultural dynamics.

The orthodox paradigm assumes that human nature is primarily concerned with buying and selling. Because people are viewed as producers and consumers, the market is the logical physical extension of this theory of human nature. People are understood to be interested in maximum consumption of the goods and services that are bought and sold in the market, and they have or can accumulate the wealth and income necessary to maximize their consumption. Orthodox theory assumes that profit maximization through market activity is the primary rational economic behavior. Consequently, the orthodox paradigm assumes the centrality of the market in social life. It assumes the autonomy of the political and cultural spheres as it primarily focuses on the analysis of market functions. Neoclassical economic theory has been the mainstream, or orthodox, theory in the United States since the eighteenth century.

A radical stream in social theory has also been present

since the classical period. It views human labor, not market exchange, as the central economic activity. The radical social model focuses on labor power and the social reproduction of class conflict between the majority who produce surplus value (and more broadly all nonowners of capital) and those few who control labor power and appropriate the wealth of society. Rather than propose a specific theory of human nature, radical theory focuses on how the social relations of capitalist societies shape what people do and think.

Radical theory is based on a structural analysis of political economy as a single, interlocking socioeconomic system that has developed historically in the service of the system of private capital accumulation. Structural analysis was used by theorists in the eighteenth and nineteenth centuries and particularly by the classical political economist Karl Marx. In the twentieth century, the radical stream in economic theory finds its logical conclusion in critical forms of neo-Marxism and socialist feminist and antiracist analysis. The radical theorists I draw on contend that socialist feminist theories that argue against exploitation in the spheres of reproduction as well as production and place the situation of women, especially poor women of color, at the center of their economic analysis are essential to complete a Marxist economic theory.[13]

As "minority reporters" in opposition to the reigning paradigm, radical theorists use a wide range of empirical studies to support their claims. As a result of their critical analysis of both capitalism and historical forms of socialism, radical theorists have formulated alternative policy proposals.[14] These proposals, however, are always viewed as tentative because radical theorists (for example, Marxists) believe that there is no way to project what forms alternative, noncapitalist societies will take. Radical theory is not a theory of socialism; it is a critical theory of capitalism.[15]

Radical theory exists in the United States despite great social intolerance. Although their number has grown significantly since the mid-1970s, relatively few economists in the

United States work within the radical tradition. Indeed, radical economists and social theorists are frequently barred from key positions in this society, and the radical tradition has enjoyed less social support in the United States than in almost any other country.

As such social problems as poverty, unemployment, and underemployment remain seemingly intractable, orthodox models have appeared increasingly inadequate to many. We live in "a time when the assumptions and methods of [orthodox] economics are being challenged almost as never before." [16] What has been called "the emergent paradigm competition" [17] between orthodox and radical theories is evident even in Catholic social teaching. It can no longer be ignored.

Competing sets of theories about society and about the way social structures interrelate exist because social theories are the products of worldviews. The concepts in social theories embody the perspectives, norms, or assumptions about society contained in a particular worldview or ideology. For example, radical and orthodox economic theories have different assumptions about the nature of work and how society ought to be organized. They focus on different phenomena in capitalist society. The structures of these social theories determine different questions as the relevant ones to ask and different problems as the significant ones to solve. Indeed, the way political economy does or should function—one's worldview or ideology—directs both the guiding principles and the organization of the theory. The origin of this social vision lies in the experience its shaper has as an active agent within a given socioeconomic context. The research that shapes a social or moral theory, therefore, is grounded in concrete activity. As Beverly Harrison argues, "What we do influences what we perceive and therefore what we come to know, which means that our human projects fate-fully determine our world view. That is why moral arguments always are as much about what *is* the case as about what *ought* to be the case." [18]

Theorists of both paradigms have realized that disinterested social theory does not exist. Every theory contains normative assumptions about the way society "should" be organized. These assumptions or norms flow from the society in which the theorist lives and his or her position therein. Ideas, theories, and values are social products because social circumstances condition social consciousness. Some theorists point out that while everyone has a worldview or ideology, not everyone recognizes the interaction of one's worldview with one's social circumstances. To fail to recognize the relative character of a worldview, or the assumptions and norms that are assumed by it, is to be ideological in the pejorative sense.

It has been acknowledged, for example, that "the perpetual game of hide-and-seek in economics consists in hiding the norm in the [economic] concept."[19] Indeed, normative assumptions about the social order are often the primary consideration in the acceptance or rejection of a given social theory, even to the exclusion of the theory's explanatory power. As the economist Phyllis Deane explains:

> Political economy, born out of philosophy and ethics has always been a discipline with strong normative implications in spite of a persistent effort on the part of its practitioners to develop its scientific and objective aspects. The philosophical and ideological premises of an economic theory play an important role in its initial acceptance and in its tenacity.[20]

Economics, like all other disciplines, is a field struggling with its own internal disagreements and operative visions. In countries dominated by western capitalism, and this is particularly true of the United States, the orthodox or neoclassical stream has informed people's most basic assumptions about the economy. Therefore, it is important to state that there are *two* major economic theories, in profound disagreement with each other, that compete for serious attention in the world today. Indeed, it has been estimated that over one-third of the world's population lives under governments influenced in various ways by the alternative radical stream in economic theory.[21]

This economic debate is reflected in Catholic social teaching when the hierarchy manifests different understandings of why some people are affluent and why increasing numbers suffer poverty. Popes and bishops propose different strategies concerning how to remedy poverty and unemployment, for example, depending on which theory's operating assumptions they have adopted to analyze capitalism. They will support different policies for social change depending on whether they see private enterprise as the problem, as in radical theory, or the solution, as in capitalist theory, to the socioeconomic realities that cause human misery and suffering. Social policies are shaped very differently depending on which economic theory informs them.

Normative Assumptions of Orthodox Theory

Orthodox theory is based on the dominant traditions of classical and neoclassical economic theory that have developed from the eighteenth to the twentieth centuries. The origins of what has become economic orthodoxy lie in the classical economic tradition, particularly in the market-centered theory of Adam Smith's *An Inquiry into the Nature and Causes of the Wealth of Nations* (1776). Smith, like other major classical political economists, was concerned with a wide range of issues such as economic value, distribution, monopoly, and the political relations of class conflict.[22] As a result of the long transition out of feudalism, which saw restrictions on production by government-granted monopolies and guild prohibitions, Smith believed that the primary economic problem was scarcity. He argued that unleashing economic initiatives in society through the unfettered and fully competitive market was the way to remedy scarcity and the social disharmony it caused.[23] But the wide range of issues in political economy debated by these classical thinkers was abandoned in the neoclassical tradition, which developed between 1870 and 1930, for the neoclassical paradigm focuses almost exclusively on market exchange.

Orthodox social theory traditionally includes two major perspectives: the laissez-faire or conservative view and the social-welfare or liberal view. It is also true that within orthodox economic theory, as in radical theory, there is "considerable doctrinal controversy and a wide variety of theorists, concepts and assumptions in continuous dispute."[24] There are some orthodox economists, for example, who are persuaded that the positive features of the capitalist market system may not outweigh their negative social costs in some nations.[25] Others approve of state-socialized ownership and control of some sectors of the economy. The range in perspectives of these economists goes from a high degree of government intervention to extreme laissez-faire. I treat the two major perspectives, conservative (laissez-faire) and liberal (social welfare), as opposite ends of the same orthodox continuum.

Both liberal and conservative orthodox views have the same underlying assumptions that support their definition of socioeconomic reality. These assumptions concern human nature, the nature of economic activity, and the function of capitalistic institutions. They were first articulated for a wide audience by Adam Smith in 1776.

Smith replaced an ethic of paternalistic benevolence and a communitarian vision of a shared life, which was grounded in the Christian view of an organic society, with an ethic of the individual pursuit of self-interest.[26] This ethic was based on the liberal understanding of human nature held by Enlightenment thinkers who believed that self-interested motives were the primary motives that informed human activity. In the marketplace these self-interested motives were understood to be desires to maximize pleasure, that is, desires for more rather than less of any good or service. People were to be free of economic restrictions by the state in order to participate in competitive market exchange so that they would maximize their consumption.[27] This would significantly enhance human happiness because creating and consuming wealth through the capitalist system was thought to be what is most in harmony with basic human nature.

This competitive and free capitalist market system necessitated private property and the ability of each citizen to own, buy, or sell their own resources and produced goods as well as the absence of monopoly control by anyone. As Smith described capitalist institutions, the free market would insure that capital and labor would be put to their most productive use. The structure of the competitive market, in which producers compete for consumer's money, would guarantee that what was produced was what people wanted most and were willing to pay for. The market serves as the social site where the interaction of buyers (human wants or preferences) and sellers (people's productive abilities) meet. All individuals work together through the market, the natural mechanism for determining price and value. The market process of perfect competition, said Smith, also operates with a beneficent "invisible hand" that guides resources to their most efficient use (maximum output) and distributes the proceeds of the market in a reasonably just manner (optimum allocation). In the capitalist marketplace, people discover a way to translate their natural self-interest into public benefit and into achieving their maximum productive and consumptive potential. Smith contended that the competitive market, not moral intentions, best served the commonweal. "It is not from the benevolence of the butcher or the baker that we expect our meal," says Smith, "but from their regard to their own interest."[28] If left to itself, this socioeconomic order would maximize production, consumption, and social welfare and create an ideal society. Smith, a theist, believed that God would work through the economic arrangements of his time, and that restraints on this divine plan were subversive of God's intentions for human society.[29]

Smith and his contemporaries were aware of the potential of capitalism to create monopoly, uneven distribution, and other forms of social oppression. Smith saw the need to restrain unbridled economic power and he believed this could be done through religious and other cultural sanctions.[30] Yet this sensitivity to capitalism's potential to allocate unjustly was lost as the orthodox tradition used Smith to justify the elimination of the paternalistic ethic inherent in organic social theory. Consequently, an unfettered capitalist economic order was absolutized. If it became evident that private industry sometimes did not serve the common good, explanations focused on personal aberrations, because the system itself conformed to the natural order, to a divine intent. Smith's work has been used to give pivotal significance to the social organization of capitalism—to landlords, laborers, and capitalists. His assumptions and policy orientations have remained intact to this day.[31]

In the late nineteenth century, neoclassical orthodox theory jettisoned classical reservations about the capability of the market to always allocate justly, further absolutized the current economic order, and focused on the individual economic actor who was divorced from cultural and community practices. Using the mathematical methodology of marginal analysis developed by economists after Smith, the orthodox social model became concerned almost exclusively with the study of microeconomic market process. It gradually centered on a theory of optimal exchange, or price and resource allocation, through the laissez-faire market. Using mathematical formulations thought to indicate a "hard" science in accord with nature or what is universally true, orthodox theory demonstrates how, under conditions of competitive markets with individual freedom to own and dispense with property and other resources, human satisfaction could be socially "optimized." Conversely, marginal analysis is also interested in showing how market interference, by whatever means, can thwart the natural drive of human beings to optimize their economic welfare.

In short, orthodox theory assumes that market exchange is optimally determined by the capitalist mode of production in which the last unit employed in each category of productive forces (land, labor, and capital) is presumed to be paid an amount equal to the value of its marginal contribution to the productive process (rent, wages, and profits). Thus, what is paid to capital and labor is their own contributions and can be ethically justified.[32] By narrowing economics to problems that could be addressed by logical mathematical reasoning, neoclassical theory limited the range of what could be considered by economic theory.[33] As theory was developed in conformity to method—and not vice versa—orthodox economics became a discipline uninterested in asking the classical questions about such broader socioeconomic processes as value, distribution, monopoly, and class relations, as well as their implications.[34]

The Orthodox Understanding of Capitalist Market Function

Orthodox economic theory, as it has developed out of the classical and neoclassical traditions, assumes the "given" nature of the capitalist institutional environment.[35] Orthodox theorists insist that the privately administered market is the best tool available for creating and distributing social wealth and for sustaining social harmony. Because the market process solves production and distribution needs automatically, it maximizes human freedom, virtually eliminates the need for social regulation, and is predisposed to achieve a stability that will accomplish the greatest advantage for all.[36] The reality of poverty is best addressed by capitalism because under this economic system there will be fewer poor than under any other economic system.[37] Orthodox economists generally believe that the high standard of living of most Americans, especially since World War II, is due to the profit-oriented market system of contemporary capitalism.

Orthodox theory assumes that individual economic units (households, firms, and workers) are all able to enter the market, have access to credit, and have a wide variety of choices within the market so that their present situations are freely chosen. Such an analysis shows how the choices of these individual economic units, presumed to be voluntary, tend toward a "harmony of interests," a "natural equilibrium" in which the most number of human desires that society is capable of satisfying will indeed be satisfied.[38] Thus, orthodox theory believes that maximum profits indicate and are necessary for the maximum happiness of individual consumers. Since market transactions are presumed to be mutually beneficial, unfree markets or lack of markets will create less social welfare and therefore be less just. When this happens—as in the Third World—orthodox theorists blame "traditionalism." They assume that people in "irrational" political and institutional arrangements are unable to make the individual choices that will ensure their economic advancement. Or they blame poverty on a "lack of political stability" in the region.[39]

Many proponents of orthodox theory in its neoclassical form have come to see that the free-market economy needs reforms in the sphere of distribution, by means such as taxation, in order to prevent vast differentials in income and wealth. Liberal economists argue that the welfare state "through redistributive taxation and through educational opportunity . . . has moved the system a bit toward greater equality."[40] Some economists observe that, while the market generally seeks the advantage of all persons, there is unequal access to the market, which creates such problems as monopoly, unequal distribution of income and wealth, and too much unemployment. They argue that the efficiency of the market system can finance the government to mitigate these problems.[41] But orthodox economists argue that it is important that significant income disparity be maintained as an incentive for work effort and productive contribution. They contend that since government altruism does not motivate people to work, the tool of the market would be underutilized and social wealth would decrease. As economist Arthur M. Okun has said, "for the vast majority an equal slice of a shrunken pie would be no bargain."[42] In this view, government interference is not necessary in the spheres of production and exchange because market forces will work themselves out to common advantage.[43] In the face of problems, orthodox theory always asserts that the market is working toward optimal social welfare "in the long run."[44]

Orthodox theory understands market exchange to be essentially private exchange, which means it does not involve an exercise of power that has consequences beyond the mutual satisfaction of the exchangers. That is, in the perfectly competitive market, the buyer and the seller, and the employer and the employee, have free and equal access to the market. In the orthodox view, business enterprises are responses to available technologies and consumer preferences. Businesses have no more power or freedom than the power of consumers and employees, capital has no more power or freedom than labor.[45] Social problems such as unemployment, racism, sexism, and pollution are traced to past mistakes, ignorance, individual perversity, disturbances of free exchange by labor unions, government interference, or other temporary distortions in the market.

Because markets do not always achieve perfect equilibrium, and are not always perfectly competitive, there is a wide spectrum of opinion within orthodoxy regarding the actual relationship between the capitalist market system and human freedom. Some economists insist that human liberty is achieved only through the privately organized market, and that without capitalism there is no freedom.[46] Other orthodox economists maintain that capitalism promotes human freedom only with competitive modification and improvement.[47] Still others understand a more limited role for the market, and claim that capitalism is a bulwark of liberty for those who own capital.[48]

Since monopoly and oligopoly (a situation where one or a few firms control the market sufficiently to raise prices and cut supply when demand is lower) are not supposed to exist in the competitive market, orthodox economists dispute their magnitude and character. Some say that industrial monopoly is difficult to determine and is inconsequential for the economy as a whole.[49] Others say that while monopoly is a problem, since as much as 60 percent of manufactured goods in the United States are produced by enterprises that set prices according to a few dominant firms, consumers still have some control since they are able to substitute another supplier.[50] Some economists have argued that since monopoly brings security to the enterprise, it frees it to contribute to innovation and growth.[51] Whatever their view, orthodox economists generally contend that corporations are accountable to stockholders, employees, and customers and are responsible to the public welfare.[52]

Despite problems with market exchange, the market remains the center of the orthodox social model and is presumed to be working toward an equilibrium that serves the commonweal, at least in the very long view. The privately controlled market efficiently utilizes resources; satisfies consumers' needs; and returns rent, wages, and profits in proportion to the contributions made by landlords, workers, and capitalists to the creation of social wealth. Consequently, orthodox theory is centered on market relations that are thought to insure the benevolence of most other social relations.

Orthodox Analysis of Poverty

According to the orthodox model, social problems arise when the market is operating at less than maximum efficiency. Orthodox theorists argue, for example, that variations in income distribution, including poverty, are due to the variations in the marginal products of workers as influenced by the laws of supply and demand. These are supposedly always tending toward market equilibrium where supply equals demand because human desire is increasingly being satisfied by the best productive capabilities of the society. Orthodox theorists contend that, under capitalism, wage and income differentials, and thus social stratification and poverty, will narrow in the very long run because individuals will make schooling and other investment decisions rationally and competitively. They argue that discrepancies in the job market—the sectors of which are fluid and mobile—will erode over time as a result of competitive pressures that are indigenous to capitalism. This will contribute to increasing social efficiency and optimum social well-being.

In addition to believing that it is only a temporary malfunction in the market that diminishes the available decent jobs, liberals believe that the causes of poverty, unemployment, and underemployment (and the racism and sexism associated with these) are due to factors outside the economy. These are discrimination (individual ignorance or psychological prejudice, both past and present) or human capital deprivation (lack of education, job training, or experience).[53] If joblessness or poverty is due to human capital deprivation, one increases income by simply increasing investment in job experience or education so as to increase productivity.

Conservative orthodox economists argue that, since market pressures themselves tend to erode discrimination because productive workers will be hired to maximize profit, there are many opportunities for social and economic mobility open through the market. They argue that a "rough" justice is always operative because individual effort is rewarded. Some conservative economists add that all societies are stratified, and there are very few social problems that can really be solved. Capitalism, however, mitigates what is an inevitable phenomenon.[54] Poverty, unemployment, and underemployment, then, must be due to the unwillingness of workers to accept the market remuneration for their services. Some conservatives assume that the personal characteristics of the poor (including genetic inferiority) are the main causes of poverty.[55] Whatever their differences with regard to the origins of poverty, both liberals and conservatives assume that social change can and should be nondisruptive of the basic system.

Orthodox Policy Prescriptions

Just as they differ in their analyses of the origins of socioeconomic problems, liberal and conservative orthodox theorists have different policy prescriptions. These differences in recommended policy reflect their different views of the proper role of the state.

Liberals, following in the tradition of the economist John Maynard Keynes, mandate greater interference in the economy on the part of the state.[56] Liberals, as do all orthodox theorists, believe that the cultural and political spheres are relatively independent from the economic sphere. They assume that in a political democracy the state reflects the common will of the society and can compensate for assaults on the market that cause it to malfunction. The state's visible hand can modify individual and institutional excesses and will for power by laborers and businesses. It can help secure private property and help restore competitive markets. This will help achieve full employment equilibrium. Liberals also argue that government can attack discrimination and human capital differences through policies such as busing, affirmative action, and programs of educational assistance. It can redistribute income and create new jobs by the wise use of fiscal and monetary policy. It can intervene and break the vicious cycles in which social structures have trapped people. Some orthodox theorists advocate state-socialized ownership and control of some sectors of the economy. Assuming the basic viability of the capitalist system, they view a form of democratic socialism, or the socialized market within capitalism, as a natural extension of the presumed success of Keynesian economic policy.[57]

When confronted with social problems generated by stagflation, the simultaneous escalation of unemployment and inflation, most liberals usually admit that they are stuck in the "zero-sum" trade-off between unemployment and inflation. But liberals traditionally have been optimistic about the possibilities of reform and erasing "imperfections" in the market because they believe that education and job training increase individual productivity and increases in productivities bring increases in individual income.

Orthodox theorists also warn that liberal welfare policies may not be able to change what they believe to be nonmarket or exogenous forces like discrimination, and they presume that noneconomic institutions like schools and religion as well as persuasive methodology must address these.[58] Because Keynesian intervention has not been able to insure continuous economic growth, some liberal economists, Paul

Samuelson, for example, have become cautious about welfare economics. Other liberals like Lester Thurow, who acknowledges a torn safety net in the capitalist welfare state, continue to argue that the real issue for liberal economics is to "unscramble good and bad forms of state intervention" so as to make for a healthy capitalism.[59]

Conservative theorists concede fewer flaws in the capitalist market system and traditionally have opposed most state welfare programs. If liberals tend to see the state as a solution, conservative economists see it as a problem. In general, the only government interference conservatives have allowed in the past is in monetary policy, adjusting interest and tax rates. Conservatives argue that since the state serves almost no one's interests the market is more reliable, especially with regard to social spending and labor regulation. Conservatives assume that increasing levels of high unemployment are "natural" for the present stage of capitalism.[60] Along with most liberals, conservatives see no escape from a cycle of inflation and unemployment, but they contend that unemployment for some is invariably better than inflation for all.

Since the 1960s two other schools have developed in the orthodox mainstream, the neoconservative and the neoliberal. Neoconservatives argue that economic problems are chiefly the result of the overbearing weight of the public sector (social security, medicare, low-income housing, and education) on private business. Liberals, they say, are destroying the economy by transferring wealth from the productive (private) to the unproductive (public) sectors. They argue that liberals have created an inflationary welfare state by supporting widespread government intervention and the erroneous expectation that everyone has the right to an equal outcome, rather than an equal opportunity. Neoconservatives contend that capitalism will never be able to create an equal society—in this they agree with radical theorists—and that people's expectations of the government must be diminished, their self-

reliance increased.[61] However, while most economic neoconservatives believe that state intervention must be drastically
reduced in the social arena in order to limit inflation, except
for enforcing high interest rates and military expansion, some
also support the cultural conservative agenda. This includes
state funding of military, police, and business expansion, and
state intervention in such areas as censorship, mandatory
prayer in the schools, and the prohibition of abortion.[62]

If neoconservatives want to solve the current problems
of capitalism by reducing the role of government—except in
the case of the military and those exceptions noted above—
neoliberals want to solve economic problems by increasing
its role. Neoliberals advocate an odd mixture of conservative
and liberal measures. As liberals they believe that government has an important role to play. But unlike traditional
liberals (either New Dealers or advocates in the 1960s of the
Great Society programs), they do not believe that government should produce goods and services, except insofar as
they endorse the further militarization of the economy. Rather,
they advocate centralized economic planning so that the government can better orchestrate private spending for meeting
social needs. They would support policies that reward corporations for "creating" jobs. Economic growth, a vehicle for
trickle-down, is thought to be the real engine for social justice.
Thus neoliberals support the continued and expanded public
subsidization of private enterprise and a program of centralized economic planning in the interests of the big corporations
and the major unions.[63] In the meantime, government can
help those left out of the market by such liberal measures as
welfare reform, including a negative income tax.[64]

Despite their differences, most theorists in the various
groups of the orthodox mainstream agree that capitalist culture exhibits certain fundamental features. While liberals and
neoliberals may argue for fairly frequent state intervention,
and conservatives and neoconservatives for less frequent,

they all share a common worldview. They are in agreement about the basic viability of the capitalist system; the autonomy of politics, culture, and other social systems from the economic system; the benevolence of privately controlled economic activity; the ability of politics and culture to regulate economic activity; the real possibility of upward mobility for all individuals; and the necessity for some income inequality for the sake of efficiency. They agree that the institutions and social relations of a capitalist market economy could not be changed without increasing human suffering. Orthodox analysts believe that if a better system does not exist now, it is highly improbable that it ever will. Indeed, orthodox theorists believe that, given political freedom, people will always choose capitalist institutions because they best conform to the basic features of our common human nature.

Introduction to Radical Theory

While orthodox theory has assumed since the classical period that capitalist society is "natural" and serves the common welfare, radical theory, also with roots in the classical period, does not. Radical theorists argue that since economic theory has been developed by people who are sustained by structures within the society, there are strong social and institutional reasons why any social theory reflects the worldview of those who hold power in the society. According to these radical theorists, orthodox economic theory developed as an apology for capitalists, their markets, and their institutions.[65] The British economist Joan Robinson has said that economics "has always been partly a vehicle for the ruling ideology of each period as well as partly a method of scientific investigation."[66] For this reason, many radical theorists believe that those who inhabit the centers of western capitalism will be the last to fundamentally change exploitative social relations and the assumptions of liberal economic theory.

Because these radical theorists believe that values permeate economic science, they are persistent in their demand for a discussion of the role of values. They argue that valuations are "the driving power of the analytic engine" and that the closest we can come to a bias-free study of economics is to abandon the claim to absolutism and acknowledge the relativity of the values and the particular point of view that shapes economic theory and the policy it generates.[67] For what is deemed feasible in economic policy flows directly from what is valued in the theory.

Contemporary radical theory, with its origins in Marxism and the structural analysis of political economy of the classical period, differs from orthodox theory in its view of what constitutes human nature and economic value. Radical theorists disagree with the orthodox paradigm that holds that there is an indigenous human nature that is primarily concerned with owning, buying, and selling. They disagree that profit maximization is the essence of economic activity, and that market exchange is the central source of economic value and the distinctive feature of capitalism. They argue that while many of the most important social outcomes are generated by the market, those who participate in markets are sorted out by undemocratic processes produced and reinforced by the private ownership and control of capital.

Radical theory focuses, not on human nature, but on the social relations in capitalist society that shape what people do and think. It contends that the market is a facade that hides the true nature of social relations in a capitalist society. Indeed, the goal of Marx's social theory, a major stream from which these contemporary radical theorists draw, was to identify the actual character of concrete social relations under an economic system in which the means for producing social wealth was controlled by fewer and fewer people and labor was exploited as the means of accumulating capital.

Marx argued that the system of the private ownership of the means of production broke up the traditional feudal patterns of control over land, resources, and labor power and commodified them, making them products to be sold on the market. Consequently, capitalism changed the nature of property and of human work as it created the structure called class. The social relations in capitalist society are social relations organized around commodity exchange and the reality that most people are exploited, that is, produce more than they are allowed to keep. Their surplus goes to enrich the owners of capital who control the means of producing wealth in the society. Radical theory believes that all the other social interactions in the political economy are in reciprocal relationship with this capitalist structure called class. That is, what is distinctive about capitalism is not the market but the reality of class, and this relationship of dominance and subordination informs all other social relations in the society. That is, radical theory holds that indirect class relations like those exhibited by the family, the police, the military, and educational and religious systems all support and encourage this fundamental class process where capitalists appropriate the surplus labor of workers.

Contrary to orthodox theory, radical theory places labor power, not market exchange, as the origin of economic value, and it views production for use as the basic economic activity. Radical theorists claim that capitalism distorts human work by changing it from production for personal and social use into a commodity—production for profit. The central problem of capitalism is that people come to depend only on wage labor for value and meaning in life, and social relations centered around the market subsume all others in the society. This organization of production around the private ownership and control of land, resources, labor power, and machines, and the organization of society around the relations of commodity production and exchange, is not in accord with essential economic "reality," contend radical theorists, but is a distortion of it. According to radical theory, it is the class structure that causes economic suffering in the exploited class and economic privilege in the ownership class.

Radical theorists contend that orthodox economic theory, by focusing on the market, diverts attention from what is actually going on in the capitalist system. They deny that the market seeks equilibrium and argue that this assumption conceals a bias for laissez-faire social policies.[68] They claim that, by focusing solely on market process, orthodox theorists are able to ignore the reality of great economic inequality and remain silent on the structural ramifications of classism, including the structural legitimation of racism and sexism that is necessary to support classism. They disagree with orthodox theory's assumed valuations that only through capitalism can social utility and social welfare be maximized. The central argument of these radical theorists is that the means of production in any society cannot maximize social welfare unless it is thoroughly democratized.

Contemporary scholars who claim adherence to radical theories are a diverse group who hold a wide range of divergent positions.[69] The formulation of twentieth-century radical theory that follows relies on those scholars who acknowledge the values and commitments that emanate from the Marxist tradition, as well as those from socialist feminist theory that include antiracist analysis. This radical theory critiques and revises classical Marxism in response to modern socioeconomic change. It utilizes Marxism as "an organic and ongoing intellectual tradition constantly in need of criticism and creativity."[70] Socialist feminist theory, an analysis within a larger body of feminist theory, locates the origins of women's oppression not only in the capitalist mode of production but in the patriarchal mode of reproduction (sexuality, home, family) and seeks to transform them both. This feminist methodology insists that the cultural systems of patriarchy and racism predate capitalism. While socialist feminism seeks to understand the concrete ways in which racism and sexism benefit the owners of capital, it critiques Marxism and the practice of most socialists and argues that unless the structures of male dominance and white supremacy are also transformed, democratic control of the means of production will not liberate white women or people of color. Many socialist feminists insist that social analysis is to be judged by how well it clarifies the sources of oppression of poor women of color.[71] Contemporary radical economic theory utilizes socialist feminist theory insofar as it is concerned with the economic ramifications of male dominance and racism.

In addition to a critical Marxism and socialist feminist theory, twentieth-century radical theorists acknowledge their origins in movements of those struggling for social change. Radical theory is not only an academic affair. It roots its development in the concrete struggles of the labor movement, the civil rights movement, the feminist movement, the peace movement, and community and other grassroots organizations working for social change in the United States and elsewhere. Obviously, however, not all people who work in these groups come to radical conclusions.

These radical theorists have become a socially identifiable group in the United States. While there are many variants of the radical paradigm indebted to the above sources, this study will describe only the major characteristics of this body of theory that are in fundamental conflict with orthodox theory.

Normative Assumptions of the Radical Theory of Capitalism

Radical theorists adhere to a Marxist understanding about the centrality of production as the most important determinant of who controls the political superstructure and how social power relations are shaped throughout the society. They affirm the importance of Marxist dialectical analysis in understanding the centrality of production to all other social relations.

As a critical, historical methodology, dialectical analysis examines social realities in terms of their internal structural relationships to other realities as they develop together over time. According to this methodology, a reality is known insofar as it can be analyzed in terms of all the other realities with which it is historically and structurally related. Dialectical analysis is opposed to a literal, mechanistic, or deterministic understanding about the relationships between entities. Rather, dialectical analysis affirms that social structures—including the cultural superstructure of a society as well as its economic base—form "a system of organically and mutually interacting elements." [72] Radical theory holds that it is impossible to understand the economic mode of production without also understanding custom, religion, and politics, including the gender and racial division of labor and the institutionalization of sexuality to which the mode of production is mutually related. Conversely, one cannot understand the culture of a given society without understanding the economic mode of production, which is a central factor in determining existing social relations in that society. Dialectical analysis involves the balancing of all social structures as interrelated systems, not one of which can be understood by itself. Thus radical theorists claim that they are careful to distinguish a simplistic economic determinism from a Marxist dialectical analysis that assumes that nothing determines other things without also being determined by them. E. K. Hunt and Howard Sherman remind us that:

> To argue that Marx believed the economic base determined completely and rigidly every aspect of the superstructure is grossly inaccurate (although it is often done). He did assert, however, that the mode of production was the most important single aspect in determining not only the present social superstructure, but also the direction of social change.[73]

Assuming that all social structures are dialectically related, radical theory also assumes that all social problems are similarly dialectically related. Under capitalism, each social problem is both reinforcement and cause of the other social problems, and *all are a consequence of capitalist economic and political arrangements*. The primary characteristic of capitalist society is social alienation, the reduction of all human relations to commodity relations. These theorists argue that a system that is centered on the accumulation of private capital needs to support such structures as racism, sexism, heterosexism, increased military spending, and environmental destruction. These are viewed as autonomous problems by orthodox theorists, but as dialectically interconnected and a consequence of the capitalist system by radical theorists.[74]

Critical Marxism is not the only contributor to the dialectical methodology utilized by twentieth-century radical economic theory. Much within feminist theory also informs contemporary radical theory with a dialectical methodology. Like twentieth-century developments in quantum theory in science, and like process philosophy (including such philosophers as Alfred North Whitehead), feminist theory insists that all knowledge is affected by participation, and that no one reality may be defined apart from its relationship to others. Josephine Donovan points out that "entities . . . can show different properties . . . depending on the environmental context within which they exist and are subject to observation. . . . What is needed is a holistic, contextual approach to reality. Such is the approach proposed in the new feminist moral vision."[75]

Because women have been the victims of objectification, many feminists reject the complete disjuncture between the knowing subject and the known object.[76] They affirm a world that is "a contextual network in which every discrete entity is defined relative to its environment and subject to the positional relativity of the observer."[77] Thus there is no universal observer of static reality. The dialectical analysis in this feminist theory affirms the radical interconnectedness and dynamism of all reality and the importance of acknowledging from whose perspective reality is perceived and whose interests are operating.

In addition to its emphasis on the organic interaction of the various structures in a society, another component of dialectical analysis is its emphasis on the struggle of dialectical opposites. Conflict and change are seen as the major dynamic force in history, thus challenging the orthodox view that there is a tendency toward harmony and equilibrium in the world.

For example, radical theory assumes that capitalist relations of production are not based on immutable natural laws whose existence is presumed for all time. Radical theorists have argued that capitalist relations of production are not any more absolute than were the relations of production of slavery or feudalism. Samuel Bowles and Herbert Gintis note that, "just as the philosophers of ancient Greece could not conceive of society without master and slave, and the scholastics of medieval times without lord and serf, so today, many cannot conceive of society without a controlling managerial hierarchy and a subservient working class."[78]

Radical theorists assume that capitalist society is part of a continuum that includes precapitalist economic structures and will include postcapitalist ones. They believe that the power conflict within the mode of production between those who own and control capital and those whose labor is exploited sets the stage for disruptive social change.[79] In addition, some see conflict between classes and tendencies toward disequilibrium not only in the social relations of production, but in the contradiction between private ownership of the means of production and democratic personal rights. The so-called property rights of capitalism, that is, the refusal to allow democratization of the control of production, and the personal rights of democratic liberalism are not ultimately harmonious. They are, in the final analysis, contradictory. For democracy that does not extend to the economic sphere is no democracy at all, and unless class structure is changed, social justice cannot exist.[80]

To explain power conflict and disruptive change in capitalist society radical theorists contend that conflict between those who own and control the means of production and those who do not—and, more extensively, those who have sex and race and other cultural privilege and those who do not—produces a dominant class with dominant institutional structures that monopolize economic and political power. These class structures in turn reproduce and perpetuate the racism, sexism, heterosexism, and class privilege that are essential to their maintenance. These forms of unjust social relations are a consequence of the ongoing functioning of capitalist institutional structures and are all related. That is, while orthodox theory sees these realities as discrete social problems primarily due to the limits of individual human nature, radical theory views them as interlocking and due to the capitalist need to produce and reproduce inequality. Radical theorists claim that racist, male-dominant capitalism is indigenously resistant to democratization *for its very survival*. Problems associated with class, race, and gender are not peculiar to autonomous "special interest groups," as in orthodox theory, but rather such structures as classism, racism, and sexism are "organizing mechanisms" for the political and economic system itself.[81]

Class helps organize a hierarchical capitalist society and aids in the legitimation of race and gender inequality and privilege in this way. Radical theorists believe that wage or income differentials depend not only on individual productivity, as stated by orthodox theory, but also on access to class power. Class power both determines and is shaped by access to market power, social status, and control of the various benefits bestowed by the state. Each of these facets of class power affects not only access to wage income, but more importantly, access to capital assets (wealth), the means of social power. There are two discrete systems of circulation, wages and capital, and their distribution is governed by whether one owns or controls the means of production or only does wage work for those who do.

Market power, an aspect of class power, affects income because sellers and buyers are not equal in bargaining power. Thus the terms of sale reflect the market power or lack of it—in terms of ownership and control of capital—that sellers and buyers bring to the marketplace.[82] Social status, including race and gender privilege, affects income by affecting the allocation of social resources, such as education, and the access to different kinds of capital, such as inherited wealth.[83] Access to state benefits affects income since the state, in order to protect vast amounts of property for relatively few capitalists, manages a tax and social expenditure system that functions regressively. That is the higher the income, the lower one is taxed proportionately, and the more one has access to various loopholes, benefits, contracts, franchises, licenses, and services.[84] Disproportionate access to market power, social status, and benefits from the state enable the dominant capitalist class to be freer from labor themselves and to exercise control over the labor of others who are without capital assets.[85]

Contrary to orthodox theory, radical theory argues that

increased productivity does not automatically result in increased real wages. Rather, since employers must always seek to increase profits and minimize the wage factor, increased wages depend on the power that employees can wrest from employers. Advancement in wages "depends primarily on attitudes and on the state of economic conditions, and much less on worker merit or productivity in its narrow traditional sense."[86]

There are many ramifications of class domination of the economic structures of society. For example, production is governed by what capitalists think will best generate profit. It is not governed by what a majority of people might democratically decide they need most: housing, healthful food, medical care, and day care.

Another ramification is that class domination of the political structures of capitalism insures that the state is militarized in order to protect capitalism from political control, that is, the democratization of production, and to protect the property and wealth of capitalists.[87] Radical theorists understand the basic dynamic of capitalist political economy in this way. At best, capitalism mitigates unjust social relations through trickle-down, which only works when the economy is expanding by pulling other parts of the globe into it. This expansion process, in which labor exploitation shifts to the Third World for a time, fuels the military state when political resistance to elitist property owners increases there. The militarization of economies contributes to rising prices and higher unemployment and, as welfare measures in the First World fail to work, such Third World conditions as rising poverty, structural unemployment, and police brutality are reproduced even in the First. As discussed further, below, advanced capitalist economies must also be militarized in order to maintain aggregate demand and monopoly profit.

Despite the incompatibility of orthodox and radical theories with regard to such basics as their views of economic value, economic activity, and the way capitalism functions, radical theorists acknowledge a dialectical relationship with capitalism. They recognize that radical theory has been shaped by the democratic ethos of capitalism. Along with Marx, they recognize that capitalism's productive capacity is capable of relieving the problem of scarcity, and that capitalism has opened up possibilities that serve as the precondition and guide for socialism. This is so because the reality of the rich productivity of capitalism means that for the first time in history human culture and social advancement need no longer be dependent on a slave class supporting a leisure class. Consequently, radical theorists, like most postcapitalist movements, do not oppose capital accumulation and the limited use of markets. However, they insist that any genuine transformation of unjust social relations cannot happen unless democratic control of the social means of producing wealth begins to occur. Thus, radical theory also critiques so-called socialist societies where the mode of production, administered by state bureaucracies, is also not subject to democratic control.[88]

In summary, these assumptions about capitalist society guide radical theorists as they analyze the current social arena and seek to shape social policy: (1) the mode of production is a major factor in determining the social relations of the society and the capitalist mode of production and distribution is inherently hierarchical; (2) dialectical analysis is a critical methodology for understanding the centrality of production within the social system as a whole, and for understanding how various social problems are interrelated and follow from this hierarchical mode of production; (3) the dynamic of social reality is characterized by conflict and change, including the creation of a dominant capitalist class and dominant institutional structures. Capitalism dictates that production is based on profit need, not social need, and that distribution is based on access to wages or capital assets, which in turn is based on access to class power; (4) the capitalist class dominates not only the economic structures of the society but also the social and political structures. As a result, the capitalist state functions to protect the economic sphere from the process of democratization, and must be militarized in order to maintain aggregate demand, corporate profit, and Third World imperialism.

Radical Analysis of the Structural Ramifications of Capitalism

Radical theorists conclude that long-term qualitative change is impossible within the capitalist framework and that fundamental structural change—not reform leaving basic institutions intact—is necessary. In order to understand why this is so, radical theorists analyze such capitalist structures or institutions as: (1) private capital accumulation, and the necessary reproduction of class division, white-collar crime, monopoly, militarism, imperialism, and the phenomena of debtor nations; (2) labor markets and their exploitation of people by race, sex, and class; (3) the education and the welfare systems, and the institutionalization of poverty. Radical theory argues that each of these capitalist institutions is structurally interrelated and one cannot act effectively against one of them without incorporating efforts to address all the others.

The System of Private Capital Accumulation

Radical social theorists argue that the most fundamental aspect of the capitalist system is the need to make profit. Capitalists must always be acting to increase their relative share of capital, at least in the long run. Capitalists are "driven to expand profits not only because they *want to*, but also because if they are to remain capitalists, the market *forces* them to do so."[89] But it is important to see that what is at issue here is a structural reality, not the morality of individual capitalists. Ethically sensitive capitalists cannot alter the basic situation of the workplace because market constraints deprive them of the option to raise wages, keep out oppressive kinds of technology, operate with ecological care, or lower prices. If capitalists did any of these things, they would be undersold and driven from the market. As Richard C. Edwards says, *"Capitalists act as capitalists because, if they are to survive as capitalists, the market forces them to act that way."*[90] The failure to grasp sufficiently the internal logic of capitalism has led, for example, to some liberals advocating the election of more ethically aware persons to the boards of directors of large corporations. Radical theorists were not surprised when a recent study by Edward Herman of the Wharton School concluded that "the behavior of large corporations does not significantly differ no matter who is on the board."[91]

Radical theorists claim that the necessity for capital accumulation undergirds all of the dynamics of capitalist society. These dynamics include, but are not limited to, the need for both unequal income and wealth distribution, incentives for white-collar crime, monopoly, military spending, and the creation of debtor nations.

Because capitalists are in constant need of increasing their profits, there must be labor power available at a cost that does not endanger profit margins. Thus, the capitalist system must generate a downward pressure on wages with unemployment at the bottom in order to maintain or increase profit, the basis of the system.[92] This explains the long-term stability of unequal income distribution in capitalist societies. Income distribution in the United States has remained substantially unchanged and unequal in the past thirty-five years, some say one hundred years.[93] Recently the inequality of distribution has increased. Nancy S. Barrett points out the inconsistency of the notion that, as consumers, people are presumed to be hedonistic and to act in a way that maximizes their satisfaction, but as workers they are supposed to be ascetical, willing to work at monotonous tasks for low wages in unpleasant or unhealthy environments.[94]

Since the late 1960s, U.S. corporations have faced an increasingly competitive global economy. As a consequence, even greater pressure has been on them to "insure a docile, divided and poorly paid labor force."[95] We will see how racism and sexism are thought by radical theorists to aid in maintaining such a work force, enabling the share of aggregate personal wealth of the nation's top 1 percent of the population to increase from 25 percent in the 1950s to over 30 percent in the 1960s.[96] By the early 1980s, the top 2 percent of the population controlled 54 percent of the total net financial assets of the nation, with 86 percent of these assets held by the top 10 percent of all families (EJA 183).

Such increasing inequality is also shown at the lower end of the income distribution scale. Citing the U.S. Bureau of Census, the U.S. bishops—who are not radical—claim that poverty has increased by nearly a third since 1973 (EJA 171). The bishops claim there are between 53 and 63 million Americans, or about a quarter of our 227 million population, who are living below "any reasonable standard" of need (EJA 16).[97] This number of poor is also accepted by other social ethicists.[98] In terms of distribution, this means that the bottom 40 percent of U.S. families share only 15.7 percent of the total national income, which the U.S. bishops characterize as "the lowest share on record" (and income is not wealth) (EJA 184).

In addition, it is estimated by some analysts that between 1960 and 1975 the middle strata shrunk by over 23 percent, contributing to "a growing population of frustrated, insecure and potentially very angry people trying to hang on to middle class status on unstable [low] incomes."[99] Many scholars note that such increasing inequality in distribution, which includes the rapid decline of middle-income people—independent farmers, artisans, small business operators, and professionals—is eroding the traditional sources of support for the capitalist system.[100] Radical economists view the economic dependency of most of the nation's citizens on the few who have economic privilege as the fundamental social problem, and as the point where the socioeconomic debate should focus.

The need for capital accumulation means that capitalism must sustain inequality and, under conditions of the globalization of advanced monopoly capitalism, U.S. capitalism must increase social inequality and class conflict to remain competitive. In radical theory class is not defined according to people's consumption levels, as in orthodox theory, but according to whether people produce or appropriate surplus labor within the mode of production. However, class in its broadest sense encompasses not only economic domination but cultural and ideological, including racist and sexist, domination as well. Radical theorists insist that male domination and white supremacy are major sources of social oppression that are exacerbated by capitalism to sustain exploitation and class division.[101]

The specifically economic dimension of class has to do with the fact that, under capitalism, most people must sell their labor power for a wage. If one's income is primarily derived from wages from work that does not control capital, one is part of the working class. A small elite, certainly less than 10 percent of the population, receive most of their income from the ownership or control of the means of production. They constitute the capitalist class.

Contrary to orthodox theorists who believe that class interests cannot be maintained in the face of diversified individual choices—such as schooling investment decisions—in a fluid job market, radical theorists posit far more life-shaping importance and structural stability to the notion of class.[102] For these

theorists, the inequality of income distribution, which has remained consistently unequal, points in this direction. They
believe that the ramifications of class extend to the broadest
social relations. People's positions with regard to the division
of labor—both domestic as well as wage labor—as well as their
neighborhood and the educational system are determined by
their class. Class shapes their sense of personal power, be-
haviors, and attitudes such that these differ from one class to
another.[103] Thus radicals understand class to be both a cause
and a product of stratified neighborhoods, labor markets, and
schools. All these structures, according to radical theory, are
fed by the necessity for the selective allocation of resources
that characterizes an economic system based on capital accumulation and inequality.

In addition to a downward pressure on wages and the
perpetration of a class system, radical theorists believe that
another dynamic created by the necessity for ever-increasing
capital accumulation is white-collar crime. In the early 1960s,
well before American business began to feel the squeeze from
a revived European and Japanese corporate sector, a study
was made of seventy of the largest nonfinancial corporations
in the United States. It found that 60 percent of these had
been guilty of multiple criminal offenses. E. K. Hunt and
Howard J. Sherman conclude that "the pressure to acquire
ever-increasing profits is so strong on many businessmen and
managers that some persistently resort to illegal and improper
means . . . [so that] society can ill afford to turn to the managerial class for paternalistic stewardship of the social and economic welfare."[104] John S. R. Shad, former chair of the Securi-
ties and Exchange Commission, who gave $30 million to Har-
vard Business School in 1987 to finance a program in business
ethics, agrees: "I've been very disturbed . . . with the large
numbers of graduates of leading business and law schools
who have become convicted felons."[105] Revelations such as
Watergate, Irangate, the HUD scandal, the savings and loan

banking crisis, and widespread embezzlement on Wall Street all support the view that corporate leadership is not the best place to look for stewards of social welfare.

Another outcome of a system based on capital accumulation is the creation of monopolies or oligopolies. It is important to note that orthodox theory does not mention the emergence of the large business firm. This reality is an anomaly in the neoclassical paradigm, which assumes the stasis of a competitive market.[106] Radical theorists believe that monopoly is the internal logic of a system that has profit enhancement and growth without interference as its only rational goal. Because the system of capital accumulation necessitates growth, firms must seek to expand indefinitely and to control competition.[107] And so the present stage of global, monopoly capitalism has witnessed the rise of agribusiness, global multifirm and franchise enterprises, a corporate health-care delivery system, and media conglomerates.[108]

Thus, claim radical theorists, in the latter twentieth century a few oligopolistic giants, like those in the food, auto, and oil industries, have grown to dominate American business. These giant firms find that monopoly with its large-scale application of technology provides a cheaper way to produce fewer goods for higher prices. It is also a more efficient way for capital to exert control over raw materials and the labor force. Radical theorists point out that American corporations, like other corporations in the system of global capitalism, monopolize business not only in America, but throughout the world. U.S. corporations directly own a large piece of European and Canadian industry, while First World corporations own the major industrial enterprises of the Third World.[109]

Orthodox economics is based on the belief that independent, consumer preference dictates what is produced and consumed. However, the reality of capitalist production and its organization around monopoly or oligopoly, argue radical theorists, determine that advertising manipulates consumers to desire what is produced and producers often spend more on controlling consumption than on production. Advertising is a $20 billion to $50 billion a year enterprise whereby corporations seek to persuade the public that each of a few identical products is better than the other. In the radical view, advertising involves "a massive waste of resources, a continual drain on consumers' income, and a systematic destruction of consumers' freedom of choice between genuine alternatives." Radical theorists believe that the waste in time, effort, and money from selling products under monopoly "must considerably lower the rate of economic growth." [110]

Another ramification of the capitalist system is the emergence of militarism, a kind of state-managed "security capitalism." As the depression in the 1930s demonstrated, pure monopoly capitalism could not sustain aggregate demand, and so it has been succeeded by a kind of Keynesian, state-funded demand grafted onto the monopolistic or oligopolistic core of the economy.[111]

Radical theorists view the state-funded demand for military spending as the primary antidepression, policy reform required by corporate America. Only large-scale military spending has kept the United States out of major depression since the 1930's.[112] Military spending has stabilized the U.S. capitalist system because it has meant enhanced profits for corporations that can sell products that individuals could not afford to buy, such as weapons systems, to the United States and on the international market. By the mid-1970s one hundred U.S. corporations received 85 percent of all military contracts. Further, profit from U.S. foreign trade and investment,[113] and profit from the military production to defend these foreign investments,[114] amounted to about 25 to 30 percent of all corporate profits. The largest one hundred corporations received about half of this profit.[115] Meanwhile, the U.S. bishops, for example, cite government statistics to support their conclusion that "spending on the arms race means a net loss in the number of jobs created in the economy because defense industries are less labor intensive than other major sectors of the economy (*EJA* 148). But since military spending maintains aggregate demand and increases the profitability of U.S. corporations, it has become the core of the U.S. economy. Military spending is more accurately called "the militarization of the economy" because by 1971 the managers of the U.S. military system, who received $1.06 for every $1.00 of private corporate capital, had surpassed U.S. private firms in control over capital.[116] The managers of the U.S. military system, radical theorists point out, now spend more than the net income of all U.S. corporations, which is over half of all income-tax revenues. They thereby run the largest planned economy in the world outside the USSR.[117]

According to radical theory, the reality of the military industrial complex, and related corporate subsidy by the government, reveals the fallacy of orthodox theory that the capitalist economy is in the private sphere. It certainly is not subject to the norms of democracy that govern formal political processes. This complex of corporations and state agencies function for the well-being of the corporate sector, not for the general well-being of citizens. Orthodox theory considers the economy as private and therefore not involved in the socially significant exercise of power that would require democratic accountability. Radical economists contend that the economy must be reorganized so that public accountability can occur.[118]

Radical theorists also argue that military spending is a primary means of the capitalist system to worsen unequal income and wealth distribution. More socially useful public spending, on schools, public-service jobs, pollution control and cleanup, and the creation of new industry, would create far more jobs than does military spending, but would transfer money from the already established wealthy to the less so. Radical theorists argue that such reallocation is unacceptable in a system in which capitalists monopolize the power to lend, to borrow, and to invest.[119]

Militarism and imperialism—or Third World development —have worked in the past to keep the United States out of recession by providing ways to invest profit and to maintain aggregate demand. However, militarism and imperialism also serve to create debtor nations, and radical theorists assert that this is one way capitalism shows its internal contradictions and demonstrates that it is breaking down.

The United States has sustained a business upswing since the 1980s by an enormous increase in military spending and by the willingness to finance a trade deficit accompanied by tax cuts for wealthy households and corporations.[120] During the 1970s and 1980s several tax-code revisions shifted the tax burdens from corporate to individual taxes and from wealthy to middle-income taxpayers. The 1986 tax reform lowered the top corporate tax rate from 46 percent to 40 percent in 1987 and to 34 percent thereafter. In addition, people whose taxable income is over $200,000 pay lower marginal tax rates than those with smaller incomes. Contrary to popular opinion, federal taxes for all but the richest Americans rose during the 1980s. Military spending during the Reagan administration doubled from $150 billion to $300 billion. Financed in small part by a $40 billion cut in welfare relief, this military spending has been red-ink spending and is one of the primary reasons the United States has become a debtor nation. On top of a previous debt of almost $1 trillion at the end of the 1970s, the United States borrowed an additional $700 billion from foreigners to keep itself out of recession in the 1980s.

In addition to these exhorbitant military outlays, another reason for the increased U.S. debt is the trade deficit. Deficits like those of $113 billion in 1984 and $160 billion in 1987 were brought on in part by capital flight. U.S. business closed factories here in order to utilize cheaper labor in the Third World.

The United States now produces only about 20 percent of the world's goods and services compared with 52 percent in 1950. Trade deficits were also increased because one of the ways the United States fights inflation is by raising interest rates. Higher interest rates not only strangle Third World debt repayment, they make the dollar more expensive and thus make U.S. exports more expensive and less attractive. Because of capital flight and high interest rates, then, the United States is exporting fewer goods to other countries than it is importing. This situation of more buying than selling cannot go on indefinitely, however, for no economy can forever consume more than it is producing. Consequently, some economists predict a major recession in the international financial system.[121]

The United States, currently in debt over $2 trillion, may be the biggest but is not the only debtor nation created by the expansionist needs of global capital. The need of capital for profitable investment has led not only to U.S. debt but to Third World debt that has risen to $1.3 trillion. This situation has its origins in the late 1960s when world capitalism, facing a decrease in demand for goods and services in the recession-struck First World, sought to convince countries in Latin America, as well as the Philippines and South Korea to take loans because banks needed an outlet for surplus capital. This trend greatly accelerated in the 1970s as First World banks needed places to invest petrodollars from OPEC countries that were unwilling or unable to invest this money in their own countries. Some of this money became loans toward agricultural and industrial development like hydroelectric projects, but most did not.

While the extent of the corruption varies from country to country, many leaders, government officials, and other elite invested these loans in real estate or bank accounts outside the country, especially in the United States, Great Britain, and Switzerland. These investments were seen as security for the wealthy if the government failed or was deposed. Most of the surplus capital given in the form of loans to Third World countries was exported because the leaders of these countries derive their power from present socioeconomic arrangements. They have no long-range interest in disrupting the basic exploitation patterns governing the rural and urban poor by investing in local projects that might move toward more self-sufficient economies.

Meanwhile the Reagan administration, in order to help finance the rising U.S. deficit, raised interest rates on loans that had been 7 percent in 1975 to 18 percent in 1981. Consequently, loan-ridden Third World nations, trapped in export-led economies, now are close to bankruptcy because they cannot repay expensive loans from which many of them never benefited due to capital flight administered by their governments and elite. The interest alone on these loans absorbs major portions of their national budgets. While First World banks currently face the possibility of loss of payment on the principal of many of these loans, they have already made enormous profits in interest payments. For example, the profits from their investment in the Third World by the seven largest U.S. banks rose from 22 percent of total profits in 1970 to 60 percent of total profits in 1982.[122] This system of interest collecting also yields these statistics: Brazil has received $108 billion in foreign loans but has paid $157 billion in interest. As a result of being the Third World's sixth largest debtor, the Philippines have 70 percent of their population living below the poverty line in the 1980s compared to 45 percent living in poverty in the 1970s.[123]

In order to reschedule their debts, for which First World Banks charge additional massive fees, Third World countries are forced to accept the terms of the International Monetary Fund (IMF). These include such restrictions as cutting government social expenditures, imports, investments, food subsidies, wages, and jobs. These austerity measures mean that lenders, not borrowers, are rescued, while increasing numbers of children, women, and men die of hunger or suffer malnutrition.[124] And conditions worsen not only in the Third World but also in the United States. Approximately eight hundred thousand U.S. jobs have already been wiped out as export markets dry up, thus contributing to the U.S. trade deficit and its position as a debtor nation.[125]

The Segmented Labor Market

In addition to the social reproduction of class division, white-collar crime, militaristic state monopoly capitalism, and debtor nations, radical theorists believe that the capitalist engine also reproduces a stratified labor market. Radical theorists have argued that the job structure in the United States is determined not only by the most efficient job design, or combination of worker skills and current technology, but that job structure is also determined by employers' desire for worker control.[126] In a study entitled *Segmented Work, Divided Workers* (1982), David M. Gordon and his coauthors offer a systematic analysis of the connections between periods of capitalist development and U.S. working-class life. They argue that the job structure in the United States has gone through three major changes that correspond to the three major periods within capitalism: proletarianization (1820–1890), homogenization (1870–1940), and most recently, segmentation.[127]

The period of segmentation, which is beginning to break down, has had two major characteristics. The first involves the co-optation of unions by capitalists who absorb the collective bargaining process, issue elaborate grievance procedures, and make an all-out effort to stop the spread of unions and to bust existing ones.[128] The second characteristic of the most recent labor-market structure involves the increasing segmentation of the labor force by utilizing and channeling racism and sexism in order to divide workers.[129]

Radical theorists argue that capitalism separates those jobs for which stability is necessary, a primary labor-market sector, from those jobs for which stability is not necessary, a secondary labor-market sector. The primary sector includes both the more dominant (professional, managerial) and the more subordinate (semiskilled white and blue collar) segments. Primary-sector jobs are better paying with more benefits and more possibility of advancement. To supplement pay increases, this primary sector has hierarchically structured jobs with complex internal promotional systems and an intricate system of rules and procedures. This creates the illusion of mobility and status and is necessary in a work situation where incentives of status and money must replace inherent job satisfaction.

The secondary labor sector consists of the low-paying, low-benefit, dead-end jobs monopolized by teenagers, women, and minority men. Many of these jobs pay the minimum wage, less than $7,000 a year.[130] Over 70 percent of all female employment and 60 percent of all black employment are located in peripheral manufacturing, retail trade, clerical, and the lower rungs of health and education work that comprise this sector. The secondary sector provides a relatively resigned, cheap labor pool, chiefly populated by women and minority men who, unlike the previous generations of immigrant men, are least likely to identify with those in the primary labor sector.[131] Radical theorists hold that job discrimination by sex, race, and class saves capital a tremendous amount of money and has probably grown increasingly important over time.[132]

Each of the three segments in the two sectors—professional primary workers, subordinate primary workers, and secondary workers—comprises roughly one-third of the nonagricultural work force.[133] The purpose of this segmentation, which gives workers very different experiences of job security and the productive process, is not only to cut labor costs but to forestall the development of class consciousness and worker solidarity. Labor-market segmentation, contend radical theorists, conditions and reinforces stratified neighborhoods and schools and fragments political awareness and voting patterns. Professional primary workers are concerned with civil liberties and the environment. Subordinate primary workers are concerned with economic growth upon which their jobs depend. And secondary workers worry over access to government services and income support.[134] Radical economists claim that this multidimensioned division of working-class life into various social strata has thus far effectively prevented a unified working-class movement.

Orthodox economists argue that if more workers had better skills, the market would provide more skilled jobs. But radical economists contend that increasing the amount of skilled jobs would undermine the segmented job structure that serves corporations well by dividing workers and curtailing unionization.[135] Therefore, radical economists hold that price subsidies to employers to increase the availability of on-the-job training would have little effect "because [the subsidies] would not alter or affect the class dynamics governing employer choices about job structure and design."[136] Manpower programs, for example, have proved to be token programs, irrelevant to workers' needs for jobs that are not dead-ended. Studies show that government programs have not effected steadily rising unemployment since World War II, and by becoming warehouses for the poor, serve rather than alter the problematic structure of the labor market.[137]

Rather than being capable of movement toward reform, say radical economists, the labor market is capable only of further rigidification in all three labor segments. The professional primary sector is experiencing a reduction in rising wages and in opportunities for job development and job control. The relatively new phenomenon of union organizing among professional workers testifies to their feelings of increased vulnerability. Subordinate primary workers in the United States experienced capital's increased control because supervisors, who are nonunion and can maintain production during strikes, went from 13 per 100 workers in 1949 to 23 per 100 in 1969, an increase of 75 percent. This segment, like the first, has experienced increased antiunion activity, forced give-backs, job dissatisfaction, and plant closings as capital seeks cheaper labor elsewhere. The earnings of secondary workers have deteriorated faster than the subordinate primary segment. As increasing numbers of secondary workers, aided in the 1960s by increases in welfare, have refused to remain committed to the most menial jobs, the secondary market has imported foreign workers whose illegal status has probably deteriorated conditions in this sector even further.[138]

Finally, it is clear that jobs in the secondary labor market have greatly proliferated in the 1980s as jobs have been lost in the manufacturing (subordinate primary) sector. The restructuring of the U.S. economy has witnessed the continued growth of jobs in the service economy (including transportation and public utilities; wholesale and retail trade; finance, insurance, and real estate; and business and personal services) and the reorganization of work toward more part-time schedules. Recent studies by the AFL–CIO and by economists Barry Bluestone and Bennett Harrison document that almost 60 percent of the jobs created between 1979 and 1984 provide incomes of less than $7,000 a year.[139] Further, the approximately 12 million workers in these newer low-wage jobs do not include only white women and people of color, those who have traditionally held the major proportion of the worst jobs in the secondary labor market. Bluestone and Harrison document that since 1979 nearly 97 percent of the net employment gains among *white men* have been in these jobs that pay $7,000 a year or less.[140]

These recent statistics, which demonstrate an increasingly

deteriorating job-market structure, seem to support the radical view that the rigid divisions of the labor market will probably not be amenable to liberal reform because they serve employers and their ever-increasing necessity for capital accumulation. If radical analysis is correct, changes in the individual skills and educational level of most workers will make little difference to their future accessibility to better paying jobs. Changes in individuals will not change the job-market structure, which is not only segmented but rapidly deteriorating as corporations seek bigger profits in the current situation of competitive global capitalism.

Racism and Sexism

Radical economists attempt a structural analysis of racism and sexism in order to understand their functional relationship to capitalism. They believe that the institutions of racism and sexism, while hardly original to capitalism, are crucial to support the continued well-being of the American capitalist system.[141]

Orthodox theory claims that market pressure tends to erode discrimination—a factor considered to originate outside the economic system—because the most productive workers must be hired at the prevailing wage in order to maximize profits. But radical theorists point out that racism has been used to support capitalism for the past three centuries in a variety of economic circumstances. The functional role of racism changes according to the needs of the economy. Racism and ethnic prejudice, which is directed toward all non-Anglo people, can be understood by studying the black community. Blacks once served primarily as a pool of superexploited labor, first as slaves and then as tenant farmers, migrant workers, and strike breakers. Now blacks serve not only to keep the labor market highly segmented, but to buffer the white majority from unemployment, while serving as a reserve labor pool for better times.[142] Harold Baron says:

> If the various forms of disguised unemployment and subemployment are taken into account, black unemployment rates can run as high as three or four times those of whites in specific labor markets in recession periods. The welfare and police costs of maintaing this labor reserve are high, but they are borne by the state as a whole and therefore do not cut into the profit calculation of individual firms.[143]

Contrary to orthodox theory, which claims that white workers benefit from racism while capitalists lose, radical theory maintains that because a divided labor force weakens all workers' strength, racism lowers white wages as well.[144] Radical theorists assert that political and moral imperatives exist for a certain limiting of racial exploitation. But black middle-class and professional strata prosper simultaneously with a growing and increasingly isolated and impoverished black underclass, whose situation has rapidly deteriorated since the mid-1970s. The U.S. Census Bureau reported that the poverty rate for black people rose at least 15 percent from 1979 to 1982.[145] William Julius Wilson points out, for example, that the proportion of employed black men decreased from 80 percent in 1930 to 56 percent in 1983. Wilson's work attempts to show that class has become even more important than race in determining the situation of blacks.[146]

These studies have led radical analysts to conclude that racism is not only psychological and historical in nature, but is a necessity for the prosperity of capitalists. Racism is backed by institutions that prevent the formation of a broad, multiracial, revolutionary coalition.[147] Many radical theorists argue that such liberal reform measures as affirmative action further divide whites and blacks by squeezing whites out of a limited amount of jobs, and thereby increasing racism. Both affirmative action and antidiscrimination measures such as busing serve the capitalist class by channeling hostility between workers and capitalists into hostility between blacks and whites. Meanwhile, the capitalist labor-market structure that is the source of the problem, and should provide decent jobs for all people, remains intact.[148]

The radical analysis of racism seems to show that it performs these functions within the capitalist system: (1) it provides a cheap source of labor at all times and a reserve army of unemployed labor for boom times, which can be isolated at bust times because blacks are not politically powerful;[149] (2) it divides the labor force, isolates jobs no one wants to do, and keeps all wages down; (3) it provides a political safety valve for capitalism by replacing interclass conflict with interracial conflict.[150] As Michael Reich has said, racism helps answer the need for "visible scapegoats on which to blame the alienating quality of life in America."[151]

Like racism, sexism is also extremely beneficial to capitalism and there are many similarities between the ways racism and sexism function within the capitalist system. Many argue that capitalism is as interested in upholding privileges of sex as it is privileges of class in all sectors of society.[152] Radical theory uses structural analysis to understand the interconnections between the family, the labor market, and the welfare state, and to show how they shape and are shaped by the dual role of women in male-dominant capitalist society.

Sexism divides the working class by justifying the underpaid wage labor of women. A structural profile of women's participation in the work force reveals that jobs for women have been concentrated in the secondary sector, and that they are the public extensions of housework (e.g., waitresses, food preparation, maids, child care, secretaries, sales clerks, producers of nondurable consumer goods).[153] This isolation of women in the secondary labor force has yielded statistics such as the following: women with college degrees earn 81 percent of what men earn with high school diplomas; 41 percent of women with children who are below the poverty line work for pay; for the past twenty years women as a group have earned three-fifths to two-thirds of the wages earned by men. This lack of earning power reflects a slightly greater gap since the 1930s, illustrating that after forty years of economic growth, and the feminist movement, women have fallen even further behind.[154] Even orthodox economists note the declining income of women.[155]

Sex segregation in the work force, then, reveals that work has changed only minimally for women in the twentieth century. Statistics from the U.S. Bureau of Labor Statistics and the Census Bureau in 1985 show that the growth in the proportion of women in some professions is not enough to upset the overall isolation of women in the secondary labor market. Despite an increase in the number of women with doctorates, the proportion of women in tenured faculty jobs has not increased in the past decade, and two-thirds of all professional women are still in traditionally female jobs—nursing and teaching. These statistics indicate that 70 percent of working women today do the gender-segregated work in the secondary labor market, and are either single, divorced, widowed, or have husbands earning less than $14,000.[156]

Although it is impossible to fix precisely the amount of the financial benefit that women's underpaid wage labor contributes to the economy, some attempts have been made. For example, Hunt and Sherman have estimated that in 1970 American women were paid an average of about 50 percent of the wages received by men doing the same jobs, and that "approximately 23 percent of all manufacturing profits [were] attributable to the lower wages paid to women."[157]

While justifying underpaid wage labor for women, sexism also justifies the unpaid and unshared domestic labor of women across class lines. In the radical view, corporate profits would be significantly reduced if business had to pay women in full for bearing, caring, cooking, and cleaning for the work force. Not only is the physical and intellectual labor of housewives vital for the profitability of the system, but so is their psychological and emotional labor. There would be no willing and productive labor force without the work of women who help families "adjust" to harsh realities, or stay in school, or remain on the job.[158] It has been estimated that women's contribution in free domestic labor is equivalent to one-quarter of the Gross National Product.[159]

Radical economic theorists who are influenced by feminist theory acknowledge that because it is so profitable, not only in markets but in all areas of life, sexism continues even in a noncapitalist society if not confronted directly. They argue that classism is conditioned by the prior sexist division of the labor structure, and if sexism is not abolished along with classism (capitalism), authentic social change cannot occur.[160] Radical theorists argue that women's unvalued work at home is the basis for their undervalued work in the marketplace, and that the latter cannot be addressed without the former.[161]

According to radical theory, besides justifying the unpaid domestic labor and underpaid wage labor of women, sexism, like racism, functions as a political safety valve for capitalism. It does so principally in three ways: (1) sexism provides a reserve army of labor that can be utilized in expansive periods and let go during recessive periods with minimal political ramifications; (2) sexism compensates for men's lack of control and drudgery at work by allowing men control and leisure at home. This gender division of labor gives exploited men specific privilege and status and is fundamental to the survival of capitalism; (3) sexism acts as a safety valve for capitalism because it entails the economic dependence of women and children, which makes men less likely to be militant on the job.[162]

It is not surprising to radical analysts that public policy

supports sexism. Legislation with regard to divorce, child custody, welfare, state employment practices, contraception and abortion, and social security further reinforce inequality between the sexes. To cite just three examples: Antiabortion measures aid capitalism by helping to keep women out of the workplace, thus reinforcing the sexist division of labor. Antiabortion measures also help generate a surplus population that keeps wages down. Under no-fault divorce women's incomes have declined an average of 73 percent while men's have risen 42 percent.[163] Under present social security laws, elderly women who have spent a major portion of their adult lives raising people to enter the work force receive less help from these adult children who work to pay social security benefits than do retired men who have no children.[164]

Meanwhile, degrading advertising and other forms of cultural ideology about "femininity" and "motherhood" encourage women, radical theorists argue, to believe that this state of affairs is natural. They claim that the ideology of femininity and the cult of motherhood justify the marginalization, exploitation, and oppression of women.[165]

Radical theorists argue that a structural analysis of the family, the labor market, and the welfare state reveals that all three institutions are shaped to benefit the system of capital accumulation, and that all three institutions are built on the unpaid and underpaid labor of white women, people of color, and other workers.[166]

The Education and Welfare Systems

Another capitalist institution that radical theorists subject to structural analysis is the education system. Orthodox economists believe that more education will increase skills (especially reading and reasoning abilities) and therefore productivity, thus increasing wages. They argue that due to education, class stratification does not survive through generations because individuals are able to make schooling investment decisions both rationally and competitively.[167] They contend that the labor market cannot afford discrimination over the long haul because the most productive workers must be hired in order to maximize profits. Hence, they say that over time education will increase social and economic mobility. The relegation of women and minorities to lower paying jobs can be remedied by increasing their education, job experience, or "human capital" (i.e., personal resources and skills that employers are willing to pay for).

In opposition to this, radical theorists point out that, since there was little change in income distribution between 1910 and 1970, for example, it does not appear that the American education system has been promoting increasing equality. Even orthodox economist Lester Thurow says that "while the distribution of education has moved in the direction of greater equality over the post-war period, the distribution of income has not." This reality, says Thurow, "entitles us to have doubts about the value of education as a means of altering the distribution of income."[168] While differences in the amount of schooling between blacks and whites and women and men have been diminishing, income inequality has either remained constant or has been increasing.[169] While women are increasingly better educated, almost three-quarters of women workers remain isolated in the gender-segregated jobs of the secondary labor market. Similarly, radical theorists note that whenever studies have been done of blacks and whites who have equal amounts of human capital that can be measured, large wage differentials existed between them. The deteriorating situation of blacks is widely recognized.[170] From the radical perspective, this shows the inadequacy of orthodox theory's analysis of wage determination and of the efficiency of education within the market system.[171] In addition, while education per capita has increased, growth rate in the economy has decreased.[172] This situation exists, radical theorists believe, because the equality of white women and minorities with white men, even "the equal exploitation" of women and minorities with men "would require such fundamental changes . . . that it is very hard to imagine how they could be effected while capitalism survives."[173]

Radical theorists argue that increased education leads neither to increased wages, nor to increased productivity for most people because education has its roots in the very class structure it is supposed to eliminate. Unequal schooling (differences in the internal structures of schools and the content of schooling, including tracking systems, for example) reflects the segmented labor market and the segregated neighborhood surrounding each school. Financing schools locally, radical theorists argue, insures that the schools will reflect the communities surrounding them.[174]

The function of education is to reproduce those aptitudes and attitudes that are desirable for capitalist production. It is not primarily to increase reading and reasoning skills as orthodox theorists maintain. Rather, the purpose of education is to reproduce desirable personality traits such as discipline and the ability to endure repetitive and boring tasks, increase in punctuality, docility, conformity, and the ability to respond cognitively, not affectively. Samuel Bowles believes that the purpose of education is to be found "not in the content . . . but in the form, the social relations" of the school, which embody rigidity, intraclass competition, and subordination to authority.[175]

Radical theory argues that education—primarily through process but also through differences in curriculum—serves as a screening device for selecting people who have certain attitudes and traits and come from certain social backgrounds.[176] Through one's performance in this process and its curriculum, education teaches social rank and the capitalist system, thereby instilling capitalist values and supporting class divisions. For these reasons, as well as the fact that the labor market structure is fairly rigid, radical theorists contend that reforms that increase the amount of education within this system offer little chance for significant income mobility for most people, and do not alter basic class structure or impact the massive problem of poverty.

Indeed, along with capital accumulation, labor markets, and education, radical theorists understand poverty and the welfare system itself as an important institution that perpetuates capitalist society. Radical theorists do not believe that poverty can be eliminated either by letting the market take its course, with only adjustments in interest rates, as conservatives believe, or by various social programs as liberals suggest, or by state orchestrated planning of private capital as neoliberals posit.

A structural analysis reveals that poverty performs important social functions to maintain capitalist social relations. First, radical theorists note that poverty is not randomly distributed in the population in accord with individual characteristics. While abilities are normally distributed, wealth and income distribution is highly skewed. The fact that it is "nonrandomly distributed among people of color, other women and the old," roughly 25 to 30 percent of the U.S. population by most estimates,[177] makes radical theorists contend that poverty is systemic: the result of the normal functioning of capitalist institutions.[178] While orthodox theory is concerned about factors over which the individual supposedly has control, (education, job experience), radical theorists content that these factors seem not to be as important in the labor-market situation as factors over which the individual has no control (sex, race, and age).

A structural analysis of poverty also leads radical analysts to note that, in their drive for capital accumulation, capitalists cannot substantially alter either the number of jobs or the type of jobs available in order to reduce poverty. In fact, the internal dynamic of capitalism is always toward replacing human labor with machines. Further, capitalism usually chooses to tackle inflation with unemployment, and one million of the poor must be out of work for three years so that inflation can be decreased by 1 percent.[179] Under the ever-increasing pressure to increase their share of the market, capitalists cannot fundamentally reorder job hierarchies with unemployment at the bottom, because inequalities in income help workers tolerate alienating work. Unequal incomes also keep workers divided as they promote the myth of individualism. Without the threat of either a lower paying job or unemployment, who would do the unrewarding or distasteful work that is essential for the successful operation of the system?[180]

Consequently, a primary function of the welfare system, argue radical theorists, is to make the worst jobs seem more attractive. It creates an outcast class, treated with contempt, in order to manage people at the bottom and channel them into menial work. It is necessary to demean the poor, especially the welfare poor, in order to exalt by contrast even the meanest labor at the meanest wages.[181] Since the incentive to work grows weakest at the bottom of the hierarchy, radical theorists contend that the real targets of welfare prejudice are not the recipients, but the able-bodied poor who might be tempted to choose welfare over intolerable work.[182] Further, radical theorists argue that people often attain their poverty as a result of either the malfunctioning of the market or the poverty (minimum) wages it pays. It is their association with the labor market, which pays minimum wages earned by heads of households of three-quarters of the poor or has led to injury or layoffs, that is the cause of their poverty.[183]

All these institutions of capitalism—capital accumulation, segmented labor markets, the educational and welfare systems, and the institutionalization of poverty—mutually reinforce one another in providing the social glue for the maintenance of capitalist society.

Normative Assumptions of Radical Theory About a Just Society

Given the above assessment of capitalist society, how does radical theory envision a society in which democracy governs all exercise of social power, but is also a society that is grounded in historical possibility? Radical theorists find it important that a vision of a better society nurtures the creative struggle to achieve it. Because radical theorists believe that what is possible for a given society directly flows from what is valued, valuations or social vision are extremely important in the process of working for social change. Economic policy both shapes and is shaped by utopian vision. The social vision of a society "determines whether certain propositions are understood, recognized, publicly accepted." [184]

Radical theorists have a vision of a new society that cannot be separated from strategy but is not reducible to it. This vision is rooted in praxis which is "practice associated with a total dynamic of historical vision and social transformation." [185] It is both a content and a process. As a content, the vision presumes we can identify and transfer democratic accountability to every sector of society where power is exercised. With regard to the economy, this involves developing an economic democracy, or a "democratic socialism," that radical theorists believe has not yet been achieved anywhere in the world. [186]

The democratic socialism advocated by radical theory is essentially different from that endorsed by orthodox theorists. While orthodox democratic socialism would extend state control over certain sectors of the economy, it would keep basic capitalist institutions intact. Radical democratic socialism, on the other hand, would seek to empower marginalized people, to democratize the entire process of the social production of wealth in order to break the basic patterns of class exploitation and the structural legitimations of racism and sexism that are necessary to the system of private capital accumulation.

Thus, radical theory emphasizes democratic decentralization of economies not the nationalization of them. Radical theory views economic dependency on those who privately control capital, whether in capitalist economies or in state collectivist economies as no less an antithesis to freedom than is personal bondage. Democratic socialism exists when corporate bureaucracies, both private and governmental, are replaced with self-governing and self-managing people.

The goal of democratic socialism, or postliberal democracy,[187] is not abstract equality but the continual rectifying of powerful versus powerless and dominator over dominated relationships in the economic and social spheres. Anti-social behavior, natural disasters and necessary trade-offs will continue, but destructive competition, social hierarchies and maldistribution of wealth and income, radical theorists claim, would no longer be "inevitable." In a democratic socialist society, greed, alienation, racism, sexism, heterosexism, and classism would no longer have strong social-structural legitimacy.[188]

Radical theorists propose a totally different form of social, economic, and political organization because they contend that the social institutions of capitalism cannot translate capitalism's rich productive capacity into general human fulfillment and growth. Capitalism cannot solve the problems it creates, nor fulfill the needs it awakens. Radical theorists also argue that besides having a productive capacity to meet all true material needs, the United States has a highly diversified and intelligent working class capable of managing itself.[189] Given the fact that the United States has already undergone the process of industrialization, and has a strong democratic tradition, the United States may be in a position to create new forms of socialism.[190]

As a process, radical theory distinguishes between strategies that seek "palliative" change, which lull people into thinking significant reform has happened but always stop short of correcting the injustice, and strategies that seek structural, "incremental" change, which open up new possibilities within the existing order.[191] Revolutionary social change entails developing politically empowering forms of community association that lie between the individual and the state. These forms of community association can gradually let people get a taste of their own power by creating structural reforms that further extend popular control. As the participants create more democratic structures, the structures create more democratic participants and ever-more inclusive participation and solidarity.[192]

Radical theorists argue that change emerges from the grass roots because "the prime energy for systemic change is internal to the developing system, not exogenously imposed."[193] In its focus on the importance of social change emerging from below, some radical theorists follow not only currents in neo-Marxist analysis[194] but also feminist theory, which uses grassroots consciousness-raising as a major praxis for social change.[195] They believe that revolutionary social agents have usually emerged from those who are most marginalized by the present system.[196] It is the seeds of this new social order, "found in the interstices of liberal democratic capitalist societies today" and "already prefigured in today's society and discourse," that signal the potential for a new society.[197]

Radical theorists stress political organizing and building coalitions of the marginalized. Some of them urge long-term, creative struggle with accountability to communities of suffering people.[198] It is out of these struggles to concretely empower people that radical theory draws its politics of social change. Radicals assert that social change can be forged by sufficiently large numbers of people who have a common social position and who have a unified political discourse—a new vocabulary that contains critical elements of the old and that is able to bond groups together in common collective practice. They also agree that the development of this discourse—and accompanying values, attitudes, practices, and skills consonant with a new socioeconomic environment—is the work of generations.[199]

Radical theory does not promulgate a program for a new society so much as it tries to understand what is presently going on in capitalist societies, especially those of the late twentieth century. It contends that understanding how capitalism actually functions is a necessary first step in creating new strategies that move toward a more just social order. For if we are not clear about where we are, social policy will not address the reality of the present political and economic dynamics that shape people's lives.[200]

The preceeding discussion has outlined the major claims of the orthodox and radical economic paradigms, two interpretations of the way capitalism functions. For the orthodox paradigm, the private control of the means of production through a market economy allocates resources and distributes wealth in a way that maximizes social welfare. For conservative orthodox theorists, the unfettered nature of the capitalist economy stimulates innovation and versatility and is the best way to generate and sustain economic growth. For liberal orthodox thinkers, the task is to discern good and bad forms of state intervention in order to create a healthy capitalism so that individuals can realize maximum capital accumulation and consumption. In this understanding of socioeconomic reality, the political and cultural spheres are separate from the economic arena, which is presumed to be a private one that does not require public accountability. Consequently, such institutions as government and religion are supposed to reform or mitigate excesses of economic power and thus guarantee that the system of privately controlled capital continues to promote the commonweal at a level that no other form of economic organization possibly could.

In contrast, the radical interpretation of capitalist political economy argues that the private control of the means of production produces the social injustice of class exploitation as the necessary by-product of the system of private capital accumulation. It believes that the system of private control over capital necessitates the social reproduction of such structures as the segmented labor market and the poverty and welfare systems, among others. These in turn depend upon the structural legitimation of racism and sexism for their maintenance. The radical interpretation argues that since the economy is controlled by the few who are capitalists, the state must serve the system of capital accumulation through such measures as militarism and other corporate subsidies at the expense of the interests of most of the citizens. With such assumptions, radical theorists argue that "reforms" that keep this basic capitalist structure intact must always stop short of rectifying the injustice.

It is important to note that this debate between radical and orthodox thinkers concerning the nature of capitalism is basically a circular one and is therefore, by itself, unresolvable. Both groups believe that their confidence or lack of confidence in late twentieth-century capitalism is justified according to criteria developed within their particular paradigm, which reflects their particular worldview. Orthodox thinkers evaluate both capitalist and noncapitalist economies by orthodox criteria such as productivity and by consumer values such as the amount and variety of goods available on the market. Radical thinkers evaluate economies by how well they feed, clothe, house, provide medical care, and educate the poorest in these societies. From the orthodox point of view, radicals are idealists who do not recognize the destructive nature of socialism and the limits of what is economically, politically, and socially feasible. From the radical point of view, orthodox theory presupposes basic conditions of concrete physical well-being that often do not exist, and orthodox thinkers do not "hear" the radical acknowledgment that noncapitalist alternatives are human experiments that may go wrong, even as they feed, house, and educate those who were once poor.

This brief outline of the major differences between radical and orthodox socioeconomic theories has been necessary in order to set the stage for the ensuing discussion. The following chapters explore my contention that ambiguities and at times self-contradictions in the Catholic Church's social analyses are due to the presence of elements from these two incompatible paradigms. In particular, they are often due to the juxtaposition of a radical mode of structural analysis with orthodox, nonstructural policy prescriptions. This leads to an incoherent social ethic. For as the preceeding discussion has tried to show, if the radical insight into the capitalist system is correct, and social, political, and economic structures—including racist and sexist structures—form one interlocking system in the service of private capital accumulation, then this would render liberal policy prescriptions ineffectual. If wealth, social power, and the state are all interstructured in the service of capitalists, then socioeconomic institutions, including the state, will participate in the social reproduction of injustice in order to maintain the capitalist system. I argue that an analysis is not coherent if it views poverty as a result of this interstructuring, but also assumes the effectiveness of reforms that keep this basic interstructuring intact.

Coherent social analysis is also important because the values advocated by Catholic social teaching, such as dignified social participation, democracy in the workplace, and what Catholic documents call an option for the poor, have different meanings depending on the social theory out of which these values operate. Norms of social justice typically embody the values assumed in a particular social model as this model articulates a worldview or ideology. I argue that the premodern social theory of the Church, as well as its allegiance to the historical struggle of those who have been marginalized by capitalism, have predisposed the Roman Catholic hierarchy to assume conflicting values from both orthodox and radical social models. If it is true that incompatible social models, and therefore conflicting ideologies, are indeed present within the Roman Catholic social-justice tradition, it is imperative, as I argue in the final chapter, that moral values resolve what would otherwise remain an irreconcilable debate.

Notes

1. David Hollenbach, S.J., "Modern Catholic Teaching Concerning Justice," in *The Faith That Does Justice*, ed. John C. Haughey (New York: Paulist Press, 1977), p. 220.

2. See the preface to the "Pastoral Constitution on the Church in the Modern World," in *The Documents of Vatican II*, ed. Walter M. Abbott, S.J. (New York: America Press, 1966), pp. 199–200.

3. The term "social teaching" has come to be used about all pronouncements that popes and bishops make on issues in political economy. Although these may include such topics as marriage and family, or war and peace, this book focuses on social teaching in the specifically economic sense.

4. David Hollenbach points out that in emphasizing the congruity of Christian perspectives on justice with what can be expected from all people, the Church has methodologically minimized conflicts about justice. See *Claims in Conflict: Retrieving and Renewing the Catholic Human Rights Tradition* (New York: Paulist Press, 1979), p. 118. As we will see, this is in harmony with the cooperative values of organic social theory.

5. Organic social theory in the Roman Catholic sense frequently compares society to the human body. That is, as the organism of the body has priority over its individual limbs, so the needs of the community have priority over the needs of its individual members. Catholic organic social theory places emphasis on the temporal welfare of the community as a whole, as well as the dominance of the

spiritual over the temporal. Jacob Viner, *Religious Thought and Economic Society*, ed. Jacques Melitz and Donald Winch (Durham, N.C.: Duke University Press, 1978), p. 5. See further discussion of organic theory in Chapter Two.

6. Gregory Baum, "The Shift in Catholic Social Teaching," in *Ethics and Economics: Canada's Catholic Bishops and the Economic Crisis*, ed. Gregory Baum and Duncan Cameron (Toronto: Lorimer, 1984), pp. 67–68.

7. The hierarchical organic theory of the Catholic Church is also in conflict with a perspective found in strains of a contemporary theory, also called organic, that stresses the harmony of mutual and egalitarian relationships, especially with regard to the environment.

8. See E. Ray Canterbery, *The Making of Economics*, 2d ed. (Belmont, Calif.: Wadsworth, 1980).

9. National Conference of Catholic Bishops, "*Economic Justice for All: Catholic Social Teaching and the U.S. Economy*," Origins 16, no. 24 (November 27, 1986): 409–55 (hereafter *EJA*).

10. Beverly W. Harrison, "Response to David Hollenbach" (Paper presented at the Symposium on Theology, Ethics, and the Church, Episcopal Divinity School, Cambridge, Mass., May 5, 1986), p. 9.

11. The documents I have chosen are those statements, whether papal encyclicals, synod documents, or the letters of national bishops, that scholarly consensus has recognized as primary to the tradition of Catholic teaching on economic justice since the Industrial Revolution. These are statements that have the discussion of "the social question," or the reality of economic marginalization, clearly at their center and have been issued by either papal or episcopal bodies, often on an anniversary of the first of these documents, *Rerum novarum*. They also illustrate the ambiguities and self-contradictions I wish to explore.

The term "the social question" was coined by John XXIII in *Mater et magistra* and made popular by Paul VI in *Populorum progressio*. The papal documents central to this question are: *Rerum novarum*, *Quadragesimo anno*, *Pacem in terris*, *Mater et magistra*, *Populorum progressio*, *Octogesima adveniens*, *Laborem exercens*, and *Sollicitudo Rei Socialis*. The episcopal documents are: *Justice in the World*, the Medellin documents, the Puebla documents, *Ethical Reflections on the Economic Crisis*, and *Economic Justice for All: Catholic Social Teaching and the U.S. Economy*.

For a discussion of the classification of papal and episcopal documents see Christine E. Gudorf, *Catholic Social Teaching on Liberation*

Themes (Washington, D.C.: University Press of America, 1981), pp. xv–xviii.

12. David M. Gordon, ed., *Problems in Political Economy* (Lexington, Mass.: D. C. Heath, 1977), p. xiv.

13. Journals that contribute ongoing radical analysis include the *Review of Radical Political Economics, Monthly Review, New Left Review, Radical America, Insurgent Socialist, Socialist Review, Contemporary Marxism*. For works in socialist feminist theory see especially Carol S. Robb's delineation of this stream in feminist ethics, "A Framework for Feminist Ethics," in *Women's Consciousness, Women's Conscience*, ed. Barbara Hilkert Andolsen, Christine E. Gudorf, and Mary D. Pellauer (New York: Winston Press, 1985), pp. 229–33. See also Nancy C. M. Hartsock, *Money, Sex, and Power: Toward a Feminist Historical Materialism* (New York: Longman, 1983); Zillah R. Eisenstein, ed., *Capitalist Patriarchy and the Case for Socialist Feminism* (New York: Monthly Review Press, 1979); and Rosalind Pollak Petchesky, *Abortion and Women's Choice: The State, Sexuality and Reproductive Freedom* (New York: Longman, 1984).

For works in antiracist analysis see Manning Marable, *How Capitalism Underdeveloped Black America: Problems in Race, Political Economy and Society* (Boston: South End Press, 1983); and Cornel West, *Prophesy Deliverance: An Afro-American Revolutionary Christianity* (Philadelphia: Westminster, 1982).

14. Radical theorists offer criticisms of existing so-called socialist societies as well as capitalist ones. For example, most people writing in the major left journals in the United States and Europe like *Review of Radical Political Economics, Socialist Review*, and *New Left Review* among others have offered negative critiques of Soviet society. See also critical studies by these leading Marxist analysts: Ernest Mandel, *Marxist Economic Theory* (London: Merlin Press, 1968); Herbert Marcuse, *Soviet Marxism: A Critical Analysis* (New York: Random House, 1961); and Charles Bettelheim, *Class Struggle in the USSR: 1917–1923*, trans. Brian Pearce (New York: Monthly Review Press, 1978).

However critical they are of the USSR and other efforts to move beyond capitalism, radical theorists believe there is something to learn from these societies when they situate them in their historical contexts. Because revolutions are always historical embodiments, Marxist revolutions in peasant societies have tended to follow the contours of the prevailing culture and traditions.

15. Karl Marx analyzed capitalism. He had relatively little to say

about socialism. Works that address the goals of Marxist theory and are important in light of the prevailing misconceptions of Marx's views, especially his views of history and science, include: Karl Marx, *A Contribution to the Critique of Political Economy*, ed. Frederick Engels, trans. Samuel Moore and Edward Aveling (New York: Modern Library, 1936); Karl Marx, *Grundrisse*, ed. and trans. David McLellan (New York: Harper Torchbooks, 1972); G. A. Cohen, *Karl Marx's Theory of History: A Defense* (Princeton, N.J.: Princeton University Press, 1978), see especially pp. 326–44; Alfred Schmidt, *The Concept of Nature in Marx* (London: New Left Books, 1971); and Nicholas Lash, *A Matter of Hope: A Theologian's Reflections on the Thought of Karl Marx* (South Bend, Ind.: University of Notre Dame Press, 1982).

16. John G. Gurley, "The State of Political Economics," *American Economic Review* 61 (May 1971): 53.

17. David M. Gordon, *Theories of Poverty and Underemployment* (Lexington, Mass.: Lexington Books, 1972), p. 136. Thomas S. Kuhn explains how knowledge functions within a paradigm, or disciplinary matrix, of shared assumptions, values, and techniques. The paradigm determines which questions will be asked, and what form acceptable answers must assume. A time of crisis occurs when the paradigm cannot accommodate new data and the shared matrix begins to break down. See *The Structure of Scientific Revolutions*, 2d ed. (Chicago: University of Chicago Press, 1970).

18. Beverly W. Harrison, *Our Right to Choose: Toward a New Ethic of Abortion* (Boston: Beacon Press, 1983), pp. 94–95.

19. Gunnar Myrdal, *The Political Element in the Development of Economic Theory* (London: Routledge and K. Paul, 1953), p. 192. Myrdal also says that norms or value premises should be chosen because they are relevant to what the majority of people actually experience. He says that norms should be introduced openly, not kept hidden as tacit assumptions. Because norms or values are an essential condition of thought and affect the structure of all theory, we can only be rational "by facing our valuations, not by evading them." Bias he defines as "being directed by unacknowledged valuations." See Gunnar Myrdal, *Value in Social Theory*, ed. Paul Streeten (London: Routledge and K. Paul, 1958), pp. 51–54. For another critical evaluation of "objective" or "neutral" social science, see C. Wright Mills, *The Sociological Imagination* (New York: Oxford University Press, 1959).

20. Phyllis Deane, *The Evolution of Economic Ideas* (New York: Cambridge University Press, 1978), p. xiii. For another orthodox econo-

mist's similar analysis see Leonard Silk, *Economics in Plain English* (New York: Simon and Schuster, 1978), pp. 42–43.

21. L. S. Stavrianos, *Global Rift: The Third World Comes of Age* (New York: William Morrow, 1981), p. 455.

22. Unlike such other classical economists as David Ricardo and Karl Marx, who viewed labor power as the central source of economic value, Adam Smith argued that the source of economic value was the market. Like Ricardo and unlike Marx, Smith argued that the private ownership of the means of production within a system of free competition was the solution to class conflict. See Deane, *Evolution of Economic Ideas*, pp. 70–75, 125.

23. Karl Marx claimed that capitalism, as a way to conquer poverty, was a precondition of socialism.

24. Deane, *Evolution of Economic Ideas*, p. 215.

25. See for example, Charles E. Lindblom, *Politics and Markets* (New York: Basic Books, 1977).

26. See discussion of the organic view of society in Chapter Two

27. Max Weber later proposed that this liberal view of the nature of economic activity, and the Industrial Revolution that it condoned, also gained support from a Protestant view of sinful humanity whose redemption was evidenced in the discipline of diligence and hard work. See Max Weber, *The Protestant Ethic and the Spirit of Capitalism* (New York: Charles Scribner's Sons, 1958).

28. Adam Smith, *An Inquiry into the Nature and Causes of the Wealth of Nations*, ed. Edward Cannan (New York: Modern Library, 1937), p. 421.

29. See Deane, *Evolution of Economic Ideas*, p. 8; and E. K. Hunt and Howard Sherman, *Economics: An Introduction to Traditional and Radical Views*, 3d ed. (New York: Harper and Row, 1978), p. 199.

30. Indications of Adam Smith's critical eye toward capitalism and the oppressive roles of landlords and capitalists include his observation that "rent and profits eat up wages and the two superior orders of people oppress the inferior one." Smith also spoke against monopoly in favor of small industrial competitive capitalism. "People of the same trade seldom meet together," he said, "but conversation ends in a conspiracy against the public or in some contrivance to raise prices" (*Wealth of Nations*, vol. 2, p. 67 quoted in Deane, *Evolution of Economic Ideas*, p. 10). Denis O'Brien notes that: "While the classical writers were the earliest fully to appreciate the allocative mechanism of the market, and the power, subtlety and efficiency

of this mechanism, they were perfectly clear that it could operate only within a framework of restrictions. Such restrictions were partly legal and partly religious, moral and conventional; and they were designed to ensure the coincidence of self and community interest" (in Samuel Bowles and Herbert Gintis, *Democracy and Capitalism* [New York, Basic Books, 1986], p. 143).

31. Deane, *Evolution of Economic Ideas*, pp. 15–16. Donald F. Gordon notes that the orthodox view of the world has remained fundamentally unchanged since the eighteenth century. See "The Role of the History of Economic Thought in the Understanding of Modern Economic Theory," *American Economic Review*, May 1965, p. 124.

32. It is evident that the theory of optimal exchange is a largely unexamined presumption in the writings of orthodox economists. C. E. Ferguson says that "placing reliance upon neoclassical economic theory is a matter of faith. I personally have the faith; but at present the best I can do to convince others is to invoke the weight of . . . authority." See *The Neoclassical Theory of Production and Distribution* (London: Cambridge University Press, 1969), pp. xvii–xviii. Lester C. Thurow says that it is an "unverified assumption" that labor is paid its marginal product. But Thurow chooses to retain it because without it, "much of [orthodox] economic theory falls apart," especially theory related to human capital and its uses. See *Investment in Human Capital* (Belmont, Calif.: Wadsworth, 1970), pp. 20–22.

With regard to the orthodox view that profit is the marginal product of capital, Paul Samuelson observes that extra profits beyond the marginal product are made by monopoly. See *Economics*, 9th ed. (New York: McGraw Hill, 1973), p. 800.

33. In becoming the guiding light of orthodox theory, neoclassical economics abandoned the philosophical concerns of the classical economists (especially Adam Smith and David Ricardo) with regard to value and distribution, which included a critical eye toward the exploitation of workers by capitalists and landlords. This tradition was developed instead by Karl Marx and his followers. Deane, *Evolution of Economic Ideas*, pp. 10, 86, 106, 121, 131–33, 136.

34. Josef Steindl, "Reflections on the Present State of Economics," *Monthly Review* 36 (February 1985): 35–48.

35. Most orthodox economists insist that economics is a "pure" science and therefore ethically and politically "neutral." See George Stigler, "The Politics of Political Economists," *Quarterly Journal of Economics* 73 (November 1959): 522.

36. Milton Friedman, *Capitalism and Freedom* (Chicago: University of Chicago Press, 1962), p. 24.

37. Neoconservative apologists for orthodox theory make this a central point of their argument. See for example Michael Novak, *The American Vision: An Essay on the Future of Democratic Capitalism* (Washington, D.C.: American Enterprise Institute, 1979); Peter Berger, *The Capitalist Revolution* (New York: Basic Books, 1986); and Robert Benne, *An Ethic for Democratic Capitalism: A Moral Reassessment* (Philadelphia: Fortress Press, 1981). Novak and Benne not only argue that capitalism is the best economic system they also use the legacy of (Protestant) Christian realism, which believes that political and social power can keep economic power in check, to buttress another argument that there is a natural liason between Christian morality and capitalism. See Michael Novak, "On Needing Niebuhr Again," *Commentary* 15 (September 1972): 52–62; and Benne, *An Ethic for Democratic Capitalism*.

38. For an introduction to these views see Samuelson, *Economics*.

39. Walter W. Rostow, *The Stages of Economic Growth: A Non-Communist Manifesto* (New York: Cambridge University Press, 1960). For orthodox theory, those not in the market, either because they cannot enter it or have fallen out of it, become irrelevant. It is presumed that they are incapable of rationally allocating resources and participating in or meeting consumer demand.

40. Samuelson, *Economics*, p. 804.

41. Arthur M. Okun, "Equality and Efficiency: The Big Tradeoff," *New York Times Magazine*, July 4, 1976.

42. Ibid.

43. The best expositions of orthodox economic theory include Milton Friedman, *Essays in Positive Economics* (Chicago: University of Chicago Press, 1953); Friedman, *Capitalism and Freedom*; Ferguson, *Neoclassical Theory of Production and Distribution*; Walter Heller, *New Dimensions of Political Economy* (Cambridge: Harvard University Press, 1966); and Samuelson, *Economics*. Friedman is one of the best representatives of the laissez-faire, or conservative, movement within orthodoxy. Samuelson was until recently a proponent of "liberal-welfare" capitalism, of government intervention to mitigate the failures of market equilibrium. However, since Keynesian forms of intervention have also not answered the need for continuous economic growth, Samuelson has become more cautious about welfare economics.

44. John Maynard Keynes, who has been selectively appropriated by orthodox theory and is rarely read in toto, remarked in *The General Theory of Employment, Interest, and Money* (1936) that, while the market may be working toward the optimal advantage of all in the long run, "in the long run we are all dead!"

45. See Joseph Schumpter, *The Theory of Economic Development: An Inquiry into Profits, Capital, Credit, Interest and the Business Cycle* (Oxford: Oxford University Press, 1934), p. 21. See also Paul Samuelson, "Wages and Interests: A Modern Dissection of Marxian Economics," *American Economic Review* 47 (1957): 894.

46. Friedman, *Capitalism and Freedom*, pp. 13–15.

47. Lester Thurow, "Who Stays Up with the Sick Cow?" review of *The Capitalist Revolution* by Peter L. Berger, *New York Times Book Review*, September 7, 1986, p. 9.

48. Lindblom, *Politics and Markets*, pp. 45–50.

49. Friedman, *Capitalism and Freedom*, p. 121.

50. Lindblom, *Politics and Markets*, pp. 149–51.

51. Joseph A. Schumpter, *Capitalism, Socialism and Democracy*, 3d ed. (New York: Harper and Brothers, 1950).

52. Carl Kaysen, "The Social Significance of the Modern Corporation," *American Economic Review* 47 (May 1957): 313–14.

53. For a study of human capital analysis see Gary Becker, *Human Capital*, 2d ed. (New York: National Bureau of Economic Research, 1974).

54. Edward C. Banfield, *The Unheavenly City Revisited* (Boston: Little, Brown, 1974), chap. 4.

55. Edward C. Banfield expresses this conservative view when he says: "Our devotion to the doctrine that all men are created equal discourages any explicit recognition of class-cultural differences and leads to 'democratic'—and often misleading—formulations of problems: for example poverty as a lack of income and material resources (something external to the individual) rather than as the inability or unwillingness to take account of the future or to control impulses (something internal) (ibid., p. 60). For a similar analysis, see Arthur R. Jensen, "How Much Can We Boost I.Q. and Scholastic Achievement?" *Harvard Educational Review* 39 (Winter/Summer, 1969): 449–83; and Richard J. Herrnstein, "I.Q." *Atlantic Monthly*, September 1971, pp. 43–64.

56. In the 1930s, the systematic reality of widespread monopoly and unemployment led to the incorporation of Keynesianism into orthodox theory. Keynesianism was an attempt to deal with some-

thing less than perfect competition and full employment by using the government to help control supply and demand. Since 1936 there has been great controversy over the meaning of Keynes's work and its implications for neoclassical theory. Phyllis Deane points out that the Keynesian "heresy" was that there was no "invisible hand" to create a tendency toward self-adjustment or equilibrium in the market system, or to translate private interest into the commonweal. Keynesian macroeconomics, however, did not replace, but instead was absorbed by orthodox microeconomics and became the "special case" of the role of the government in influencing effective demand. With the new economic situation generated by World War II, orthodox microeconomic theory gained a new lease on life. In the United States, the orthodox mainstream became a marriage of laissez-faire neoclassical and Keynesian ideas without the criticisms and uncertainties that Keynes exhibited about market benevolence. See Deane, *Evolution of Economic Ideas*, pp. 182–87.

57. For a discussion of social market capitalism see J. Philip Wogaman, *The Great Economic Debate* (Philadelphia: Westminster Press, 1978), pp. 98–124.

58. Conservative economist Milton Friedman argues against government intervention and for persuasion within the free market system as the best way to attack discrimination (*Capitalism and Freedom*, pp. 108–18).

59. Thurow, "Who Stays Up with the Sick Cow?" p. 9.

60. Hunt and Sherman, *Economics: An Introduction to Traditional and Radical Views*, p. 486. Milton Friedman is known for his statement that the "natural rate" of unemployment is the rate that does not increase inflation.

61. For example, neoconservative Michael Novak wishes that Catholic social teaching would encourage people to develop the discipline they need to create wealth through capitalist institutions. See *The Spirit of Democratic Capitalism* (New York: Simon and Schuster, 1982), p. 248.

62. Zillah R. Eisenstein, "The Sexual Politics of the New Right: Understanding the Crisis of Liberalism for the 1980's," in *Feminist Theory: A Critique of Ideology*, ed. Nannerl O. Keohane, Michelle Z. Rosaldo, and Barbara C. Gelpi (Chicago: University of Chicago Press, 1982), pp. 81–84.

63. Studies that articulate neoliberal policy include: Lester C. Thurow, *The Zero Sum Society* (New York: Basic Books, 1980); Seymour Zucher et al., *The Reindustrialization of America* (New York:

McGraw Hill, 1982); and Felix Rohaytyn, *The Twenty Year Century: Essays on Economics and Public Finance* (New York: Random House, 1983).

64. Randall Rosenberg, "The Neoliberal Club," *Esquire*, February 1982, pp. 37–46.

65. Gerald E. Peabody, "Scientific Paradigms and Economics: An Introduction," *Radical Review of Economics* 3, no. 2 (July 1971): 7–8.

66. Joan Robinson as quoted in Ronald L. Meek, *Economics and Ideology and Other Essays* (London: Chapman and Hall, 1967), p. 196.

67. Paul Streeten, Introduction to *Value in Social Theory*, by Gunnar Myrdal (London: Routledge and K. Paul, 1958), p. xlii.

68. Myrdal, *Value in Social Theory*, p. 231.

69. There are various groups that identify themselves with the "radical" position and are anti-Marxist, such as left anarchists, left environmentalists, left spiritualists, utopian socialists, radical feminists.

70. Joe Holland, "Marxist Class Analysis in American Society Today," in *Theology in the Americas*, ed. Sergio Torres and John Eagleson (Maryknoll, N.Y.: Orbis, 1976), p. 327. Some of the ways twentieth-century radical theory draws upon Marxism will be evident in the subsequent discussion.

71. Carol S. Robb outlines the diversity in feminist theory with regard to defining the structures that are the sources of women's oppression. Besides socialist feminism, she delineates three other divergent feminist social–political theories: radical feminism, which posits the source of women's oppression as the system of male dominance that is to be dealt with by withdrawal into a matriarchal society; sexrolism, which posits the cause of women's oppression as culturally created gender roles that are to be dealt with through education and achieving legal rights within the current system; Marxist–Leninist feminism, which posits the dominance of the advanced capitalist system as the main source of women's oppression, but does not wish to see the sphere of reproduction as a secondary cause. Unlike socialist feminists who advocate democratic coalition building, Robb says this group has not sufficiently critiqued the bureaucratic centralism in Marxist–Leninism. Robb argues that the analysis of women's oppression fundamentally affects the way the problem is posed and dealt with, and that feminist values have different meaning depending on the social–political theory out of which they operate. See "A Framework for Feminist Ethics," pp. 211–33.

72. Arthur F. McGovern, *Marxism: An American Christian Perspective* (Maryknoll, N.Y.: Orbis, 1980), p. 72.

73. Hunt and Sherman, *Economics: An Introduction to Traditional and Radical Views*, p. 60. See also Gordon, *Theories of Poverty and Underemployment*, pp. 54–55; Deane, *Evolution of Economic Ideas*, p. 126; and Richard D. Wolff and Stephen A. Resnick, *Economics: Marxian versus Neoclassical* (Baltimore, Md.: Johns Hopkins University Press, 1987), p. 21.

74. Gordon, ed., *Problems in Political Economy*, pp. xiv–xv. Some orthodox thinkers, Peter Berger, for example, also operate with explicit theories of politics and culture. But contrary to the radical analysis of capitalist political economy as one system of organically and mutually interacting elements, Berger's orthodox analysis of capitalist culture claims to demonstrate that capitalist economic relationships exist in relative isolation from most other social relations and institutions. See Berger, *The Capitalist Revolution*. For an analysis of how heterosexism is utilized by capitalism, see Gerre Goodman, George Lakey, Judy Lashof, and Erica Thorne, *No Turning Back: Lesbian and Gay Liberation for the 80's* (Philadelphia: New Society Publishers, 1983), esp. pp. 37–44.

75. Josephine Donovan, *Feminist Theory: The Intellectual Traditions of American Feminism* (New York: Frederick Ungar, 1985), p. 183. Perhaps the most well-known demonstration of how women's moral processing is contextually oriented is found in Carol Gilligan's *In a Different Voice* (Cambridge: Harvard University Press, 1982). Gilligan argues that women see a humanly interconnected world and reason according to the logic of relationships. This is in contrast to the mainstream view that sees the world in terms of separation, individual rights, and a hierarchical system of rules and privileges.

76. Catharine A. MacKinnon, "Feminism, Marxism, Method and the State: An Agenda for Theory," in *Feminist Theory: A Critique of Ideology*, ed. Keohane, Rosaldo, and Gelpi, p. 22.

77. Donovan, *Feminist Theory*, p. 180. See also Rosemary Radford Ruether, *New Woman, New Earth* (New York: Seabury Press, 1975), pp. 194–96.

78. Samuel Bowles and Herbert Gintis, "Socialist Revolution in the United States: Goals and Means," in *The Capitalist System*, 2d ed., ed. Richard C. Edwards, Michael Reich, and Thomas E. Weisskopf (Englewood Cliffs, N.J.: Prentice-Hall, 1978), pp. 522–23.

79. Gurley, "State of Political Economics," pp. 53–68.

80. Bowles and Gintis, *Democracy and Capitalism*, p. 36.

81. Gary W. Nickerson, "Introduction," *Review of Radical Political Economics* 16, no. 4 (Winter 1984): iv.

82. Hunt and Sherman, *Economics: An Introduction to Traditional and Radical Views*, p. 173.

83. Gordon, *Theories of Poverty and Underemployment*, p. 64.

84. Hunt and Sherman, *Economics: An Introduction to Traditional and Radical Views*, p. 294; and Gordon, ed., *Problems in Political Economy*, p. 341.

85. Gordon, ed., *Problems in Political Economy*, p. 25.

86. Gordon, *Theories of Poverty and Underemployment*, p. 50.

87. Various neo-Marxist understandings of the role of the state include the state as instrument of class rule, as organizationally autonomous but necessary guarantor of capital accumulation, or as arena for political class struggle. For overviews of these debates see Bob Jessop, "Recent Theories of the Capitalist State," *Cambridge Journal of Economics* 1 (1977): 353–73; and Martin Carnoy, *The State and Political Theory* (Princeton, N.J.: Princeton University Press, 1984). For an overview of the recent discussion among comparative social scientists that argues for a more independent role for the state in shaping the political capacity of the dominant class and other groups to direct the socioeconomic order, see Theda Skocpol, "Introduction," in *Bringing the State Back In*, ed. Peter B. Evans, Dietrich Rueschemeyer, and Theda Skocpol (New York: Cambridge University Press, 1985), pp. 3–37.

88. For Marxist critiques of historical Marxism, see n. 15.

89. Richard C. Edwards, "The Logic of Capitalist Accumulation," in *The Capitalist System*, ed. Edwards, Reich, and Weisskopf, p. 101.

90. Ibid.

91. Quoted in Gar Alperovitz and Jeff Faux, *Rebuilding America* (New York: Pantheon, 1984), p. 241.

92. Steven Hyman and Frank Roosevelt, "The Marxian Paradigm," in *Problems in Political Economy*, ed. Gordon, p. 22.

93. Alperovitz and Faux, *Rebuilding America*, p. 12.

94. Nancy S. Barrett, "How the Study of Women Has Restructured the Discipline of Economics," in *A Feminist Perspective in the Academy*, ed. Elizabeth Langland and Walter Gove (Chicago: University of Chicago Press, 1981), p. 106.

While much has been made of the cooperative and supposedly democratic work model of Japanese capitalism, which is thought to bypass this inconsistency, William K. Tabb argues that this "co-operation is in fact *conditioned* on a rigid adherence to hierarchy" and it functions to maintain centralized authority. In Japanese business, union officials are also part of the management structure. Tabb describes this form of worker/employer organization in terms reminiscent of the corporative social model (see Chapter Two). He also says that this work model encompasses no more than 20 percent of the work force, and that Japan has a larger "sweatshop contracting system" with the Korean minority at the bottom. Tabb argues that this secondary labor force is a clue to Japan's success. See "Competitiveness and Workers," *Christianity and Crisis* 47, no. 15 (October 26, 1987): 364–66. In addition, most Japanese women are not in the paid labor force and remain at home. Japan illustrates how structures of racism, classism, and sexism are important factors in the making of capitalist profit.

95. Nancy Bancroft, "Women in the Cutback Economy," in *Women's Consciousness, Women's Conscience*, ed. Andolsen, Gudorf, and Pellauer, p. 27.

96. David M. Gordon, "Digging Up the Roots: The Economic Determinants of Social Problems," in *Problems in Political Economy*, ed. Gordon, pp. 16–21.

97. In order to understand how the bishops arrived at such a figure, consider that the U.S. Bureau of the Census, using the Social Security Administration's "minimum subsistance income" of $5,008 as a gauge, classified 24 million Americans as poor, or nearly 12 percent of the population in 1974. However, the U.S. Department of Labor Statistics has adopted a "lower than moderate" income as an index of poverty—under $10,000 for a family of four in 1975—which was then roughly 30 percent of the U.S. population. See U.S. Bureau of the Census, "Money, Income and Poverty Status of Families and Persons in the U.S., 1974" (Advance Report), Current Population Reports, Series P-60, No. 99, July 1975; and David M. Gordon, "Poverty and Welfare," in *Problems in Political Economy*, ed. Gordon, pp. 274–75.

98. John C. Raines and Donna C. Day-Lower, *Modern Work and Human Meaning* (Philadelphia: Westminster Press, 1986), p. 131.

99. Alperovitz and Faux, *Rebuilding America*, pp. 62–63, 67. These economists also say that between 1960 and 1975 the very rich increased by 8 percent, while the poorest group increased by 17 percent (p. 62).

100. Samuel Bowles and Herbert Gintis, "Socialist Revolution in the United States: Goals and Means," in *The Capitalist System*, ed. Edwards, Reich, and Weisskopf, p. 524.

101. A radical understanding of class includes cultural as well as economic aspects of oppression. Radical theory posits that capitalism perpetuates and even worsens precapitalist sources of domination such as racism and sexism. It objects to the narrowness of the liberal concern with the despotic state and the concern of traditional Marxism of breaking economic domination through elite cadre politics that also continue and worsen these sources of domination. See Nancy Hartsock, "Feminist Theory and Revolutionary Strategy," in *Capitalist Patriarchy and the Case for Socialist Feminism*, ed. Zillah R. Eisenstein (New York: Monthly Review Press, 1979), pp. 67–73; and Iris Young, "Beyond the Unhappy Marriage: A Critique of Dual Systems Theory," in *Women and Revolution*, ed. Lydia Sargent (Boston: South End Press, 1981), pp. 44–65. Bowles and Gintis speak about the inadequacy of class (economic exploitation) as the sole location of the exercise of power in capitalist society. They prefer to speak about the "heterogeneity of power," which is not reducible to a single source or structure. See *Democracy and Capitalism*, p. 23.

102. Gordon, *Theories of Poverty and Underemployment*, pp. 88, 112.

103. Ibid., p. 91.

104. Hunt and Sherman, *Economics: An Introduction to Traditional and Radical Views*, pp. 134–135.

105. "Scandals Force Schools to Consider Ethics," *Bangor Daily News*, April 3, 1987, p. 29. Gerry Spence claims that corporate crime in America is over ten times greater than the combined larcenies, robberies, burglaries, and auto thefts committed by individuals. See his book, *With Justice for None: Destroying an American Myth* (New York: Times Books, 1989).

106. Bowles and Gintis, *Democracy and Capitalism*, p. 195.

107. Deane, *Evolution of Economic Ideas*, p. 150.

108. For an explanation of monopoly that draws on government documentation and other sources see Hunt and Sherman, *Economics: An Introduction to Traditional and Radical Views*, esp. pp. 238–51. For a brief introduction to monopoly in the food, auto, and oil industries see pp. 473–80.

109. Ibid., pp. 512–17, 546.

110. Ibid., pp. 249–50.

111. Thomas E. Weisskopf, "The Current Economic Crisis in Historical Perspective," *Socialist Review* 11 (May–June 1981): 15.

112. Hunt and Sherman, *Economics: An Introduction to Traditional and Radical Views*, p. 440.

113. In the mid-1970s the wealthiest 298 U.S. corporations earned 40 percent of their entire profit in the Third World (ibid., p. 541).

114. Since over 50 percent of the world's population cannot enter the capitalist market, the expansion of capitalist development always requires the use of force. See Lee Cormie, "The U.S. Bishops on Capitalism," Working papers of the American Academy of Religion (1985), pp. 16–19.

Likewise Richard J. Barnet and Ronald E. Müller claim that capitalist development in the Third World may enlarge the middle strata, but "60% of the world's population will be relatively untouched by the new wealth of the once poor nations." See *Global Reach: The Power of the Multinational Corporations* (New York: Simon and Schuster, 1974), p. 209. Even neoconservative Michael Novak acknowledges that the capitalist system has no way of bringing those who live on less than $1,000 annual income—a substantial and growing number of the world's population—into the capitalist market. See *Spirit of Democratic Capitalism*, p. 109. For documentation on the worsening situation of Third World women, once vital to a rural economy, with the advent of capitalist "development," see Ester Boserup, *Women's Role in Economic Development* (New York: St. Martin's Press, 1974); Jackie M. Smith, ed., *Women, Faith and Economic Justice* (Philadelphia, Westminster Press, 1985), especially pp. 13–20; and ISIS Women's International Information and Communication Service, *Women in Development: A Resource Guide for Organization and Action* (Santa Cruz, Calif.: New Society Publishers, 1987).

115. Hunt and Sherman, *Economics: An Introduction to Traditional and Radical Views*, pp. 444, 550. Other works pertinent to this discussion, and not necessarily by scholars identified as radical, include: Michael T. Klare, *American Arms Supermarket* (Austin: University of Texas Press, 1984); and Lars Schoultz, *National Security and U.S. Policy Toward Latin America* (Princeton, N.J.: Princeton University Press, 1987).

116. Seymour Melman quoted in Lee Cormie, "The U.S. Bishops on Capitalism," pp. 14–16.

117. Hunt and Sherman, *Economics: An Introduction to Traditional and Radical Views*, p. 441. The Reagan administration spent over $300 billion on the military, more than 50 percent of federal income tax revenues (Jim Hug, S.J., "UN Crisis, US Crisis," *Center Focus* 74 [August 1986]: 2). In addition, the doubling of the U.S. national debt

from $914 billion in 1980 to more than $2 trillion in 1986 results more from growth in military expenditures than any other factor. See Robert F. Drinan, S.J., review of *State of the World 1986: A Worldwatch Institute Report on Progress Toward a Sustainable Society*, ed. Linda Starke, *National Catholic Reporter*, September 19, 1986, p. 19.

118. Bowles and Gintis, *Democracy and Capitalism*, pp. 66–91.

119. Ibid., p. 438. It is interesting to note the great caution with which the U.S. government is responding to current changes in the USSR and Eastern Europe. Obviously, the government has more invested in the cold war than concern about actual Soviet expansionism. It is possible that the drug war and the war over oil are on the rise to replace the cold war as a major justification for U.S. foreign policy and continued U.S. military spending.

120. See Amata Miller, IHM, "ABC's of Taxes: A NETWORK Primer on Tax Fairness," *Connections*, May/June 1990, pp. 1–6.

121. See Richard B. DuBoff, "If a Recession Strikes, It Could Be a Whopper," *In These Times*, December 7–13, 1988, p. 7, and Drinan, review of *State of the World 1986*, p. 19.

122. For this discussion I am indebted to Walden Bello and Claudio Saunt, "International Debt Crisis, Year Five," *Christianity and Crisis* 47, no. 17 (November 23, 1987); Penny Lernoux, *In Banks We Trust* (New York: Penguin Books, 1986); and Teresa Hayter and Catharine Watson, *Aid: Rhetoric and Reality* (London: Pluto Press, 1985), pp. 22–36.

123. Jaime Wright, "Against Debt and Despair," *Christianity and Crisis* 47, no. 17 (November 23, 1987): 410.

124. Bello and Saunt, "International Debt Crisis, Year Five," p. 404. Meanwhile it is estimated that the private sector of every major Latin American debtor nation except Brazil has enough assets abroad to pay off all foreign debt. See James S. Henry, "Poor Man's Debt, Rich Man's Loot," *Washington Post National Weekly Edition*, December 19–25, 1988, p. 24.

Teresa Hayter and Catharine Watson, in their detailed study of the international system of "aid," discuss why these nations do not simply repudiate their debts or, through a debtors' cartel, use their potential collective power to destroy the western banking system in order to extract better terms from the lenders. The most fundamental reason seems to be that ruling elites do not wish to close off their well-established escape routes to lucrative jobs on Wall Street. They comment: "The absence of open defaults is in a sense merely an illustration of the pre-eminence of class over national interests" (*Aid: Rhetoric and Reality*, p. 34).

As for the International Monetary Fund (IMF) and the World Bank, which along with the private commercial banks, are the major First World institutions responsible for international short-term and long-term financing of loans, Hayter and Watson say, "There is no possibility that the World Bank and the IMF will support policies that are not at least compatible with the perceived interests of the ruling class in the major capitalist powers which finance them" (p. 249).

125. Bello and Saunt, "International Debt Crisis, Year Five," p. 407.

126. Gordon, *Theories of Poverty and Underemployment*, pp. 88–89. Bowles and Gintis show how the employer exercises significant power over the employee by comparing the situation of the employee with that of the independent contractor. In the case of the employee, the employer does not engage in a mutual exchange with him or her but determines the content of the exchange itself (*Democracy and Capitalism*, p. 76).

127. David M. Gordon, Richard Edwards, and Michael Reich, *Segmented Work, Divided Workers: The Historical Transformation of Labor in the United States* (New York: Cambridge University Press, 1982).

128. Gordon, *Theories of Poverty and Underemployment*, p. 94.

129. Gordon, Edwards, and Reich, *Segmented Work, Divided Workers*, p. 204.

130. The minimum wage has been frozen at $3.35 per hour since 1981 and will increase only to $3.80 per hour in 1990 and $4.25 per hour in 1991.

131. Gordon, *Theories of Poverty and Underemployment*, p. 74.

132. Ibid., p. 78. See also Iris Young, "Beyond the Unhappy Marriage: A Critique of Dual Systems Theory," in *Women and Revolution*, ed. Sargent, p. 58.

133. Gordon, Edwards, and Reich, *Segmented Work, Divided Workers*, p. 204.

134. Ibid., p. 214.

135. Gordon, ed., *Problems in Political Economy*, p. 61, n. 42.

136. Gordon, *Theories of Poverty and Underemployment*, p. 90.

137. Firdaus Jhabvala, "A Critique of Reformist Solutions to Discrimination," in *Problems in Political Economy*, ed. Gordon, p. 196.

138. Gordon, Edwards, and Reich, *Segmented Work, Divided Workers*, pp. 222–27.

139. During this time there was also an absolute decline of more than 450,000 jobs paying high wages. See Danny Collum, "The Crash of '87," *Sojourners* 17 (January 1988): 4; and Barry Bluestone and Bennett Harrison, "The Great American Job Machine: The Proliferation of Low Wage Employment in the U.S. Economy," Study prepared for the Joint Economic Committee, December 1986, pp. 43–44. This escalation of low-wage work, as well as the lack of available low-income housing, helps to explain some of the increase in homeless people in the United States. The homeless are estimated to be about 3 million children, women, and men, and of these 20 to 30 percent are employed. Many fully employed people cannot afford housing because since 1981 the federal government has cut revenue for low-income housing by 75 percent—from $32 billion to $8 billion. In the Lehigh Valley, which includes three typical communities in Pennsylvania (Allentown, Bethlehem, and Easton), the average two-bedroom apartment rents for $502 a month. Assuming affordability means 25 percent of a family's income on housing, a typical family must earn $25,000 to afford the average two-bedroom apartment. With jobs that pay the minimum wage even families willing to spend two-thirds of their income on housing cannot afford it. See Lucy Poulin, "Homeless in America: A Summary," *This Time* 13, no. 1 (Winter 1989): 1–10; and the Lehigh Valley Coalition on Affordable Housing, "Some Facts About Homelessness in the Lehigh Valley," 520 East Broad Street, Bethlehem, Pa. 18018, August 29, 1989.

140. Bluestone and Harrison, "Great American Job Machine," p. 6.

141. Michael Reich, "The Economics of Racism," in *Problems in Political Economy*, ed. Gordon, pp. 183–88.

142. Steven Shulman, "Competition and Racial Discrimination: The Employment Effects of Reagan's Labor Market Policies," *Review of Radical Political Economics* 16, no. 4 (Winter 1984): 125–26.

143. Harold Baron, "The Demand for Black Labor," in *The Capitalist System*, ed. Edwards, Reich, and Weisskopf, p. 378.

144. Michael Reich, "The Economics of Racism," in *Problems in Political Economy*, ed. Gordon, p. 185; and Robert Cherry, "Economic Theories of Racism," in *Problems in Political Economy*, ed. Gordon, pp. 174–75.

145. "Rise in Poverty from '79–'82 Is Found in U.S.," *New York Times*, February 23, 1983, sec. A.

146. See William Julius Wilson, *The Declining Significance of Race* (Chicago: University of Chicago Press, 1978); and *The Truly Disad-*

vantaged (Chicago: University of Chicago Press, 1987). The title of Wilson's earlier book must be understood in relative terms. His point in both studies is that specific policies, including affirmative action, benefit only middle-strata blacks while poor blacks remain increasingly isolated. In underscoring the importance of class in the discussion of racism, Wilson moves his analysis in a radical direction. However, his policy prescriptions, like increased education and retraining programs, remain within the orthodox paradigm.

147. Manuel Febres, "Racism in the U.S.A.," in *Theology in the Americas*, ed. Torres and Eagleson, p. 184.

148. Gordon, ed., *Problems in Political Economy*, p. 149.

149. For example, blacks earned 61 percent of what whites earned in 1950, but in 1962, despite the civil rights movement, black income had deteriorated to 55 percent of white income (Hunt and Sherman, *Economics: An Introduction to Traditional and Radical Views*, p. 137). The U.S. bishops report that in 1986 black income was 55 percent of whites (*EJA* 181).

150. Baron, "The Demand for Black Labor," in *The Capitalist System*, ed. Edwards, Reich, and Weisskopf, pp. 374–78.

151. Reich, "The Economics of Racism," in *Problems in Political Economy*, ed. Gordon, p. 185.

152. Even though Marx and Engel's writings acknowledge that sexual domination preceded capitalism, some Marxist and socialist feminists critique Marx's use of class oppression as being "gender blind" or unable to identify gender oppression. Hence the traditional concept of class is insufficient to explain women's specific oppression. Iris Young suggests that by using the Marxian category of division of labor, which is more accurate than class analysis, feminist theory can utilize the Marxian method in analyzing the social relations of capitalist production in a gender-specific way. See Iris Young, "Beyond the Unhappy Marriage: A Critique of Dual Systems Theory," in *Women and Revolution*, ed. Sargent, pp. 50–52.

153. Michelle Russell, "Women, Work and Politics in the U.S.," in *Theology in the Americas*, ed. Torres and Eagleson, pp. 344–45.

154. Eloise Thomas, "Myths and Facts of Women and Work," *Probe* 14 (January–February 1986): 7. While women earned 64 cents for every dollar a man earned in 1964, women earned 59.7 cents for every dollar a man earned in 1987 (*Bangor Daily News*, April 2, 1987, p. 11). See also Francis D. Blau and Wallace D. Henricks, "Occupational Segregation by Sex," *Journal of Human Resources* 14 (Spring 1979): 197–210; and Heidi Hartman, "Capitalist Patriarchy and Job

Segregation by Sex," in *Capitalist Patriarchy and the Case for Socialist Feminism*, ed. Eisenstein, pp. 206–48, for a historical analysis of women's oppression under capitalism.

155. Thurow, *Zero Sum Society*, p. 19. Meanwhile women in the Third World, once vital to a rural economy, also have experienced decline with the advent of capitalist "development." Annette Fuentes and Barbara Ehrenreich document the situation of women in the "global factory" where such places as Taiwan, Singapore, Hong Kong, and South Korea allow corporations to make huge profits through the cheap labor of sixteen- to twenty-five-year-old women. As is the usual case with uneven capitalist "development," the GNP increases while the majority of the people grow poor. See *Women in the Global Factory*, pamphlet no. 2. Institute for New Communications, 853 Broadway, Room 905, New York, N.Y. 10003.

156. Ruth Spitz, "Women and Labor: Unfinished Revolution," *Democratic Left* 14 (September–October 1986): 15–17.

157. Hunt and Sherman, *Economics: An Introduction to Traditional and Radical Views*, p. 147.

158. Donovan, *Feminist Theory*, p. 80; and Rosemary Radford Ruether, "Home and Work: Women's Role and the Transformation of Values," *Theological Studies* 36 (December 1975): 647–59.

159. Hunt and Sherman, *Economics: An Introduction to Traditional and Radical Views*, p. 315.

160. Ibid., pp. 53–54. For a historical analysis that argues that gender oppression was the primary oppression and provided the pattern for a subsequent race and class oppression see Gerda Lerner, *The Creation of Patriarchy* (New York: Oxford University Press, 1986).

161. Consequently some feminists believe that there is no true feminist movement without an anticapitalist movement that points to the injustice of women's dual role. See Wendy Darvasy and Judith Van Allen, "Fighting the Feminization of Poverty," *Review of Radical Political Economics* 16, no. 4 (Winter 1984): 96. See also Robb, "A Framework for Feminist Ethics," esp. pp. 226–31.

162. Edwards, Reich, and Weisskopf, eds., *The Capitalist System*, pp. 331–41.

163. Thomas, "Myths and Facts of Women and Work," p. 7.

164. For a revealing study of sexism in public policy see Nancy Folbre, "The Pauperization of Motherhood: Patriarchy and Public Policy in the United States," *Review of Radical Political Economics* 16, no. 4 (Winter 1984): 68–83. It is interesting to note that the family in orthodox social theory is treated as an organic whole in which

the altruism of the head is supposed to insure the equitable allocation of family resources. This is in complete contradistinction to the equitable allocation of market resources, which is dependent on individual self-interest. See Bowles and Gintis, *Democracy and Capitalism*, pp. 106–8. In this we see that orthodox theory retained the model of the family inherent in organic (feudal) social theory.

165. Sheila Rowbotham, "Woman's Consciousness, Man's World," in *The Capitalist System*, ed. Edwards, Reich, and Weisskopf, p. 356.

166. It seems that women are becoming increasingly aware of this situation. A 1986 Gallup poll found that 56 percent of the women interviewed reported that they identified with the feminist movement. It also found that 65 percent of the black women respondents identified themselves with feminism, and that as class position *decreased*, the percentage of women who identified themselves as feminists *increased*. Nancy Fraser, "Toward a New Feminist Agenda: The Primacy of Class" (Paper presented at the Philosophy Visiting Lecture Series, University of Maine, April 21, 1987).

167. Gordon, *Theories of Poverty and Underemployment*, p. 112.

168. Lester C. Thurow, "Education and Economic Equality," in *Problems in Political Economy*, ed. Gordon, p. 229.

169. Hunt and Sherman, *Economics: An Introduction to Traditional and Radical Views*, p. 289. The authors point out that there has been no reduction in inequality between these groups since 1910.

170. For example, theorists note that the perennial gap between white and black median family income widened between 1970 and 1980, even before the Reagan administration. Most blacks today remain isolated in a vast underclass where unemployment can run well over 50 percent. Reflecting the declining situation of blacks is a 1985 U.S. Census Bureau figure that put the poverty rate of black children under six at 51.5 percent—an all-time high. See Wilson, *The Truly Disadvantaged*, p. 82; John Bickerman and Robert Greenstein, "High and Dry on the Poverty Plateau," *Christianity and Crisis* 45, no. 17 (October 28, 1985): 411–12; and Jim Wallis, "America's Original Sin: The Legacy of White Racism," *Sojourners* 16, no. 10 (November 1987): 16.

171. Barrett, "How the Study of Women Has Restructured the Discipline of Economics," p. 106. Samuel Bowles and Herbert Gintis show that the correlation between education and income level is a false correlation. The real correlation, done with orthodox regression analysis, is between socioeconomic background and education

levels. See *Schooling in Capitalist America: Educational Reform and the Contradictions of Economic Life* (New York: Basic Books, 1976).

172. Thurow, "Education and Economic Equality," in *Problems in Political Economy*, ed. Gordon, p. 229.

173. Sheila Rowbotham, "Woman's Consciousness, Man's World," in *The Capitalist System*, ed. Edwards, Reich, and Weisskopf, p. 356.

174. Samuel Bowles, "Unequal Education and the Social Division of Labor," in *Problems in Political Economy*, ed. Gordon, p. 250.

175. Ibid., p. 240.

176. Gordon, *Theories of Poverty and Underemployment*, p. 126.

177. To get an idea of the number of poor people in the United States, it is important to remember that there are two ways of measuring poverty. The Social Security Administration has set a bottom line for calculating poverty (income under $5,000 for family of four in 1974), which put about 12 percent of the population (or 24 million) under that line. But the Bureau of Labor Statistics has adopted a "lower than moderate" income as an index of poverty (under $10,000 in 1975) which put about 30 percent of the population in poverty. See David M. Gordon, "Poverty and Welfare," in *Problems in Political Economy*, ed. Gordon, pp. 274–75.

The last year the Bureau of Labor Statistics calculated a lower than moderate income level for an urban family of four was 1981. After this year, the budget cuts of the Reagan administration prevented gathering these statistics (U.S. Department of Commerce, Bureau of the Census, telephone communication, May 23, 1990). In 1981 the lower than moderate income as an index of poverty was $15,323 as compared to the Social Security Administration level of poverty which was $8, 450 for a nonfarm family of four. See Ruth Sidel, *Women and Children Last: The Plight of Poor Women in Affluent America* (New York: Penguin Books, 1986), p. 10. During 1981, 44 million children, women, and men lived in families that had total incomes of less than $15,000. Out of a U.S. population of 227,157,000, this is about 20 percent of the population. It is also important to note that in 1981, 114 million people, or over half the population, earned incomes of less than $15,000 (U.S. Department of Commerce, Income Branch of the Census Bureau, telephone communication, May 24, 1990). In 1986, the U.S. bishops estimated 53 to 63 million Americans as needy or poor, or about 25 percent of the population (*EJA* 16).

Consider also that Aid to Families with Dependent Children (AFDC) payments are calculated on the (lower) Social Security Administration's index of poverty "but average only 53% of this federal poverty line." No pretense exists that AFDC is designed to keep families out of poverty. See Nancy Folbre, "The Pauperization of Motherhood," p. 82. The U.S. bishops also note that the combined benefits of AFDC and food stamps comes to less than three-quarters of the official poverty level (*EJA* 212).

178. Howard M. Wachtel, "Looking at Poverty from a Radical Perspective," in *Problems in Political Economy*, ed. Gordon, p. 308.

179. Alperovitz and Faux, *Rebuilding America*, pp. 7–8.

180. Herbert J. Gans, "The Functions of Poverty," in *Problems in Political Economy*, ed. Gordon, p. 313.

181. Francis Fox Piven and Richard A. Cloward, "Regulating the Poor," in *Problems in Political Economy*, ed. Gordon, p. 339.

182. Ibid., p. 338.

183. Wachtel, "Looking at Poverty from a Radical Perspective," in *Problems in Political Economy*, ed. Gordon, esp. pp. 309–10; and Steve Max, "New Alliance Between the Middle Class and the Poor," *Democratic Left* 17 (May–August 1987): 3.

184. Streeten, Introduction to Myrdal's *Value in Social Theory*, pp. xl, xxviii. See also Steindl, "Reflections on the Present State of Economics," p. 47.

185. Organizing Committee of Detroit 1975 Theology in Americas Conference, "Contextualization of North American Theology," *Theology in the Americas*, ed. Torres and Eagleson, p. 435.

186. For example, even the best of these efforts to build post-capitalist societies have not been able to democratize the arena of reproduction and domestic labor. Radical theorists point out that these efforts have been severely limited by the struggle to survive within a global capitalist system. Nevertheless, whatever the seriousness of their defects, radical theorists contend that some postcapitalist economies have generated alternative experiments from which people may continue to learn. Radical theorists caution against a dismissal of these efforts without a consideration of their historical context. See Harrison, *Making the Connections*, pp. 71–74.

187. Bowles and Gintis, *Democracy and Capitalism*, p. 177.

188. Ibid., p. 518. However Beverly W. Harrison cautions that while racism, sexism, and classism are relevant to every social dynamic, no construct ever exhausts reality. Since analytic categories can be reified, it is important that social theorists be accountable to concrete human suffering, never to theoretical constructs per se. See her statement in *Theology in the Americas*, ed. Torres and Eagleson, pp. 367–73.

189. Samuel Bowles and Herbert Gintis, "Socialist Revolution in

the United States: Goals and Means," in *The Capitalist System*, ed. Edwards, Reich, and Weisskopf, pp. 523, 534.

190. Indeed, the liberal tradition, while part of the problem, is also part of the solution because it nurtures a love for individual choice and agency against the authoritarianism of the state. Bowles and Gintis believe that democratic socialism may be considered a synthesis of Jeffersonian and traditional Marxian views. It is true that the former underestimated the undemocratic power of capital, and the latter underestimated the undemocratic power of collective ownership through state bureaucracy. But Jefferson was committed to the decentralized control of the productive apparatus, and Marx recognized that production is social and cannot take the form of individual private property. A synthesis of these understandings would mark the end of the "two century old debate between liberals and socialists concerning the nature of property" (ibid., pp. 177–78).

191. Denis Goulet, "Sufficiency for All: The Basic Mandate of Development and Social Economics," *Review of Social Economy* 36, no. 3 (December 1978): 243–61. Marvin M. Ellison's analysis of the body of Goulet's work, however, concludes that in the development–liberationist debate, Goulet would fall on the development side of the argument. See *The Center Cannot Hold: The Search for a Global Economy of Justice* (Washington, D.C.: University Press of America, 1983), pp. 105–53.

192. Radicals see this "democratic dynamic" as a true move toward democratic participation and a move away from representative government that is inherently hostile to decentralized autonomous communities. See Bowles and Gintis, *Democracy and Capitalism*, pp. 136, 139, 140, 186.

193. Gordon, *Theories of Poverty and Underemployment*, p. 86.

194. In this radical theorists follow such neo-Marxists as Antonio Gramsci, most well known for his understanding that authentic socialism will not occur until it achieves cultural hegemony. Against the economic determinism and class reductionism of some orthodox Marxists, Gramsci held that the economic contradictions of the capitalist system will not automatically lead to revolution. Rather, social change will only occur if people recognize their situation and act together in solidarity. See Bob Jessop, *The Capitalist State: Marxist Theories and Methods* (New York: New York University Press, 1982), pp. 142–52; and Gregory Baum, *The Social Imperative* (New York: Paulist Press, 1979), pp. 194–95.

195. MacKinnon, "Feminism, Marxism, Method and the State,"

in *Feminist Theory: A Critique of Ideology,* ed. Keohane, Rosaldo, and Gelpi, pp. 56–77.

196. This perspective of radical analysis is evidenced, for example, in the work of revisionist labor historians who are uncovering a variety of resistance movements indigenous to labor's history. Just because orthodox theory, in its focus on the individual and the state, eclipses cultural and community dynamics does not mean that they do not exist. See David Montgomery, *Workers' Control in America* (New York: Cambridge University Press, 1979); Herbert Gutman, *Work, Culture and Society in Industrializing America* (New York: Knopf, 1976); James R. Green, *The World of the Worker: Labor in 20th Century America,* ed. Eric Foner (New York: Hill and Wang, 1978); and James R. Green, ed., *Workers' Struggles, Past and Present* (Philadelphia: Temple University Press, 1983).

197. Bowles and Gintis, *Democracy and Capitalism,* pp. 26, 185.

198. See Michael Albert, *What Is to Be Undone: A Modern Revolutionary Discussion of Classical Left Ideologies* (Boston: Porter Sargent, 1974); and Michael Albert and Robin Hahnel, *Un-Orthodox Marxism* (Boston: South End Press, 1978).

199. Bowles and Gintis, *Democracy and Capitalism,* pp. 89, 154–55, 161, 163.

200. Consequently, alternative economic policies in radical social theory must always remain tentative as they emerge out of concrete movements for social change. Some of the suggested social policies that advocate new forms of politics, authority and social organization and are debated among radical theorists include: (1) Effective provision for democratic participation in which unions, parties, and other voluntary institutions would determine the common good in terms of the particular (and possibly conflicting) goods of different sectors of the citizenry; (2) Full employment (unemployment at the wartime average of 2 percent) with wage and price controls in a democratically planned economy where social investment programs directly promote workers' interests; (3) Highly progressive wage structures with differentials relating to skill and outputs during transition periods; (4) Creation of worker and community or regionally owned industry and private industry subject to public accountability (This may be accomplished through worker representation at every level and their accountability to a democratic national planning agency. The question of public versus private ownership may be resolved differently under different conditions.); (5) New national infrastructure (including housing, day care, community-based health care,

public transportation, roads, sewers, water systems, etc.); (6) Socialization of the cost of raising children (a parallel to the social security system for the elderly); (7) Creation of an education system that is freed from the task of legitimating privilege and training people for privately controlled capitalist production; (8) Federal ownership of natural resources and energy; (9) Federal laws regulating corporations and capital mobility; (10) Democratically managed foreign exchange controls (sometimes called a "macroeconomic politics of economic nationalism," which makes trading rights contingent on those countries' recognition of organizing and bargaining rights for their workers); (11) Financial Redistribution Policy—including (a) the reduction of military spending; (b) reduction of spending for advertising; (c) charge corporations for their use and destruction of natural resources; (d) creation of a highly progressive tax policy, including taxation of corporations and the unearned income of rentiers, and ending tax shelters and inheritance prerogatives for the wealthy; and (e) using public employee pension funds (16 percent of equity capital) to fund public investment (92 percent of which has been invested in the private sector). When one adds private sector and self-employed pensions, it is estimated that pensioners now "own" though they do not control 50–60 percent of equity capital. Radical theorists contend that democratic control of this money could realistically finance a socialist economy.

Radical theorists also advocate the creation of a national planning agency to coordinate democratic planning done at the local and regional levels and a national development bank to transfer above funds to democratically determined high-priority areas of the economy. They advocate the democratization of the Federal Reserve System for public control over credit to the private sector, and reducing the power of the International Monetary Fund and the World Bank, which represent corporate interests.

Radical theorists do not underestimate the immense problems in transferring the control of basic investment decisions from private board rooms to the democratic process within economies in which traditional capitalist and corporate collectivism still exist.

For studies that challenge the power and control of late twentieth-century advanced monopoly capitalism see: Samuel Bowles, David M. Gordon, and Thomas E. Weisskopf, *Beyond the Wasteland: A Democratic Alternative to Economic Decline* (Garden City, N.Y.: Anchor Press/Doubleday, 1983); Barry Bluestone and Bennett Harrison, *The Deindustrialization of America: Plant Closing, Community Abandonment and the Dismantling of Basic Industry* (New York: Basic Books, 1982); Martin Carnoy, Derek Shearer, Russell Rumberger, *A New Social Contract: The Economy and Government after Reagan* (New York: Harper and Row, 1983); Alec Nove, *The Economics of Feasible Socialism* (London: George Allen and Unwin, 1983); Carmen Sirianni and Frank Fischer, eds., *Critical Studies in Organization and Power* (Philadelphia: Temple University Press, 1984); Joshua Cohen and Joel Rogers, *On Democracy: Toward a Transformation of American Society* (New York: Penguin, 1983); Philip Green, *Retrieving Democracy: In Search of Civic Equality* (Totowa, N.J.: Rowman and Allenheld, 1985).

For summaries of alternative economic policy suggestions see: Michael Harrington, *Taking Sides: The Education of a Militant Mind* (New York: Holt, Rinehart, and Winston, 1985), esp. pp. 211, 217–19; Wendy Darvasy and Judith Van Allen, "Fighting the Feminization of Poverty," p. 100; Martin Hunt-Landsberg and Jerry Lembcke, "Class Struggle and Economic Transformation," *Review of Radical Political Economics* 16, no. 4 (Winter 1984): 98–105; and Bowles and Gintis, *Democracy and Capitalism*, p. 183.

Chapter Two. Early Modern Roman Catholic Economic Teaching: 1891–1931

THE CATHOLIC CHURCH'S OFFICIAL response to industrial capitalism began in the late nineteenth century. That the factory system had begun in England almost a century before reflects the Church's absorption with its own internal issues. These included its deteriorating influence with the newly emerging European states and the challenging legacy wrought by the Reformation, the French Revolution, the rise of science, and the Enlightenment. Consequently, until the end of the nineteenth century, the Catholic hierarchy had relatively little doctrinal interest in the temporal order and little involvement in speaking about economic life.

Since the time of the Church fathers, Catholic teaching had generally supported the economic status quo. These Christian leaders had sometimes taken the view that under the original law of nature, God intended the property and goods of the earth to be held in common by all people. Therefore, the middleman's gain was economically and morally illegitimate. Nevertheless, they were more frequently known to acknowledge that trade was permissible if conducted honestly and for acceptable ends. Indeed, Jacob Viner argues that the controversies in the early Church and the Middle Ages between the Church, the greatest of the feudal landlords, and various Christian groups named heretical was in large part due to the hierarchy's opposition to their communistic economic doctrines.[1]

From the late Middle Ages to the end of the sixteenth century, the Scholastic period of Catholic moral theology, the

Church continued to have little to say about the remodeling of social institutions. The hierarchy's interest in economic matters was confined to providing religious and ethical guidance for individual economic behavior, stressing the priority of the common good over individual good. During this period the teachings of Thomas Aquinas (1225–1274) gradually gained influence. Aquinas had maintained a closer link between private property and the natural law than had the early Church fathers. Even more than they, Thomas Aquinas and the Scholastics came to terms with the rise of trade and the commercial class. This was in harmony with their notion that the status quo was divinely ordained. Aquinas posited the ethical priority of the market scale of values, and sanctioned a just price for the trader or middleman.[2] Most Scholastics agreed that a just price was the one that would normally be achieved in a competitive market. Hence, Catholic writers during the Scholastic period were generally supportive of the economic arrangements of their time, as long as they did not involve what they considered to be monopoly, fraud, or overt usury.[3]

In the seventeenth and eighteenth centuries, reflecting the official Church's divorce from the world, and its opposition to dialogue with modern ideas, the main economic concern of the Church was its opposition to usury. It was the rise of socialism due to the Industrial Revolution, and Leo XIII's desire to respond to the commercial and working classes in an effort to avoid socialist revolution, that brought an end to the Church's relative silence on economic matters.[4]

The tradition of modern Roman Catholic pronouncements on economic justice begins with *Rerum novarum*, an encyclical, or circular letter, addressed to the entire Church. It was issued by Leo XIII in 1891. In the twentieth century, Pius XI, John XXIII, Paul VI, and John Paul II have also issued encyclicals on economic justice, often on an anniversary of *Rerum novarum*. In addition, groups of regional and synodical bishops have issued statements on economic justice in the tradition of *Rerum novarum*. This chapter considers the presence of economic theory in this encyclical, as well as in its first successor, *Quadragesimo anno*. Commemorating the fortieth anniversary of *Rerum novarum*, Pius XI issued *Quadragesimo anno* in 1931.

The economic teaching of Leo XIII and Pius XI aligned the Roman Catholic Church with some of the major assumptions of orthodox economic theory. In order to understand why this was so, it is necessary to consider both the social theory the Church had assimilated from the feudal era, as well as the historical context in which the modern teaching originated.

Premodern Catholic social theory drew on assumptions taken from Thomas Aquinas and feudal social relations. This theory is often called organic because it derives from Aquinas's appropriation of Aristotle in which the social order and the natural world are viewed on the same continuum. In organic social theory, society was compared to the human body. As the organism of the body has priority over the individual limbs, so the commonweal was thought to have priority over the needs of individual citizens. In harmony with this hierarchical view of society and nature, Catholic social theory assumed the appropriateness of feudal social relations. In this system, every relationship had a dominant and a subordinate member (lord–serf, husband–wife, rich–poor). The dominant members in the social order received their status and responsibility according to their perceived benefit to society as a whole. Organic Catholic social theory applied this dualistic view toward the cosmos as well, so that the spiritual and the eternal had dominance over the material and the historical. While communitarian values of organic social theory predisposed the hierarchical Church toward a critique of the autonomous nonrelated "economic man" of liberal theory, organic theory also predisposed the Church toward accepting capitalism and those aspects of orthodox theory that support hierarchical social arrangements.

Official teaching drew on Aquinas in developing its notions of justice. His notion of particular justice, or justice emanating from individuals, was central in developing Catholic social theory.[5] The two components of particular justice are commutative justice and distributive justice. Aquinas assumed that they both functioned in a society that was hierarchically organized.

For example, commutative justice is a type of civil justice that protects persons against arbitrariness in private agreements and social contracts.[6] These contracts were dependent on the justice of the circumstances or context surrounding the exchange.[7] The context, feudal social arrangements, were assumed by Aquinas to be divinely sanctioned and therefore just in themselves. Distributive justice is a type of economic justice that protects the right of all persons to share in the public good, or the products of the social system as a whole, according to their rank in society.[8] This type of justice depended upon an assumption of natural inequality.[9] Distributive justice mandated that one did not neglect the duties or give up the privileges of one's social role in the society because this role was ordained by God for the purpose of the just governing of the society and was part of the natural law. Even extreme need on the part of some in the society did not require wealthy persons to give away alms if it might put their social position in jeopardy.[10]

As a consequence of baptizing the feudal social order, the Church began to teach, not the disadvantage of wealth and privilege, as in the Gospels,[11] but the obligation of privilege. It held, not the gospel sense of giving out of scarcity,[12] but giving out of surplus. The Church taught that endangering one's particular status disadvantaged the whole society.[13] The medieval understanding of personal property as generating obligation, not disadvantage for the Christian, deviated somewhat from the teaching of the early Church fathers. They were sometimes negative in their attitude toward property, arguing that there was no natural right to it. They understood it at worst as a necessity because of sin, and at best a resource for charity.[14]

Thomas Aquinas deviated from this early church view and held that private property was not contrary to an eternal natural law, but is a rational addition to positive or human-made law, as long as it is always subordinate to the common good.[15] Leo XIII and Pius XI, in their opposition to socialism, deviated from Thomas. They claimed that privately owned property was an integral part of the natural law itself (RN 12, 35; QA 45), and Pius XI taught that the social use or nonuse of property was subordinate to the right to ownership (QA 47).[16] Private ownership was increasingly favored, even though it was usually assumed that the owner would use the property for the public welfare. In other words, the right to ownership, in the Catholic organic sense, does not mean the liberal right to autonomous use, or to utilize, sell, or destroy the property as one pleases.[17] The evolution of the idea of just ownership, in which a feudal social theory was adapted and extended, sheds light on the Church's predisposition to the acceptance of the right to private ownership of the means of production as understood in orthodox theory.

The understanding of property relations in the Catholic organic sense is an understanding that was, and still is, premodern. The Church has not recognized that, under capitalism, the nature of property has changed. Leo XIII hoped that private ownership of land would be universal (RN 35). However, since land and resources were commodified in the market system, traditional agrarian patterns of ownership were disrupted. New forms of capitalist ownership monopolized land and resources, and the means of production were controlled by increasingly fewer people. In its teaching about private property, as well as its teaching about socialism, the Church did not differentiate between privately owned personal goods and the private ownership of the means of production.

But it was not just the Church's failure to recognize the changing nature of property under capitalism that allowed it to view a certain consolidation of wealth and property as congenial to a just social order. Inherent to organic social theory was the notion that the privileged are capable of benevolence. Organic theory assumed not only the justice of class privilege but also the justice of male privilege. The organic view of the social order had the patriarchal family as the model for the institutional Church and all other social entities, including labor unions and the state. This model assumed that privileged (white) males would protect the rest of society in spiritual, economic, and military ways. These men would execute their social obligations in order to insure cooperation, tranquility, and relative material well-being in the social order (*RN* 14). But they would do this for a price, the subordination and servitude of those they were to protect.

This organic ethic would prevent a grossly unequal income distribution that inhibited achieving commutative and distributive justice. It would be the basis for an order and harmony that would make all conflict unnecessary. Leo XIII and Pius XI saw social hierarchy and the traditions of civil and religious authority as a remedy to the absolute autonomy of the individual as understood in Enlightenment liberal philosophy.[18]

This ethic would also prevent social equality, which was thought to be a violation of the natural law because it led to anarchy.[19] The Church viewed the existence of social stratification as natural and necessary. It looked with horror not only at Enlightenment liberalism but also at the various socialist movements that it saw as the alternative to capitalism. Consequently, while Leo XIII and Pius XI could analyze, sometimes with remarkable sophistication, the structural tensions between social classes, these conflicts were not consistently understood as integral components of the social and political structures of capitalist society. They were primarily seen as elements of class egoism that were assumed to be under the moral control of individuals whom the Church could influence.[20]

In accord with the organic perspective, which accepted the primacy of the spiritual and ideational world over the historical and material world, Leo XIII and Pius XI believed that tensions in the economic arena would erode when individuals accepted the teaching of the Church. When people rejected excessive individualism and the ruling elite recognized their social responsibility, the common good would be championed. In the meantime, the Church believed that its social principles remained universally valid because it had access to an eternal truth that was not mediated by activity in the world (QA 11, 19).[21]

Thus, key elements in organic social theory, especially its hierarchical notions of distributive justice, the right to ownership of private property, and the necessity of social stratification in accordance with patriarchal and class privilege influenced the Church's position on capitalism. Because capitalists as efficient producers of wealth were considered to be of more use to society, it was thought to be just that they controlled more property and received more monetary reward (QA 136).[22]

The Church's assimilation of this hierarchical social theory was not the only factor that predisposed it to accepting elements in capitalist social theory. Despite the Church's belief that it had access to an eternal truth that was not mediated historically, an examination of the Church's historical situation in the nineteenth century sheds light on why some orthodox assumptions were appealing to the Catholic Church as it framed its economic teaching.

Catholic social teaching was in part a response to the economic suffering generated by the Industrial Revolution. Since the middle of the nineteenth century, a small but active tradition of "social Catholicism" had struggled in various ways to make concrete responses to a new urban, poverty-stricken class. The reform goals of social Catholicism were later taken up by the Christian Democratic movements that strove to make the Church acceptable both to the liberal aspirations of the commercial classes as well as to the working class. As great numbers of the French working class, for example, joined various socialist movements, a small minority of mostly aristocratic Catholics proposed reforms and were active in social projects that were rooted in the organic social model. They ran the gamut of the more paternalistic and corporative styles of social reform advocated by men such as Félicité de Lamennais, René de la Tour du Pin, and Albert de Mun, to the less paternalistic reforms of Frederic Ozanam and Philippe Buchez. Varying degrees of paternalistic reform within capitalism were also advocated by Cardinal Henry Edward Manning of Great Britain, Bishop Wilhelm Emmanuel Von Kettler of Germany, and James Cardinal Gibbons of the United States.[23]

But Catholic teaching on economic justice was also impelled by the Church's need for social stability during a time of rapid social change. Scholars have noted that, while social Catholicism exhibited various degrees of paternalism and egalitarianism in its prescriptions for social change, "Catholic church leaders tended to measure and judge social and political action in terms of the welfare of the institutional Church."[24] For example, Leo XIII could oppose Catholic social and political movements if he thought they might adversely affect the institutional Church.[25] The Church was cautious in the latter half of the nineteenth century because it was threatened by both the rising bourgeois class and the democratic aspirations of the propertyless masses.

The commercial class threatened the Church with an anticlerical world of socioeconomic liberalism and the desire for freedom of, and often from, religion. In the last half of the nineteenth century, Italy, Spain, Belgium, Austria, and Germany had governments that closed Catholic schools, dissolved monastic orders, rescinded clerical privilege, and confiscated Church property.[26]

But perhaps the greatest challenge to the Church came

from the urban propertyless masses. During this time, when the real income of workers rose throughout the capitalist world (some estimate by as much as 84 percent between 1850 and 1900), as many as 40 percent of the working class in many areas still lived in extreme poverty.[27] After 1880, following a worldwide economic depression, various Marxist and evolutionary socialist parties rapidly developed.[28] Indicative of the growing strength of socialism is the fact that in 1890, the year before Leo XIII issued *Rerum novarum*, the Social Democratic party in Germany (followers of Marx and LaSalle) received almost one and a half million votes, despite the existence of severe antisocialist laws for over a decade.[29] In addition, trade unionism and militant socialism in France, England, and Italy were gaining in popularity during this time. Less clear, but also present, was socialist influence in the United States.[30]

Liberals, once allied with the poorer classes against the aristocracy, now began to turn to the right under working-class demands that were increasingly influenced by socialist ideas.[31] The Church began to ally itself with liberalism, since the Church also perceived the poor, illiterate, and what it thought to be easily deceived masses as a threat to itself.[32] Even though liberal philosophy and the Industrial Revolution had undermined the traditional organic Christian society, and even though the Church had been the victim of revolution during the entire previous century, these inroads into the Church's institutional privilege were much less severe than would have been the case if a socialist upheaval was successful. Thus, in the latter half of the nineteenth century, the Church was finally abandoning its exclusive alliance with the aristocracy. The Church needed to establish itself as an ally with the bourgeois class in order to absorb the socialist threat and promote the social stability so vital to them both.[33] Consequently, in Europe the Church sought to maintain its alliance with the old nobility even as it gained the support of the new middle class. In Germany, Leo XIII served the political order by reinforcing the conservative authority of Bismark against socialistic movements. In Switzerland, the old aristocracy and the most successful capitalists elicited the pope's help in thwarting Christian Democracy. In Italy, a Catholic-sponsored union of aristocracy and peasants, the Opera dei Congressi, defeated coalitions of radicals and socialists. The Revolution of 1848 in France had been implemented by a coalition of bourgeoisie and the Church against the revolutionary aspirations of workers. In the midst of this, as we have seen, a small movement of French Catholic social reformers advocated aristocratic paternalism. In Belgium, the Church supported the Parti Catholique, middle-class Catholics who thwarted workers' groups to its left.[34]

Thus Leo XIII, as well as Pius XI, moved away from the Thomistic tradition (that private property was not contrary to natural law provided it was used to promote the common good) and made private property indigenous to the natural law and a central element of their teaching (*RN* 12, 35; *QA* 45, 47).[35] For its part, *Rerum novarum* represents a fundamental decision in favor of capitalist society. In this encyclical, Leo XIII endeavored to show the civil authorities that religion could be useful because it could protect private property—which meant the private ownership of the means of production. Further, the Church could undermine the more radical socialist threat by teaching the employer justice and the worker duty and fidelity.[36] "Let it become more and more evident," said Leo XIII, "that the tranquility of order and the true prosperity flourish especially among the people whom the Church controls and influences."[37] Leo XIII, who published more encyclicals than any previous pope, wanted the capitalist world to take note òf the Church as an important actor in modern times.[38] The Church could educate the public conscience against both the tyranny of socialism and the anarchy of liberalism. It could bring the illiterate masses to obedience and both legitimate and make benevolent the authority of rulers and employers. The Church spoke out against collectivism and egalitarianism, which destroyed the hierarchies of God, Church, civil authority, economic privilege, and the patriarchal family. It drew close to the capitalist ethos when it defended a stratified social model and a doctrine of property rights.[39] The Church taught that its freedom was as indispensable to the stability of the secular capitalist order as it was to the salvation of human souls (*RN* 13, 15, 16, 39, 45).[40]

Rerum novarum

Rerum novarum originated from a desire to protect the organic model of society from socialist egalitarianism, and to safeguard the position of the Church in this turbulent historical situation. This twofold need on the part of the Church prevented Leo XIII from reaching conclusions about capitalism to which his own structural analysis logically pointed.

Leo XIII utilized the thought of the political economists of his day in the encyclical. As we saw in Chapter One, the classical economic thinkers—whether Adam Smith, David Ricardo, or Karl Marx—were preoccupied with issues concerning the whole political economy, including the nature of economic value, the process of distribution, and the political relations of class conflict.[41] As they analyzed the political economy as one interlocking system, the nineteenth-century classical economists agreed that growing concentrations of capital had accelerated social antagonism. This analytic framework was the one available to Leo, and its holistic concerns would have been amenable to a pope whose worldview was informed by the organic social model.

Reflecting the classical analysis of political economy that is concerned with class relations, Leo XIII performed a structural analysis of capital and labor that was attuned to social conflict. Wealth, he said, was concentrated in the hands of a few who had amassed "enormous fortunes" and who perpetrated "the greed of unrestrained competition." This situation existed alongside the "poverty of the masses," and the wealthy few "have been able to lay upon [them] a yoke little better than slavery itself (*RN* 1, 2).

Yet simultaneous with this analysis, Leo also argued that rich and poor are intended to live in "harmony and agreement." They should "fit into one another so as to maintain the equilibrium of the body politic" (*RN* 15). This reflection of his organic sensibility is hardly in conflict with what became a central assertion of orthodox theory, that market exchange seeks a natural equilibrium and gives optimal returns to both capital and labor. *Rerum novarum* resolved the dilemma of the simultaneous opposition and harmony of capital and labor by arguing that the educational function of the Church would be able to promote this harmony (*RN* 15–16; see also 18, 21, 22). This is not the same as teaching there is an inherent tendency toward equilibrium in the market, but neither is it in conflict with it.

According to organic theory's elevation of the spiritual over the material, Leo argued that the Church could generate moral action in history by teaching moral ideas. The Church could teach the poor that earthly gain is transitory, that Jesus himself was poor, and that economic suffering has been "sweetened" by the cross of Christ (*RN* 18). The Church taught the wealthy that Jesus Christ threatened a strict accounting of their possessions, and that the right to possession does not mean the right to all possible uses of those possessions. Indeed, personal ownership requires paternal benevolence, as long as this is not done at the expense of one's social status (*RN* 19). In this way the Church would function to "keep down the pride of those who are well off, and to cheer the spirit of the afflicted; to incline the former to generosity and the latter to tranquil resignation" (*RN* 20). Further, the exercise of Christian morality, by restraining greed and advancing charity, would bring temporal prosperity to all (*RN* 23, 24). While the document focused on the educational function of the Church, not on an inherent harmonious tendency in the market, its rejection of a necessary tension between capital and labor, and its affirmation of the possibility of equilibrium in a stratified society was very much in line with the orthodox perspective. Thus the document juxtaposed a structural analysis of conflict between capital and labor with a presumed indigenous harmony between them that could be cultivated by the Church.

Leo argued that trade unions were another means for ameliorating class conflict. He juxtaposed a structural analysis of the conflict between capital and labor with a call for trade associations that were to be deferential to employer and state authority. He argued that capital, in its conflict with labor, exerted "the cruelty of grasping speculators, who use human beings as mere instruments for making money." Capital "grind[s] men [*sic*] down with excessive labor as to stupify their minds and wear out their bodies" (*RN* 33). Capital "holds this power because it holds the wealth" (*RN* 35). Because wealth leads to greater power, capital "has in its grasp all labor and all trade." And the wealthy exert this inordinate power over labor because they are "powerfully represented in the councils of the state itself" (*RN* 35). The power of capital over labor, particularly as it is exercised through the state, allows capital to grow rich because of the labor of working people (*RN* 27). Against the power of capital, and the state which it dominates, stand the working masses who are "needy and powerless . . . sore and suffering" (*RN* 35).

Yet alongside this discernment of such tremendous power disparity between social classes, and between the working class and the state, Leo argued for the usefulness of "workmen's associations" that are not "dangerous to the state" (*RN* 38). These associations were to be Christian, and thus in rejecting secular unions would presumably divide the union movement (*RN* 40). Leo assumed that the state would "watch over these associations," which would have as their purpose the enablement of each member "to better his condition to the utmost in body, mind and property" (*RN* 41, 42). But the means to this betterment was not to include strikes, which would invoke the "imminent danger of disturbance to the public place" (*RN* 29).[42] Workers were not to harm property, or the person of the employer, or be violent in any way (*RN* 30). Leo even negated the teaching of Thomas Aquinas, that a hungry person may take from another's plenty, when he said that neither justice nor the common good allowed anyone to seize what belonged to another (*RN* 30).

Rather, workers would achieve their goals through the witness of their personal integrity. Leo argued that the honesty and industriousness of Christian workers would enable capital "to be won over to a kindly feeling" toward labor and to repent of their "inhumanity" and their subjugation of labor to "galling slavery" (*RN* 44). In arguing for the effectiveness of subordinate and deferential trade unions, Leo maintained an organic worldview and avoided conflict with the orthodox assumption that held that militant unionism interfered with the tendency of the market to reach equilibrium.

In addition to his assumptions about the potential harmony of class interests, and the effectiveness of a subordinate trade union movement, Leo entertained a third assumption that was also in tension with his analysis of the capitalist political economy. This had to do with his view of the role of the state, which he saw as the arena wherein the wealthy maintained political control over the economy. In accord with structural analysis, Leo developed a clear relationship between economic ownership and political control. "On the one side is the party which holds the power because it holds the wealth; which has in its grasp all labor and all trade; which manipulates for its benefit and its own purposes all the sources of supply, and which is powerfully represented in the councils of the State itself. On the other side there is the needy and powerless multitude, sore and suffering always ready for disturbance" (RN 35).

Yet Leo also argued that because the state existed for the common good, it could exercise a "fatherly solicitude" toward the poor, who are weak and unprotected (RN 28). In spite of his assessment that the wealthy maintain political control over the economy at the expense of the multitudes, Leo said that the state could work for the commonweal because there was no necessary conflict between private prosperity and public well-being (RN 26). The state was capable of implementing laws that would prevent strikes, ensure just wages, and induce as many people as possible to become land owners (RN 31, 35).[43]

It would seem that the Church's ties to the organic social perspective, including assumptions about the benevolent capabilities of the privileged, made it necessary for it to circumvent, and even contradict, the structural conflict between capital and labor that it analyzed so well. It made it necessary for Leo to propose the possibility of social change by those very agents, the wealthy and the state apparatus they dominated, who were at the root of the conflict and were benefiting from it. In view of Leo's desire to make the Church indispensable to government, it was convenient that the Church's organic assumption that the state could transcend class interests and work for the common good was in harmony with the orthodox view.

Despite a structural analysis that illuminated the deep conflict between capital, the state, and labor, Leo argued for the possibility of a resolution of this conflict through these three agencies: the teaching of the Church; the witness of honest, industrious, and nonmilitant trade unions; and state intervention on behalf of the working poor. These remedies seemed viable to Leo because he believed in the benevolence of hierarchy. However, in light of the encyclical's structural analysis of the depth of the conflict between labor and capital, especially as this is played out within the arena of the state, none of his remedies offers a historically possible agenda for achieving Leo's vision of a just society.[44]

It seems that Leo XIII knew that the rich could use their monopoly of political power to continue to promote their interests in the economic sphere.[45] But in upholding the role of the state and the wealthy who controlled it, Leo was upholding the traditional organic social model even though he had done a structural analysis of the political economy that demonstrated the impossibility of the state being able to function in this capacity. It is likely that the democratic rhetoric of the commercial classes and the egalitarian views of the socialist, communist, and Masonic "sects" of his time, which were advocating greater economic democracy, made traditional hierarchical lines of authority seem especially appealing to Leo.[46] Thus he struggled to maintain an organic worldview and to secure a stable position for the Church and its inherited doctrine.

Likewise Leo XIII rejected socialism, not only because he did not understand its teaching about the changed nature of property (which he misunderstood to be advancing the total community of goods) but because he understood it to reject "paternal authority."[47] He also rejected the egalitarian basis of socialism because he thought it was dangerous to want to be relieved from the suffering of inequality (RN 14). Leo believed that inequality was essential for social stability and that suffering was humanity's inheritance from original sin and the reason for reward in heaven (RN 14, 18).

Rerum novarum made other evaluations that were incompatible with the orthodox model. Leo rejected a central tenet of capitalism that labor is a commodity to be sold at market price. He argued that people are not free to decide whether they will work; and because work is a necessity, people have a right to a work contract that allows them to live in dignity (RN

34).[48] While in the United States *Rerum novarum* was viewed primarily as an antisocialist document, in Europe it was interpreted by Catholics and others as a call to massive social reform.[49] It can be argued that this document specified that a just society has obligations to its members beyond charity.[50] It envisioned that a just society is one in which all people own property, and in which all have a right to participate in the shaping of their society (limited, of course, by their status) (*RN* 27, 35).

Rerum novarum was, in part, an attempt by the Church to gain the allegiance of the new industrial working class. But the simultaneous needs of the Church to uphold an organic model of society, to gain influence among capitalists and their new political orders, and with them to thwart socialism limited the extent to which the Church could follow through on its analysis. These other interests limited what the Church could actually champion within the arena of economic justice. Indeed, Leo XIII's commitment to an organic social model allowed him to ignore the conclusions of his own structural analysis of capitalist political economy.

Quadragesimo anno

The encyclical *Quadragesimo anno* (1931) celebrated the fortieth anniversary of *Rerum novarum* and was an attempt by Pius XI to apply the economic teaching of the 1891 encyclical to the situation of worldwide depression and massive unemployment in 1931 (*QA* 40, 74). Written during one of the worst crises of industrial capitalism, this document was no longer as anxious to align the Church with the liberal forces of capitalism as was *Rerum novarum*.

But Pius XI was as preoccupied with the socialist threat as Leo ever was, and he was as concerned as Leo about the prosperity of the institutional Church. Anti-Catholic persecutions by leftist governments in Eastern Europe, Russia, Spain, and Mexico impelled Pius XI to develop a new agenda for social change (*QA* 112).[51] He warned that unless the distribution of the fruits of production was made more equitable, violent revolution would surely ensue (*QA* 62).

As a middle way between capitalism and socialism, both of which seemed incapable of addressing the ills of the time, Pius XI proposed restructuring the social order along lines that had prevailed in medieval Christianity. Examples of this medieval structure had been kept alive in a guild system in Germany that had functioned well into the nineteenth century.[52] In this corporative system, groups based on vocational or professional orientation would reconstruct the economic order. These groups would cut across class lines and, while maintaining class hierarchy, would include both workers and employers in the ownership and management of business. This moderate corporatism, where harmony would exist regardless of one's place in the labor market, was a full-blown example of the organic social model that linked the ownership of property with social responsibility (*QA* 65).[53] The corporative model was supposed to eliminate social conflict "by the creation of a functionally differentiated and hierarchically stratified social organism . . . to be held together by the coordinating authority of the state."[54] The elaboration of a moderate corporate model was thought to help defend the Church against accusations that it was aligned with capital against workers (*QA* 44, 124). However, while wishing a return to the past, Pius did not intend a rejection of the capitalist system.

Like *Rerum novarum*, this encyclical included a structural analysis of political economy. The capitalist class was a wealthy group enjoying practically all the comforts of modern life; the laboring class was an immense multitude that "struggle[d] in vain" against "the galling yoke" of slavery in capitalist institutions (*QA* 3, 4). Even though the conditions of the workers had improved since Leo's day, Pius XI said that there still existed dispossessed laboring masses "whose cries mount to heaven" and who "have no hope of ever obtaining a share of the land" (QA 59). Pius XI protested the orthodox view that the market distributes goods and services efficiently among social classes when he deplored the "economic supremacy" that created "the superabundant riches of the . . . few," and the "immense number of propertyless wage earners" whose lot was "hand to mouth uncertainty" (QA 60, 61, 88). These numerous workers, who had only their labor to sell were "engaged in combat" with capital, and this conflict was "leading society to ruin" (QA 83).

True to the hierarchy's understanding that right practice will follow from right ideas, Pius XI argued, as did Leo, that Church teaching would reconcile this immense conflict. Pius said that the mutual cooperation of labor and capital "must be accepted in theory and reduced to practice" (QA 110). Capital and labor must be brought together "in mutual harmony and mutual support" (QA 69). It was possible for "mutual understanding and Christian harmony [to exist] between employers and workers" if both accepted the Church's teaching that capital and labor need each other (QA 73). Social harmony would prevail when each side gives up its unjust claims, and labor recognized capital's right to a just profit and capital realized labor's right to a just wage (QA 53, 58).

With regard to specifying the components of just profit and just wage, the encyclical dealt only with what might constitute a just wage. Supporting the orthodox view against the socialists, Pius XI said that a just wage should not be determined with regard to the amount of value created by the labor (QA 68). Rather, it should be determined according to what was necessary to meet "ordinary domestic needs," and to enable the laborer to attain "a modest fortune" (QA 71, 74). Except in some exceptional circumstances, the document rejected a wage contract that was an "equitable partnership," and argued that due shares were to be apportioned according to one's social class (*QA* 58, 64). It assumed that everything over and above what was sufficient to meet ordinary needs of the worker's social station and attain modest savings for the worker was appropriately relegated to the employer as a just profit.

Agreeing with *Rerum novarum*, Pius XI argued that this equilibrium between capital and labor would occur through the educational function of the Church, not through inherent tendencies of the market. Writing during particularly desperate times, Pius XI was more critical of the market than Leo XIII. He said that the market, when left to itself, creates "economic dictatorship" (*QA* 109). But he agreed with Leo that only insofar as people returned to the teaching of the Church would "the fatal internal strife which rends the human family" be mitigated (*QA* 39). Through the Gospel, the Church taught the value of poverty and the accountability of all according to their conduct (*QA* 126). Pius XI argued that "Christianity alone can apply an efficacious remedy to this strife" (*QA* 129; see also 15, 17, 96, 126). He asserted that moral choice could maintain an equitable relationship between wages and prices (*QA* 75, 76).

Even though Pius rejected the market, he still maintained the possibility of justice within the present system. Like Leo, he was in harmony with the orthodox perspective when he denied any necessary tension between capital and labor, and when he affirmed the possibility of harmony in a stratified society. He was also in accord with orthodox theory in rejecting the Marxist labor theory of value, that capitalist profit is unjust because it is taken from the workers who produced it (*QA* 55).

Pius not only assumed the harmony of class interests, he also assumed the effectiveness of nonmilitant unions and vocational groups. While Pius's description of legitimate labor union activity was a degree stronger than Leo's, nevertheless, like Leo, his analysis of the class system would seem to render unions powerless.

Pius also drew upon a structural analysis of political economy. Capital, said the pope, "has long been able to appropriate to itself excessive advantages." Capital has constantly shown a tendency to claim "all the products and profits and [leave] to the laborer the barest minimum necessary to repair his strength and to ensure the continuation of his class" (QA 54). As a consequence, the labor market was the arena of "two armies engaged in combat" (QA 83). Meanwhile, governments were willing to recognize and protect employer associations, but denied "the innate right of forming associations to those who need them the most for self protection against oppression by the most powerful" (QA 30).

At the same time, Pius XI affirmed the innate right of workers "to defend their temporal rights and interests energetically and efficiently" as long as they retained "due respect for justice and a sincere desire to collaborate with other classes" (QA 33, 37). This openness toward reconciliation with capital could be maintained by Christian unions; "neutral," or secular unions, must be associated with a parallel Christian group that promotes "a thorough religious and moral training" (QA 35).

So despite an analysis of the structural conflict between capital and labor that sees them as warring armies, Pius assumed the possibility of their cooperation (QA 83). He placed fewer restrictions on unions than did Leo (RN 28, 30), because Pius assumed that a more primary agent of social change would be, not the unions, but corporations or vocational groups that would cut across class structures. Pius endorsed these groups, which were modeled on the medieval guild system. They were utilized not only by the Italian state at that time, but in varying degrees were revived in Austria, Portugal, and Spain in the 1930s as a right-wing reaction against democracy.[55] These corporate groups would consist of both employers and employees of the same trade, or would extend even beyond the limits of a single trade (*QA* 82–87, 93). Despite Mussolini's utilization of a corporate model in creating a fascist state, Pius argued that similar corporate groups, rather than unions, would replace conflict with cooperation by joining capital and labor together. Pius rejected an extreme corporatist position, which relies on a bureaucratic state, and argued for a moderate corporatism, with decentralized authority, in which some workers would share in ownership and management (*QA* 65, 95).[56] He argued for this despite his structural analysis of the capitalist political economy, and in the midst of Mussolini's creation of a totalitarian corporatism.[57]

In addition to Pius XI's assumptions about the harmony of class interests that could be cultivated by the Church, and his assumptions about the effectiveness of a moderate corporatism, there was a third assumption made by *Quadragesimo anno* that seems uncalled for in view of the encyclical's analysis of the structural conflict between capital and labor. Like *Rerum novarum*, this had to do with the effectiveness of state intervention on behalf of social justice.

Capitalism and unrestrained free competition, said Pius XI, had as its "natural result" the creation of tremendous concentrations of wealth. Those few who command this wealth also command "immense power" because "they hold and control money, . . . govern credit and determine its allotment," and thus have power over the "life-blood [of] the entire economic body" (*QA* 105–107). This control over the economic arena leads to a "fierce battle to acquire control of the state," and then, finally, a struggle to gain international power (*QA* 108). This occurs as each country promotes the economic activities of its leading citizens and they use their financial supremacy to decide international controversy. In view of this reality, said Pius, there is no true "free market," there is only "economic dictatorship" that leads to international class struggle and war (*QA* 107–109). The state had "become a . . . slave"; its resources and authority were undermined by its domination by the wealthy (*QA* 107–109).

Thus to an even greater extent than Leo, Pius XI recognized the interstructuring of wealth, power, and government within the capitalist system. He clearly delineated the relationship between economic ownership and political control. He acknowledged the existence of a class society in which the dominant class controls the state to its own advantage.

But also like Leo, Pius juxtaposed this structural analysis with the organic view that the state can function to humanize the conflict if it had the help of the Church. Pius argued that a correction of morals through a return to the teachings of the Church would lead to a reform of institutions, especially to a reform of the state (*QA* 77, 78). He argued that the state which had become an instrument of economic dictatorship could bring free competition "under effective control" (*QA* 110; see also 88). Consequently, *Quadragesimo anno* gave an even wider endorsement of the state's role in regulating private property than did *Rerum novarum* (*QA* 114).[58] Since Pius believed in the possibility and effectiveness of the conversion of individual capitalists by the Church, even though he said that the "natural result" of capitalism was "economic dictatorship," he still held that "the system [of capitalism] as such is not to be condemned" (*QA* 107, 109, 110).

Written during the Great Depression, Pius went even further than Leo in detailing the cause of economic misery within the structures of capitalist society—in the conflict between capital and the state with labor.[59] Pius located the agents of social change within those very structures that he thought were at the root of the conflict, capital and the state. However, Pius XI resolved the conflict between capital and labor through the same basic agents: the Church, nonmilitant unions or corporate vocational groups, and an altruistic state. These agents, however, do not seem feasible in view of Pius XI's even more extensive structural analysis of the conflict between labor, capital, and the state.[60] Like Leo XIII, Pius XI did not render a historically possible agenda for addressing what Pius called "despotic economic domination" or "the fatal internal strife that rends the human family" (*QA* 39, 105).

Quadragesimo anno acknowledged splits in the socialist movement, and differentiated between socialism and communism (*QA* 112–113). Pius XI came closer to an accurate understanding of socialism than *Rerum novarum* when he demonstrated an awareness that socialism is concerned, not with personally owned goods, but with the ownership of the means of production (*QA* 55). He also recognized that at least some forms of socialism condemn violence and allow private property. Pius XI acknowledged that socialism's goals of social justice "often strikingly approach the just demands of Christian social reformers" (*QA* 113). But even though socialism was not to be condemned as severely as the economic oppression that gave rise to it (*QA* 112), socialism, because of its philosophical base, could never be brought into harmony with the teaching of the Roman Catholic Church and its spiritual concerns. This was because socialist movements were grounded in concerns of "efficient production" and "temporal cares in which they are too much involved" (*QA* 117, 119, 139). Pius condemned the nationalizing of production and the radical view that the value that labor creates belongs to labor (*QA* 55). The Church's commitment to an organic social model, including the hierarchical dominance of the spiritual over the temporal,[61] made Pius XI pronounce that " 'religious socialism' was a contradiction in terms," and "no one can be at the same time a sincere Catholic and a true socialist" (*QA* 120).

Even as Pius XI rejected socialist perspectives on property and labor, it seems that he did not understand the socialist explanation about the changed nature of property, particularly productive property in the capitalist system. When Pius spoke about private property, he was usually not referring to the private ownership of the means of production, but to the individual ownership of land. Like Leo, Pius XI, despite great evidence to the contrary, still hoped for universal individual ownership of land (*QA* 59; see also *RN* 35). At a certain level he may have observed the structural opposition between capital and labor, but he did not see that capitalism was changing the traditional patterns of ownership of land and resources. When Pius spoke about the relationship between capital and labor, he saw this relationship in terms of "one'[s] toil" making an "alliance" with "his neighbor's property" (*QA* 53). He did not understand how new forms of ownership of land and resourses under the capitalist system not only made this explanation of the relationship between capital and labor unrealistic but also was the cause of his own lamentation that there was such an "immense army" of people who were without hope of ever "obtaining a share of the land" (*QA* 59).

Ironically, in their struggles against socialism, Leo XIII and Pius XI made arguments to support the universal individual ownership of land that supported the orthodox view of the necessity for private ownership of the means of production. Pius XI, like Leo XIII, modified traditional Church teaching about private property as it had been articulated by the early Church fathers and Thomas Aquinas. Pius and Leo taught that ownership is indigenous to the natural law, and that the right to ownership of private property, including the right to the transmission of property through inheritance, is more fundamental than the responsibility for the social use of that property (*QA* 47; *RN* 10, 12, 35).[62] Although the public aspect of ownership is important, Pius XI argued that right use is a moral not a legal obligation (*QA* 47).[63] These teachings emanated, however, from an agrarian experience and an organic worldview and their target was a misunderstood socialism. Their purpose was to promote widespread individual owner-

ship of land, even as the reality of capitalist property relations was precluding this possibility for increasing numbers
of people. Yet, in the United States, *Quadragesimo anno*, like
Rerum novarum, was known essentially for its affirmation of
the capitalist system, and the private ownership of the means
of production.[64]

If Pius XI did not understand the nature of property under
capitalism, he also did not understand what was possible
within the limits of capitalism. For example, Pius believed that
it was possible to pay life-supporting wages even if business
was unprofitable due to its own mismanagement or to an un-
favorable social context. He also believed that it was possible
to have other goals than "to make clear profits with the least
labor" (*QA* 72, 132).

Both encyclicals emphasized the organic model of the
patriarchial family where women belong at home in economic
dependency. Domestic labor and childrearing were thought
to be more suited to their nature. Since orthodox social theory
assumes the organic or feudal model of the family, there was
no conflict between these encyclicals and the orthodox perspective (see *RN* 33; *QA* 28, 71).[65]

Due to its wedding to organic social theory, *Quadragesimo
anno*, like *Rerum novarum*, was unable to draw up an agenda for
social change that was responsive to its own structural analysis of the capitalist political economy. Despite his discernment
of the intense conflict between capital and labor, Pius XI remained ambivalent with regard to capitalism. His ambivalence sometimes led him to believe that reform was possible,
at other times it led him to advocate a more conservative corporate social ordering. He sanctioned a moderate corporatism
that stressed the decentralization of authority (not the totalitarian corporatism of fascist states in Europe).[66] Pius rejected
free market competition (*QA* 88), but his arguments for the
universal individual ownership of property served to support

the system of private ownership of the means of production. He believed in a graded sharing of the fruits of production according to one's social class (*QA* 57, 58, 61, 136).

Nevertheless, this encyclical can be said to have made a contribution to a social vision beyond the status quo. It extended Leo XIII's assertion that labor is not a product along with any other to be sold at market prices (*QA* 83).[67] Pius XI, while agreeing with Leo that the wage contract as a system is basically just, nevertheless advocated the partnership of capital and labor in ownership, management, and profit sharing "when possible" (*QA* 65). He conceded the possibility that some private ownership might "injure the community at large" (*QA* 49, 114). He also extended the implicit view of Leo XIII that charity cannot substitute for justice. When Pius XI said that "charity cannot take the place of justice unfairly withheld," he argued that charity is not intended as something interchangeable with justice. Rather, charity is a recourse toward those whose economic suffering is not the result of structural injustice (*QA* 137).[68]

In both *Rerum novarum* and *Quadragesimo anno* the popes could recognize economic suffering as a ramification of the capitalist system. They performed an analysis of the interstructuring of capital and the state against labor as a means of perpetuating this suffering. They also recognized the inadequacy of a liberal social theory that affirms individual autonomy apart from social responsibility.

But as long as the socioeconomic hierarchies that capitalism created both in the family and in the market were not too pronounced, they were congenial with the organic social theory promulgated by the hierarchy, and the structural analysis in official Church documents was compromised. These hierarchies, which were coherent with the Church's notion of distributive justice, kept the Church from condemning capitalism systemically. On the other hand, socialism, which was more in contradiction with organic social theory, *was* condemned systemically.[69] As a consequence of both the need to preserve a social order in which an organic notion of justice could function, and the need to maintain institutional stability in times of rapid socioeconomic change, the Catholic Church "was afraid of the conclusions to which [its] own principles [and analysis] led."[70]

Notes

1. Jacob Viner, *Religious Thought and Economic Society*, ed. Jacques Melitz and Donald Winch (Durham, N.C.: Duke University Press, 1978), pp. 45, 107–8.

2. *Summa Theologica* IIa, IIae, q. 77 as quoted in Viner, *Religious Thought and Economic Society*, p. 83.

3. Viner, *Religious Thought and Economic Society*, pp. 84–85. The Church's opposition to usury did not spring primarily from the situation of the rich exploiting the poor, but from Aristotle's notion that the use of a thing for something other than its purpose was not legitimate. Since the proper function of money is to act as a medium of exchange, to use it to acquire more money is to engage in improper use. See ibid., pp. 87–89.

4. Ibid., pp. 34–38, 45, 49, 62, 67, 69, 82–85, 111–12.

5. Aquinas also posited a second form of justice: legal justice, or the justice of the state. Legal justice was gradually absorbed by the term "social justice" at the end of the nineteenth century. This referred to the obligations of citizens, not just the state, to address the economic "social problem" and to build a just and participatory society. See Richard L. Camp, *The Papal Ideology of Social Reform* (Leiden: E. J. Brille, 1969), pp. 99–100; and Christine E. Gudorf, *Catholic Social Teaching on Liberation Themes* (Washington, D.C.: University Press of America, 1981), pp. 2–3.

6. *Summa Theologica*, IIa, IIae, q. 58.

7. Gudorf, *Catholic Social Teaching on Liberation Themes*, p. 21.

8. *Summa Theologica*, IIa, IIae, q. 58.

9. See Gudorf, *Catholic Social Teaching on Liberation Themes*, p. 22.

10. Viner, *Religious Thought and Economic Society*, pp. 24, 74.

11. See especially Luke 1: 46–55; 6: 24; 16: 14, 19–31; 18: 24–26; Mark 10: 23–26; Matt. 6: 19–21.

12. Mark 12: 41–44. See also Matt. 5: 40; 14: 13–21; Mark 6: 34–45; 8: 1–10; 12: 41–44; John 6: 1–15.

13. Clement of Alexandria, who is indicative of the medieval church tradition, wrote a treatise entitled *The Rich Man's Salvation* in which wealth is not considered an obstacle to union with God as long as the wealthy person is concerned with its paternalistic use. See Viner, *Religious Thought and Economic Society*, pp. 44, 108. Viner argues that this treatise, as well as the evolution of Church doctrine in favor of private property, was in part a response to the Church's need to attack the communistic economic doctrines of the various heretical groups (p. 45).

14. Ibid., pp. 21, 67–69.

15. *Summa Theologica* IIa, IIae, q. 66. Aquinas bases his teaching that private property is not against the natural law on his view that men are superior creatures and have a "natural dominion over all things" (J. Y. Calves and Jacques Perrin, *The Church and Social Justice* [London: Burns and Oates, 1961], pp. 19–21).

The "common good" as defined by medieval theoreticians has priority over individual good and is thought to be self-evident (Viner, *Religious Thought and Economic Society*, p. 51).

16. *Rerum novarum* (*RN*) and *Quadragesimo anno* (*QA*) are found in *Seven Great Encyclicals* (Glen Rock, N.J.: Paulist Press, 1963). See also Camp, *Papal Ideology of Social Reform*, p. 55; and Viner, *Religious Thought and Economic Society*, pp. 15–29, 67–74.

17. Gregory Baum, *Catholics and Canadian Socialism* (Toronto: Lorimer, 1980), p. 77.

18. John Courtney Murray argues that Leo XIII's quarrel with continental liberalism, as well as with socialism, was due to their rejection of the authorities of natural law and religion. See especially Leo XIII's encyclicals *Libertas* and *Immortale Dei*. John Courtney Murray, S.J., "Leo XIII: Two Concepts of Government, II. Government and the Order of Culture," *Theological Studies* 15 (1954): 3–10.

Similarly, as we shall see, Pius XI, along with other European right-wing secular and religious reformers of the 1930s, believed that a return to a medieval corporatist (organic) ordering of society would remedy the ills of both capitalist and socialist orders. See Camp, *Papal Ideology of Social Reform*, pp. 36–37, 65, 97.

19. Camp, *Papal Ideology of Social Reform*, p. 30. John Courtney Murray argued for a continuous line of philosophical development from Rousseau to Marx. He argued that Leo XIII believed that Marxist collectivism was an extension of Latin rationalist individualism, and

that both were components of a unified movement. See "Leo XIII: Two Concepts of Government," p. 21.

20. Kuno Fussel, "Theoretical Aspects of Class Struggle," in *Christianity and Socialism* (Concilium), ed. Johan Baptist Metz and Jean Pierre Jossua (New York: Seabury Press, 1977), p. 58.

21. See Gudorf, *Catholic Social Teaching on Liberation Themes*, pp. 6, 11–15; and David J. O'Brien and Thomas A. Shannon, eds., *Renewing the Earth: Catholic Documents on Peace, Justice and Liberation* (New York: Image Books, 1977), pp. 20–21.

22. See also Gudorf, *Catholic Social Teaching on Liberation Themes*, pp. 38–39.

23. Camp, *Papal Ideology of Social Reform*, pp. 4, 80. See also Charles Pichon, *The Vatican and Its Role in World Affairs* (New York: E. P. Dutton, 1950), pp. 110–20. For a detailed study of social Catholicism, which founded Catholic mutual aid societies, labor unions, and political parties, including the various movements of Christian Democracy, see Joseph N. Moody, ed., *Church and Society: Catholic Social and Political Thought and Movements, 1789–1950*. (New York: Polyglot Press, 1953); Hans Maier, *Revolution and the Church: The Early History of Christian Democracy* (South Bend, Ind.: University of Notre Dame Press, 1969); and Roger Aubert, *The Church in the Industrial Age* (New York: Crossroads Press, 1981). For a study that argues for Cardinal Gibbons's paternalistic participation in U.S. labor conflict see Henry J. Browne, *The Catholic Church and the Knights of Labor* (Washington, D.C.: Catholic University Press, 1949).

24. O'Brien and Shannon, *Renewing the Earth*, p. 33.

25. In 1885 Leo XIII inhibited a Catholic party in France founded by Albert de Mun. In 1901 Leo issued the encyclical *Graves de communi* in which he warned that Christian Democracy could be dangerous because its advocacy of democracy might place the Church at a disadvantage with other forms of government. For studies of the Vatican's relationship to nineteenth-century social Catholicism and Christian Democracy see works cited in note 23 above.

26. Camp, *Papal Ideology of Social Reform*, p. 9.

27. E. K. Hunt and Howard Sherman, *Economics: An Introduction to Traditional and Radical Views*, 3d ed. (New York: Harper and Row, 1978), pp. 95–96. See also Camp, *Papal Ideology of Social Reform*, p. 78. Third World economist L. S. Stavrianos claims that capital was able to pay unionized European workers higher wages because unionization paralleled the colonization and exploitation of the Third World by the major European capitalist powers in the late 19th century (*Global*

Rift: The Third World Comes of Age [New York: William Morrow, 1981], p. 439).

28. Camp, *The Papal Ideology of Social Reform*, p. 12.

29. Hunt and Sherman, *Economics: An Introduction to Traditional and Radical Views*, pp. 95–96.

30. Camp, *Papal Ideology of Social Reform*, p. 49; and Neil Betten, *Catholic Activism and the Industrial Worker* (Gainesville: University Presses of Florida, 1976), p. 11.

31. Samuel Bowles and Herbert Gintis, *Democracy and Capitalism* (New York: Basic Books, 1986), p. 44.

32. John Courtney Murray documents European illiteracy statistics of between 30 and 88 percent of the population at this time. He argues that Leo XIII thought he faced an organized conspiracy against the moral basis of society by both liberal anarchists and totalitarian socialists through their deception of the illiterate masses. See "Leo XIII: Two Concepts of Government," pp. 1–33.

33. Camp, *Papal Ideology of Social Reform*, pp. 48, 54. See also Baum, *Catholics and Canadian Socialism*, p. 92.

34. See Roger Aubert, *The Church in the Industrial Age*; and Maier, *Revolution and Church*.

35. See also Camp, *Papal Ideology of Social Reform*, p. 55; and Viner, *Religious Thought and Economic Society*, p. 70.

Christine Gudorf points out that while Leo XIII claimed that private property was part of the natural law because it was reasonable and universal, Pius argues that it is part of the natural law even though it is not universal but has been a relatively recent historical development. See QA 49; *Catholic Social Teaching on Liberation Themes*, p. 117.

36. Donal Dorr, *Option for the Poor: A Hundred Years of Vatican Social Teaching* (Maryknoll, N.Y.: Orbis, 1983), p. 43.

37. Quoted in O'Brien and Shannon, *Renewing the Earth*, p. 34.

38. Charles Pichon, *The Vatican and Its Role in World Affairs* (New York: E. P. Dutton, 1950), p. 100.

39. Dorr, *Option for the Poor*, p. 261; Gudorf, *Catholic Social Teaching on Liberation Themes*, p. 39; and David Hollenbach, S.J., "Modern Catholic Teaching Concerning Justice," in *The Faith That Does Justice*, ed. John C. Haughey (New York: Paulist Press, 1977), p. 222.

40. Leo XIII's other writings indicate that he equated civil order with godliness and even counseled allegiance to governments that harrassed the Church. He saw socialism, which was violently opposed to many of the sensibilities in organic social theory, as the root of all evil and the source of all revolution. Contrary to Thomas

Aquinas, he held that active resistance to tyrannical power (such as some socialists proposed) could never be justified. People were to endure injustice rather than revolt. Leo thought that the only remedy against socialism was a coalition of Church and national states wherein religion would comfort the poor, ameliorate the tensions between classes, and support and maintain the state in power. See Dorr, *Option for the Poor*, pp. 30–33, 38, 41, 46; and Murray, "Leo XIII: Two Concepts of Government," pp. 1–33.

41. In the mid-nineteenth century the broader analysis of political economy present in the earlier classical period was continued by Karl Marx and his followers. In the late nineteenth and early twentieth centuries, the neoclassical preoccupation with market exchange involved a narrowing of economic theory from the broader concerns of the classical economists. For neoclassical economists, economic activity is linked to market exchange and politics and culture are viewed as separate spheres. See Phyllis Deane, *The Evolution of Economic Ideas* (New York: Cambridge University Press, 1978), pp. 10, 86, 106, 121, 131–33, 136. Leo XIII however, drew from a unified classical discourse on political economy before the clear emergence of the neoclassical stream.

42. Gudorf notes that many who read *Rerum novarum* 31 saw an implicit affirmation of the right to strike (*Catholic Social Teaching on Liberation Themes*, p. 179).

43. The ultimate goal of Leo's wage policy was to make all workers owners of private property. See Camp, *Papal Ideology of Social Reform*, p. 83. It is evident that Leo XIII did not understand that the nature of property had changed under the capitalist system.

44. The phrase "historically possible agenda" is inspired by Samuel Bowles and Herbert Gintis. They point out that a social agenda that "displaces historical concerns and simply develops an ideal structure that meets favored normative standards" is utopian in the worst sense of the term. See *Democracy and Capitalism*, p. 186. I argue in Chapter Five that this is exactly what Catholic economic teaching often does.

45. See Dorr, *Option for the Poor*, p. 49.

46. John Courtney Murray notes that Leo XIII's writing repeatedly indicts these "sects" as the locus of organized conspiracy against the established order. See "Leo XIII: Two Concepts of Government," p. 21.

47. John Courtney Murray justifies Leo XIII's extension of the police power of government in his encyclical *Libertas*, for example. Murray says it was appropriate for government to serve *in loco paren-*

tis given that popular sovereignty could not occur in conditions of 30 to 88 percent European illiteracy ("Leo XIII: Two Concepts of Government," pp. 20–27).

48. The papal insistence on "dignity" and a "living wage" was the one exception to the blanket assumption that the status quo reflected a situation of potential social justice. However, attention to a "living wage" did not change the relative power of worker and employer (Gudorf, *Catholic Social Teaching on Liberation Themes*, pp. 30, 34). Similarly, the concept of "dignity" is hierarchically organized and has no relation to capitalist profit.

49. See Pichon, *The Vatican and Its Role in World Affairs*, p. 114; and Betten, *Catholic Activism and the Industrial Worker*, p. 23.

50. Dorr, *Option for the Poor*, p. 51.

51. See also Camp, *Papal Ideology of Social Reform*, p. 64.

52. See R. H. Bowen, *German Theories of the Corporative State* (New York: McGraw Hill, 1947).

53. See also Camp, *Papal Ideology of Social Reform*, pp. 65, 97.

54. David Hollenbach, S.J., *Claims in Conflict: Retrieving and Renewing the Catholic Human Rights Tradition* (New York: Paulist Press, 1979), pp. 161–62.

55. See Camp, *Papal Ideology of Social Reform*, pp. 36–37.

56. See also Camp, *Papal Ideology of Social Reform*, p. 37; Dorr, *Option for the Poor*, pp. 64–65; and Gudorf, *Catholic Social Teaching on Liberation Themes*, p. 7.

57. As a consequence of the corruption of corporatism by fascism, which made these groups artificial instruments of a centralized totalitarian state, the corporate model was abandoned as a Catholic ideal. See Arthur F. McGovern, *Marxism: An American Christian Perspective* (Maryknoll, N.Y.: Orbis, 1981), p. 106.

58. See Camp, *Papal Ideology of Social Reform*, p. 147.

59. Dorr, *Option for the Poor*, p. 58.

60. Dorr's study, to which I am indebted, does not recognize the contradiction between the economic power of the state on behalf of the wealthy (*QA* 108, 109) and the responsibility of the state for the commonweal (*QA* 110) in Pius's encyclical as it does in Leo's (*RN* 35, 28, 37). Compare *Option for the Poor*, p. 49, with n. 28 on p. 286.

61. Viner, *Religious Thought and Economic Society*, p. 5.

62. See also Camp, *Papal Ideology of Social Reform*, p. 66.

63. Richard L. Camp points out that here Pius is opposing those corporatists who, like the socialists, said that unused land could be forfeited and used for the commonweal (ibid.).

However unclear the Church may have been regarding the nature of private property under capitalism, the principle of right use has been a strong one in the Catholic social tradition. Contrary to this tradition, which has mandated the moral if not the legal obligation to use property for the commonweal, accounts of the Vatican's financial dealings argue that the institutional Church pays no attention to right use. They claim, for example, that since the Vatican received 750 million lire, or $81 million from Mussolini in the Lateran Treaty of 1929, Vatican financial administrators have given priority to making profit through the capitalist system regardless of religious, doctrinal, or moral considerations. See Nino LoBello, *The Vatican Empire* (New York: Trident Press, 1968); and David A. Yallop, *In God's Name: An Investigation into the Murder of Pope John Paul I* (New York: Bantam Books, 1984), especially pp. 91–92, 98–99, 129–130, 174, 191–195, and Penny Lernoux, *In Banks We Trust* (New York: Penguin Books, 1986), pp. 169–222.

64. Betten, *Catholic Activism and the Industrial Worker*, pp. 22–23.

65. Despite some movements in the direction of supporting equal rights for women in public life, every pope, including John Paul II, has understood women's primary role as that of childrearing and housekeeping. See Gudorf, *Catholic Social Teaching on Liberation Themes*, pp. 249–328.

For a discussion on how the liberal social contract assumes feudal social relations within the family because it is a contract between fathers and sons, not one between men and women, see Carole Pateman, *The Sexual Contract* (Stanford, Calif.: Stanford University Press, 1988). Samuel Bowles and Herbert Gintis offer a similar insight that liberal theory holds an organic view of the family, even though a patriarchal overlord of the family's resources is in direct contradiction to the tenets of liberal economic theory (*Democracy and Capitalism*, pp. 106–8).

Pamela Brubaker points to the same reality when she offers evidence that refutes the assumption of neoclassical and some radical theory that an increase in family income benefits all family members. She says that this assumption is evident in all of Catholic social teaching. See "Rendering the Invisible Visible: Methodological Constraints in Economic Ethics in Relation to Women's Impoverishment" (Ph.D. diss., Union Theological Seminary, 1989), chaps. 1, 2.

66. See Camp, *Papal Ideology of Social Reform*, pp. 40, 148, 149; and Dorr, *Option for the Poor*, pp. 64–65.

67. However, when the just wage is calculated it has no relation-

ship to the amount of profit or "increased public riches" made, as does the income of employers (*QA* 136).

68. See Camp, *Papal Ideology of Social Reform*, p. 100. Camp notes that, Pius XI, in his encyclical against Communism, *Divini redemptoris* (1937), says, "The wage earner is not to receive as alms what is his due in justice" (p. 100). Christine E. Gudorf notes that in the encyclical *Ubi arcano* (1922), Pius XI is also explicit about the evil of preferring charity to justice. She notes, however, that he spiritualizes both justice and charity so that they depend not so much on what people do as upon their spiritual seeking. Gudorf says that the shift from the concrete to the spiritual is common in papal social teaching before Vatican II (*Catholic Social Teaching on Liberation Themes*, pp. 4–6).

69. Gudorf notes that since the Church believes that the order of creation that God intended was a graded order, the basis for the papal attack on Marxism in the twentieth century is that it destroys the hierarchy of God, Church, civil powers, and patriarchal family that the Church thinks are necessary to safeguard the common good. She also points out that, while the modern popes place increasing emphasis on the need for justice for workers, they are, at best, silent about equality of the classes (*Catholic Social Teaching on Liberation Themes*, pp. 44–45, 175–76).

70. Baum, *Catholics and Canadian Socialism*, p. 83.

Chapter Three. *Economic Teaching from John XXIII to Puebla: 1961–1979*

LEO XIII AND PIUS XI were concerned with making the Church relevant to those who were undergoing the throes of capitalist industrialization in the West. The papacies of John XXIII and Paul VI saw the Church engaged in a struggle for relevance in a world community in which "great masses of workers," especially those living in the southern half of the globe, received "too small a return for their labor" and "live[d] in conditions completely out of accord with human dignity." John XXIII and Paul VI addressed a situation in which "the acute disquiet" of the world's poor was measured against "a type of capitalism [that had] been the source of excessive suffering, injustices and fratricidal conflicts" (*MM* 68; *PP* 9, 26).[1]

The social teaching of the Church continued its efforts to identify the structural dynamics by which poverty is perpetuated and to propose strategies for the eradication of such widespread economic suffering. The economic teachings of the institutional Church continued to mix an orthodox analysis with increasing elements of structural analysis. This period also saw the hierarchy at times proposing policy prescriptions that could be aligned with the radical paradigm.

While the social encyclicals of Leo XIII and Pius XI were concerned with the relationship between owners and workers, those of John XXIII and Paul VI, as well as *Gaudium et spes* of Vatican II, focused on the relationship between the First World and the Third World.[2] In the words of Paul VI, the "social [justice] question" had become "worldwide" (*PP* 3; *OA* 5).[3] What liberal reform within First World nations was to Pius and Leo, liberal development within Third World nations was to John and Paul and the Second Vatican Council. Development was thought to be a way to remedy the distortions of capitalism, even though at times their own analyses called into serious question its efficacy as a remedy.

John XXIII

John XXIII issued two encyclicals pertinent to this study, *Mater et magistra* (1961), which dealt primarily with economic society, and *Pacem in terris* (1963), which was concerned with the national and international communities. Writing in the post–World War II economic boom, one of the most prosperous times in modern history in the West, John was decidedly less critical of capitalism than his predecessors. John followed an orthodox analysis in his affirmation of private property and the wage system, and in his belief that genuine social betterment could occur through the application of western modes of technology to economic and political activity.

Affirming a central tenet of economic orthodoxy, John stated that "in economic affairs first place is to be given to the private initiative" of individuals or groups pursuing common interests (*MM* 51; see also *PT* 65).[4] John asserted that doubts concerning the natural-law right to private property, including the right to own productive properties, had no foundation (*MM* 108–109). Indeed, he said, the very right to own property, and exercise private initiative concerning its productivity, was necessary to prevent "political tyranny" and to meet the basic needs of body and spirit (*MM* 57; *PT* 21). In short, if people were without the consumer goods they needed, it was because of a lack of capitalist development.

Even though he referred to them separately, John XXIII, like Leo XIII and Pius XI, did not differentiate the nature of private ownership of land and other goods from the nature of private ownership of the means of production. John's optimism about capitalism was further demonstrated in his belief that the system of private property was not only a means to promote the efficient generation of material surplus through the capitalist market, it was also a means to enable universal family ownership of land (*MM* 112–115). While Leo XIII and Pius XI had desired it (*RN* 5, 9, 10, 35; *QA* 61),[5] universal private ownership of land was not considered a possibility until the time of John.[6] John XXIII believed that capitalist development would promote widespread individual ownership of land. John said, "it will not be difficult . . . for widespread private possession" (*MM* 115). John saw the existence of social security and insurance programs, as well as "human capital" accumulation, as modern substitutes for private property that would assure material well-being (*MM* 105–108). John also believed in the basic justice of the wage system, and he believed that unions had gained enough power that would allow them to work in harmony with management (*MM* 32, 97; *PT* 40).

John XXIII's optimism concerning what capitalism could do for the poor was grounded in his trust in the potential of western technology. John's encyclical, *Mater et magistra*, was issued in 1961, the same year that the United Nations launched the First Development Decade. Many people believed that poverty would be eradicated through the application of First World technology to the "underdeveloped" Third World. The rich nations could initiate social progress in the poor ones through technological management of economic and political activity. John shared completely in the assumption that the misery of the masses was due to a lack of modern industrial techniques. Capitalist methods of production, he said, could create vast amounts of goods in an efficient way (*MM* 68, 94). John stated that the underlying causes of poverty were due to the "primitive state" of Third World economies, and that science and technology held the key to the alleviation of poverty and the creation of human solidarity (*MM* 163).[7]

John called an important result of modern developments in science and technology "socialization," or the increasingly complex "interdependence of citizens" (*MM* 59; see also *MM* 200). When interdependence did not inhibit freedom through the bureaucratic systems it often created, John saw it as a positive development because it aided human solidarity (*PT* 130–131). He did not connect the positive development socialization with the imbalances of dependence that he also observed (*MM* 157).

John also agreed with liberal orthodoxy in viewing the state as a responsible agent of commonweal. States were capable of working for the "common good," that is, establishing conditions whereby the entire human family could satisfy needs of both body and soul and "achieve perfection" (*MM* 65; *PT* 57, 98; see also *PT* 54, 69, 72, 77, 82, 84, 136). In particular, national and international authorities were capable of serving the common good by reducing "imbalances" within countries and providing "disinterested aid" to poorer countries (*MM* 20, 37, 40, 52, 58, 99, 134, 137, 147, 150, 151, 165, 173, 183). They could "set up relations of mutual collaboration facilitating the circulation from one [nation] to the other of capital, goods and manpower" (*PT* 101). The authority of states to regulate and oversee the common good must not "restrict the freedom" of private citizens or individual states (*MM* 55; *PT* 141). John was equally in harmony with liberalism and with organic social theory when he promoted the duty of economically privileged persons and nations to help the poor, *as long as* this is not at the expense of their own development and as long as it does not disturb structures of class (*MM* 119, 158–165, 228; *PT* 121–125).

John retained a traditional understanding of the function of the Church as an agent of social change. It made known the ideas through which social change and social harmony could be achieved. The Church's task was to issue social teaching that was evidence of both the Church's teaching and its action

(*MM* 6–7). The purpose of John's teaching was to enable individual Christians to apply the principles against unregulated competition and Marxist class struggle enunciated by Leo XIII and Pius XII to the changed social conditions of the early 1960s (*MM* 42, 50). These principles, John said, were part of a permanent and universally valid moral law that transcended the laws of all the states and was the most important resource for the achievement of world peace (*MM* 218–221, 225, 228, 257, 262; *PT* 37–38). The actual implementation of the principles was the work, not of the hierarchical Church, but of the laity, who were to "reduce" these principles to action. The laity were to "take an active part in various organizations and influence them from within" (*MM* 238).[8]

While some of John's teaching was in line with orthodox theory, it also included elements that were decidedly at odds with orthodox assumptions and policies. This was evident in his discussions about private property, economic rights, the wage system, and the democratic control of business. John also made observations about the capitalist world that called into question the possibilities that large-scale private ownership and western forms of development could be the keys for genuine social progress. As much as he affirmed traditional sources of social agency in the pursuit of justice, he also called them into question and held out the possibility of new sources.

John's concern with poverty led him to reemphasize the Thomistic teaching that the right to private property includes the duty of the just social use of that property. He said that it was prohibited by the will of God that the ownership of property should "obstruct the flow of 'material goods created by God to meet the needs of all.'" Recalling a radio broadcast of his predecessor, Pius XII, John said that the right of human beings to adequate sustenance is prior to all other economic rights, including private ownership (*MM* 43; see also *MM* 111, 120 and *PT* 22). Here John abandoned Pius XI's distinction between the legal and moral imperative to just social use of property (see *QA* 47).

John's concern for the just social use of property and material goods led him to enunciate a new order of human rights. He affirmed basic civil rights characteristic of liberal orthodoxy: freedoms of religion, assembly, democratic participation, and information. He also affirmed socioeconomic rights traditionally identified with socialism, such as rights to a job, food, shelter, clothing, and medical care regardless of sex, race, or class (*PT* 11, 18, 44, 64).[9]

With regard to the wage system, John moved beyond his predecessors, who made wages dependent on "what is required in order to live" or what constitutes an "ample sufficiency" (*RN* 34; *QA* 61).[10] Rather, John made observations that show that he held capital accountable to the claims of orthodox economic theory; namely, that labor is paid according to the value of its contribution to the productive process, and that there is an automatic transfer from increased labor productivity to increased real wages. John emphasized Pius XI's view that capitalist enterprise did not demonstrate this theory so that the wage system took "inhuman and unjust forms" (*MM* 31). John agreed with Pius XI that capital was allocating to itself part of the contribution of labor so that more than an equitable share of the fruits of production were being accumulated by the wealthy (*MM* 76–77). In other words, labor was not being paid according to what it produced. John observed that some companies experience rapid growth without paying workers more than the minimum wage (*MM* 75). Thus, there was no automatic transfer from increased labor productivity to increased real wages. John was aware of the "many and great difficulties" experienced by labor as it sought to achieve its rights (*MM* 100).

John also called even greater attention than his predecessors to what constituted just partnership in business. He repeatedly advocated that workers become partners not only in the ownership of industrial, agricultural, and craft enterprises but in their control and management (*MM* 32, 75, 84, 91–93, 99). He said that this requirement accords both with developments in modern society and with the dignity of human nature (*MM* 93). Through the development of intermediate groups and bodies, all citizens should participate in the shaping of socioeconomic life (*MM* 65, 151; *PT* 24, 34, 64, 69). Citizens "have the right to play the leading part in the process of their own development" (*PT* 92).

Despite his basic optimism with regard to capitalist development and its potential for eradicating poverty, John issued many warnings. Many of his observations about the modern world were in conflict with this optimism. He noted, for example, the increasing social inequality and military spending with capitalist expansion. He saw signs that western development led to "domination" and "another form of colonialism" (*MM* 171–173). John noted that social and economic advances grew in tandem with "increasingly pronounced imbalances," and that "inequalities between citizens tend . . . to become more and more widespread" (*MM* 48; *PT* 63). Western development could increase class differences, creating economic, cultural, and political imperialism (*MM* 73, 170, 171; *PT* 88). John noted that the most economically developed countries spent vast amounts of intellectual and economic resources on stockpiling armaments (*PT* 109). He warned against the havoc in economic and social affairs rendered by a development that "militate[s] against justice and humanity" (*MM* 94).

John's concern about a development process that was controlled by small groups of powerful elites led him to modify the principle of subsidiarity. Both Pius XI and Pius XII had used the principle of subsidiarity to deny the right of civil authorities to interfere in the operations of organizations closer to the grass roots (including the Church), or to change the relative power of bargaining units by redistributing material goods.[11] John now used the same principle, "small is beautiful", to emphasize the need for public authority to intervene when power was too great to be left in private hands without damage to the common good, especially the poor. John's modified principle of subsidiarity held that "small is beautiful but big whenever necessary" (MM 53–54; PT 56). Originally promulgated to deny collective ownership, John restructured this principle to demand, for example, that the state collectivize property if the common good requires (MM 58, 116–117; PT 57).[12]

John also used the principle of subsidiarity to applaud the formation of the United Nations and its various agencies, which he saw as essential for a modern complex society in its search for the commonweal (MM 103, 156, 202; PT 145). The central theme of the encyclical *Pacem in terris* is the need for the establishment of public authorities that can act for the commonweal on a worldwide basis (see esp. PT 7, 134, 135, 137, 138, 140).

But at the same time that John put his trust in the ability of governments and international agencies to work for the common good, John called into question the abilities of states and governing elites to be agents of justice. John observed that public authorities often served the interests of the wealthy (MM 36). Or, if they might have the commonweal at heart, they were powerless because they were at the mercy of capital investment decisions (MM 104). Internationally, authorities from the powerful nations might impose one-sided interests, such as interests of the wealthy for economic and political domination (PT 138) and unjust activity in the temporal sphere. John observed that those with responsibility for public life were unable to accomplish their just aspirations, and that "the energies of man and the resources of nature are very widely directed by peoples toward destruction" (MM 203–204). John puzzled over the inconsistency he found between religious belief and unjust activity in the temporal sphere throughout the traditional Christian nations (PT 152). He saw that economic greed and power constantly impeded the demands of social justice as it sought political control on behalf of that power (*MM* 36).

While John believed that this inconsistency between religious faith and injustice could be remedied primarily by a solid Christian education (*PT* 152–153), he also advocated putting limits on the state, as he had tried to limit the power of private interests by the state. Quoting Thomas Aquinas, John affirmed that the state represented God's will only when its laws corresponded to the moral law. If the state's laws were unjust, they were not binding because they represented "a kind of violence" that is no less violent or unjust because it is legal (*PT* 51, 52). John said that if a government either fails to acknowledge the rights of people, and for John rights included economic rights, or violates these rights, "it not only fails in its duty, but its orders completely lack juridical force" (*PT* 61). While an acknowledgment of violence in capitalist institutions was present in the structural analysis of Leo XIII and Pius XI, John XXIII explicitly opened up the subject of structural or institutionalized violence.[13]

John also broke new ground in the area of social agency when he championed the possibility of dialogue with non-Catholics, even Marxists, in the struggle for social change (*MM* 239; *PT* 159). Contrary to Pius XI, who allowed no differentiation between socialist movements and their philosophical base (*QA* 120), John implied that collaboration between Christians and Marxists or other socialist movements may be permitted when these movements are more influenced by "evolving historical situations" than by static teachings in the past. Historical situations may influence these movements profoundly and Christians should be open to elements in them "that are deserving of approval" (*PT* 159). This was a noteworthy move, even though John was careful to state that "violence has always achieved only destruction," and the Church always reserves the right to decide whether a social system or movement is in accord with God's will (*PT* 162; *MM* 42; *PT* 160).

Perhaps equally groundbreaking was John's seeming support in *Pacem in terris* for the equality of women with men in domestic and public life (*PT* 41). But this affirmation must be read in light of his other writings that clearly show that he understood woman's nature and primary responsibility to be that of childrearing and housekeeping within the patriarchal family.[14]

The bulk of John's teaching was framed within the orthodox and organic theoretical models. He was less critical of the evils of capitalism than were his predecessors because he believed in the potential of western methods of development. He accepted the orthodox view that capitalist economic growth is the best way to eradicate poverty, both within and between nations. Beyond this, his organic sensibilities are manifest in his belief in the possibility of an ordered, hierarchical society in which every social class knows its proper duty, and in which all can be motivated by a common will inspired by the Church (*MM* 228; *PT* 31, 37, 38). Like the popes before him, he believed in a justice proportional to one's social location (*PT* 56).

Nevertheless, a careful reading of his work makes it possible to say that John XXIII contributed to a movement away from mainstream economic analysis in at least four ways. First, he shifted the teaching's emphasis away from concern about private property to concern about poverty.[15] This included a movement from concern about the rights of ownership to concern about the obligations and limitations of ownership. It included the declaration of a new order of individual economic rights.[16] It also included a noticeable shift from concern about collectivism to concern about strengthening political structures so as to deal adequately with the commonweal, and correct the new imbalances appearing within current economies.[17] John implemented this concern by a modification of the principle of subsidiarity, "small is better," to include, "but big whenever necessary." John could thus defend a social-welfare model of society that sought to restrict capitalist interests that failed to provide for the needs of people in an increasingly complex world. While a social-welfare model of the state was new to Catholic social teaching, the understanding that government could stand above the conflict of the classes was part of traditional organic social theory. Still, *Mater et magistra* was called "warmed over Marxism" by conservative critic William Buckley, who coined the phrase "mater si, magistra, no."[18]

A second way in which John moved Catholic social teaching away from the orthodox mode of economic analysis was by assuming that labor had a right to participate in the ownership, management, and control of enterprise. A third teaching at odds with orthodox theory was John's affirmation that the Marxist agenda might have some worth for Christians seeking social justice. It seemed that in John's view, human integrity was related to the exercise of social responsibility, not to ideological purity.[19] Finally, John moved away from mainstream economic analysis when he affirmed that violence was present within the socioeconomic structures of any state that did not acknowledge or that violated a holistic sense of basic human rights, including economic rights.

What John XXIII did that was noteworthy was to move Catholic social teaching away from concerns for private property and against socialism, and toward concerns for the majority poor and possibly even for collaboration with the Left. According to John, the common good required both more centralization than in the past, and more pluralism in political alliances than in the past.[20] The Church's vision of society was marked by John's acceptance of the world as a pluralistic realm in which philosophical agreement was subordinated to the value of living together in historical community.[21] It has been noted that John's pontificate "began the process of breaking the long alliance between Roman Catholicism and socially conservative forces."[22] The Second Vatican Council, especially its document, *Gaudium et spes*, continued this movement.

Gaudium et spes

Gaudium et spes, the Pastoral Constitution on the Church in the Modern World, was signed by Paul VI and was issued by the bishops of the Second Vatican Council in 1965. As a document of an ecumenical council, *Gaudium et spes* perhaps has more authority than a papal encyclical;[23] it merits a separate discussion here.

One can find in this Pastoral Constitution traditional affirmations about the economy that emanate from orthodox and organic assumptions. The bishops of Vatican II continued the hierarchy's habit of blending individual ownership of land and goods with the private ownership and control of capital, reifying private property into one, ahistorical entity. Though the document did not use natural law arguments with regard to private property, it did affirm that private ownership is important for the "expression of personality" and for some measure of independence and freedom (*GS* 71).[24] Goods may be transferred to the public domain only by competent authority and with compensation (*GS* 71). It affirmed that capitalist production and exchange are "apt instrument[s]" for meeting human needs (*GS* 63). It assumed that poor people want western development, and that they need to abandon, for example, traditional methods of farming (*GS* 6, 66, 87).

In harmony with orthodox liberalism, this document assumed that public authorities, both national and international, and other privileged elites could be the source of solutions to pressing social problems. They could guard against misuse of private property and coordinate efforts of individuals and other groups for the common good (*GS* 65, 70, 71, 74, 83, 84,

88). They could feed the poor, remove all forms of discrimination, and enable individuals and governments to redistribute goods (*GS* 29, 66, 69).[25] Present authorities were further sanctioned when the document linked guerrilla warfare with "methods of deceit and subversion (*GS* 79).

Gaudium et spes also included a traditional understanding of the role of the Church. Since human solidarity is problematic because of the reality of sin, people need the Church to dispense grace and moral teaching that will give "soul" to society (*GS* 3, 10–13, 17, 23, 37, 40–41, 43, 58, 76, 88, 89). The Church has "no proper mission" in the political, economic, and social order save to teach the principles that foster solidarity and enable the laity to do the works of mercy (*GS* 42, 21, 76). Justice happens when the laity as individuals work with appropriate institutions (but not the Church!). These are "secular" duties that belong to the laity; the function of the hierarchy is to govern the Church (*GS* 42–43, 72).

Traditional also was the document's view of women. This was so despite its stance against sexual and racial discrimination, and its affirmation of the "active presence of the father" in the rearing of children. This document taught that women may participate in cultural life but it added the traditional qualifier "in accordance with their own nature." Elsewhere the document said that "the domestic role [of women] must be safely preserved," thus endorsing gender segregation and the injustice of women's double day of work in the marketplace and at home (*GS* 29, 52, 60).

Gaudium et spes expressed less optimism about the capitalist world than the encyclicals of John XXIII. At the same time that it championed western development, it also supported policies opposed to capitalist expansion like the expropriation of land, support for liberation and economic independence, and democratic control of production and investment. Even more than the teaching of John XXIII, what it conceded to capitalist expansion with one hand, it took away with the other.

Gaudium et spes was written out of an awareness that the world was in "grave crisis" because the majority of its people were still suffering from "hunger, disease and every kind of misery" (*GS* 82, 88). The bishops of Vatican II emphasized not only the just social use of private property, but, contrary to Pius XI, they specifically advocated that public authorities redistribute land to those who will make it productive if it is either kept idle or used to exploit tenants (*GS* 71).[26] This document held that private ownership was not opposed to "the right inherent in various forms of public ownership" (*GS* 71). Affirming the economic rights described in *Pacem in terris*, this document supported the right of every person "to have a share of earthly goods sufficient for oneself and one's family . . . [even if this means taking] from the riches of others what he himself needs" (*GS* 69, 26, 67).

Gaudium et spes also relinquished the organic teaching of the previous popes that held that charity was to be given out of surplus, for it was not to disturb one's social position.[27] Rather, this document affirmed "the ancient custom of the Church" and the gospel sense of giving "out of the substance of [one's] goods, and not only out of what is superfluous" (*GS* 88, 69). Further, one of the strongest statements that the document made was against those who neglect duties of social justice (*GS* 43).[28]

Gaudium et spes declared that western development often increased inequalities because it was done for profit and domination. As a consequence, "the contrast between the economically more advanced countries and other countries is becoming more serious day by day" and an "enormous mass of people still lack the absolute necessities" (*GS* 63). The document said that the "practices of modern business" create "excessive desire for profit, nationalistic pretensions, the lust for political domination, militaristic thinking and intrigues designed to spread and impose ideologies" (*GS* 85). The document said that economic development leads to "collective greed" and the crisis of war (*GS* 8). It linked the vast expenditure on armaments to the need to dominate other nations, which extends human misery (*GS* 79, 81, 83). It also pointed out that political independence often exists simultaneously with economic dependence and it stated that poor nations need their own form of economic liberation before they need "outside help" (*GS* 86). Therefore, the document mandated "vigorous efforts" to remove "immense economic inequalities" and sanctioned the need for a new political, social, and economic order based on justice and economic independence (*GS* 9, 66, 85–87).

Like the writings of John XXIII, *Gaudium et spes* affirmed the right of all people to participate in shaping the socioeconomic life of the society (*GS* 60, 65, 75, 86, 87). It affirmed unions, strikes, and the partnership of capital and labor. It extended the content of partnership to include, not only co-ownership and comanagement, but also worker control of higher institutions and authorities that regulate individual firms (*GS* 68). This would significantly increase the movement toward democratic control of production and investment.

The contradiction evidenced in this document's advocacy of capitalist forms of development as well as forms of economic democracy is paralleled in its assessment of the proper agents of social change. Alongside the traditional emphasis on the state as the mediator of the commonweal, this document also observed that the state can oppress people. It included the assertions that public authorities are motivated both by "the very grave peacemaking task" and "national selfishness and ambition" to oppress others (*GS* 82). When the latter happens, it is lawful for people to defend themselves (*GS* 74). *Gaudium et spes* thus modified the assumption of commutative justice that the status quo represents a situation of potential justice. The document emphasized this further when it referred to Thomas Aquinas and implied that laws against stealing are not valid when the hungry take from the surplus of others (*GS* 69).

Gaudium et spes continued the ecumenical stance of *Pacem in terris* when it said that Christians should engage in dialogue with people "of all shades of opinion" in search of solutions to social injustice (*GS* 90, 43, 16). It noted that atheism often resulted from a violent protest against evil in the world, and a desire for the economic and social emancipation of people (*GS* 19–21). Scholars have noted the significance of this first acknowledgment by the Church of the sincerity of Marxist efforts to relieve suffering in the world.[29]

Finally, in tension with the statement that the Church has "no mission" to the socioeconomic order, the document also said that the Church has "the right to pass moral judgements, even on matters touching the political order" (*cf. GS* 42 with *GS* 76). This means that the Church must be ready for reprisals when it falls out of favor with the political order. These may include loss of "privileges" and other "legitimately acquired rights" (*GS* 76). Thus, the teaching of *Gaudium et spes* supported the Church in an alliance with the poor, even at the expense of its wealth and status. This is faithful to the document's opening mandate that Christians be attuned to "the joys and the hopes, the griefs and anxieties of the [people] of this age, especially those who are poor, or in any way afflicted" (*GS* 1).

Gaudium et spes moved away from the economic assumptions of orthodoxy in several ways. Like the teaching of John XXIII, it affirmed the just social use of property and the legitimacy of economic rights. But it continued to move further to the left when it explicitly sanctioned such policies as the expropriation of land and the more equitable distribution of property, even at the expense of social hierarchies.[30] Like John, it affirmed the partnership of capital and labor, but it went on to mandate worker representation at every level of the economy. It continued to call attention to the need for "the practices of the modern business world [to] undergo a profound change," and affirmed that true economic progress "begins and develops primarily from the efforts and endowments of the people themselves" (*GS* 85–86). Finally, it acknowledged the sincerity of Marxist efforts on behalf of social justice, and called on the Church to do likewise, through its teaching, even at the expense of its own privilege. Scholars have noted that *Gaudium et spes* marked the first time the Church took an official stand challenging those in power.[31]

Paul VI

An examination of the writings of Paul VI reveals that his orthodox assumptions, like those of his predecessors, are often in conflict with a sensitivity to structural realities that also informs his analysis. Because Paul was faced with mounting evidence of the failure of developmentalist policies as the Third World churches became more deeply involved with the struggle of the poor, he developed an analysis that was at times reflective of radical social theory.[32] But Paul was also faced with alarm in Vatican circles over the revolutionary momentum in the Southern hemisphere, as well as extreme polarization between the Right and the Left in the region itself. This caused him to reiterate positions on industrialization, women, and on social agency that may be aligned with orthodox and organic perspectives. His positions on Marxism and on the use of force may possibly demonstrate a retreat from important movements to the left that had already been made.

Echoing the urgency of Pius XI's *Quadragesimo anno*, Paul's two letters, *Populorum progressio* (1967), an encyclical letter, and *Octogesima adveniens* (1971), an apostolic letter to Cardinal Roy issued on the thirtieth anniversary of *Rerum novarum*, depicted with great alarm the problems evident in capitalist industrialization. Very few have power and wealth, Paul said, "while whole populations destitute of necessities live in a state of dependence" (*PP* 30; *OA* 2). The oppressive social structures that caused this injustice are due to "abuses of ownership or to the abuses of power" (*PP* 21). "Modern economies," if "left to [themselves] work rather to widen the differences" so that the rich grow richer and the poor languish (PP 8, 29, 57). Paul condemned the "limits" and "misdeeds" of economic growth. Quoting Pius XI, Paul said, "unchecked liberalism" has created the "international imperialism of money" with "excessive suffering, injustices, and fratracidal conflicts" (OA 41; PP 26).

Paul showed an orthodox analysis, however, when he stated that problems such as these incurred by the process of industrialization, are due to peasant "flight from the land" and are necessary for the "advance of industrial civilization." Thus, in harmony with the liberal sector of the orthodox mainstream, Paul assumed that social dislocation and misery are either necessities of the industrial process, or "abuses" that can be remedied by the liberal agenda (see OA 8–10).[33]

With regard to the position of women, Paul continued the assumptions of both organic and orthodox social theory regarding the family. Women may have "equal rights" in economic, social, and political life. But this is not to be confused with a "false equality" that would deny their "nature" and "proper vocation" as child raisers and domestic workers (OA 13).[34] Women may have access (however limited) to the "public" male world, but the "private" domestic world is not subject to change. Papal social teaching continued to assume that norms of justice were not violated when women work a double day.

Another area in which Paul appropriated liberal orthodox theory is that of agency for social change. Paul carefully restricted the agency allowed to trade unions. Unions were not to demand more than is economically feasible, and they were not to be involved in political activity (OA 14). Rather, national and international public authorities and powerful elites were to be the sources for social change. They could reform and regulate the world market; "encourage, stimulate, coordinate, supplement and integrate" the work of individuals and groups; and "give of their own possessions" (*PP* 33; see also 32, 64, 78). They could pay higher taxes and higher prices for imported goods from poor countries, give technical assistance, and establish a world fund of money usually spent on armaments (*PP* 47, 51). They could restructure the international division of production, the structure of exchanges, the control of profits, and the monetary system—all without violating "human solidarity" (*OA* 43, 49). As agents capable of "great generousity, much sacrifice and unceasing effort," national authorities, business elites, and other "experts" were the primary agents of authentic development (*PP* 35, 47–49, 71, 83–84). Paul described the social encyclicals as "anguished appeals" to elites and public authorities on behalf of social justice (*PP* 46).

Paul's move away from the left included adamant warnings against Marxism in both his encyclicals. While he included John XXIII's differentiation between ideologies and actual historical movements, his quote from *Pacem in terris* was placed in a context highly critical of these movements (*cf. OA* 26–34 with *PT* 159).[35] Against the thrust of John's analysis, Paul warned that people can accept "totalitarian and coercive" ideologies without being aware of their true character. Generous people could be deceived, even into violent activity (*OA* 28). He said it is wrong when Christians "refuse to recognize the limitations of the historical socialist movements which remain conditioned by the ideologies from which they originated" (*OA* 31). In his view, there was an inescapable link between the best in these movements that seek a just society and their unacceptable ideology. Christians needed to remember this even if they were able to distinguish four "aspects" or levels of Marxism. Some, including possibly Paul himself, may have been drawn to the fourth level: that is, Marxism as "a rigorous method of examining social and political reality, and as the rational link . . . between theoretical knowledge and the practice of revolutionary transformation" (*OA* 33).[36] But, said Paul, it would be "illusory and dangerous" to ignore "the intimate link" that binds Marxism as a useful tool of social analysis with other aspects of Marxism, including Marxism as a theory of class struggle—and therefore violent activity—and Marxism as a denial of transcendent reality (*OA* 34; see also 26, 28). Paul qualified, perhaps to death, John's assertion that Christians can make a distinction between Marxist movements and Marxism as an ideology.[37]

Another movement to the left from which Paul retreated, this time a move to the left within his own writing, had to do with the use of force. In *Populorum progressio* Paul was sympathetic to a revolutionary uprising when there was "manifest, long-standing tyranny which would do great damage to fundamental personal rights and dangerous harm to the common good of the country" (*PP* 31).[38] Four years later in *Octogesima adveniens*, Paul's reference to the use of force said that it leads to extreme violence and abuses (*OA* 43). Since a footnote in the original text of *Octogesima adveniens* refers to the passage just cited from *Populorum progressio*, it is possible that Paul was retracting his support for revolution.[39]

Finally, Paul's writing included a traditional understanding of the role of the Church. The Church's role is to link traditional social teaching and gospel precepts to the "signs of the times" so that Christians will know what is expected of them with regard to the poor, and they won't be deceived by false ideologies of Marxism and liberalism (*OA* 5, 36, 41). The hierarchy teaches and interprets, while the laity implements this teaching in the social order.[40]

On the other hand, like all the teaching before him, Paul's analysis also used elements that may be aligned with the radical paradigm, and are decidedly at odds with his orthodox analyses. Paul engaged in a structural analysis of the causes of the divisions between the wealthy and the poor. He said that poverty in the Third World was due to the legacy of colonialism, especially to the establishment of one-product economies. Despite political independence, nations were still kept in economic dependence through the current practices of neo-colonialism (*PP* 7, 52). Paul said that "under cloak of financial aid or technical assistance" there often lurked neocolonialist concerns for "maintaining or acquiring complete dominance" (*PP* 52). Paul gave an economic interpretation of the sources of war, saying that peace grows out of just economic and social structures in which all can participate (*PP* 49, 76, 87). Thus, said Paul, what is called for is social and economic liberation, or "a fitting autonomous growth" (*PP* 6).

In addition to a structural analysis that made a distinction between political independence and current economic dependence because of neocolonialist patterns, Paul included a structural analysis of power. He said that, given the wide disparity between prices for the raw materials of poor nations and prices for the manufactured goods of more affluent nations, the promotion of "free trade" as a means to equity was ludicrous (*PP* 57–58). Here Paul manifested a radical critique of orthodox theory. He implied that the terms of sale reflected the market power, or lack thereof, that sellers and buyers brought to the marketplace. Income depended not only on productivity, as in orthodox theory, but on the relative power of the group to which one belonged, a postulate of radical theory. He identified "glaring inequities . . . in the exercise of power" and said that trade is only free when "the parties involved are not affected by any excessive inequalities of economic power" (*PP* 58, 61, 9). Ultimately, Paul said, economics is dependent on political power. Consequently, a shift from a focus on economics to a focus on political power is necessary (*OA* 46).

A structural analysis of power led Paul to evaluate global corporations. He viewed them as "largely independent" structures that "conduct autonomous strategies" that are beyond the control of public authorities (*OA* 44). In recognizing that advanced global capitalism was not accountable to individual

nation-states, he saw how economic power was not accountable to political power as orthodox theory maintained. He
questioned all models of socioeconomic organization, and
condemned both "bureaucratic socialism" and "technocratic
capitalism" not as systems full of abuses, but as systems that
have failed "in their roots" (OA 45, 37, 35).

Because of the need for "bold transformations," "comprehensive structural changes," and "innovations that go deep,"
Paul moved to the left in his consideration of method and
agency (PP 32). The Church could no longer presume to enunciate the specifics concerning what was appropriate in this
area. Rather, the methods of change would have to be determined by an analysis of the specific situation by the local
community (OA 4).[41] If one interprets Paul's analysis of John's
dialogue with Marxism in a positive light, Paul leaves room
for some "degree of commitment" with Marxists, and "a legitimate variety of possible options" (OA 31, 50).

Another way Paul moved to the left in his consideration of
method and agency was his advocacy of the utopian imagination. Paul was careful not to describe it as a fleeing from
historical reality nor to replace it with an ideal.[42] Rather, Paul
understood the utopian imagination as "perceiv[ing] in the
present the disregarded possibility hidden within it" and
directing it "towards a fresh future" (OA 37). Human misery
was linked to injustice, which must be "faced with courage"
and "fought against and overcome" (PP 32). Paul was calling for a visionary yet historically possible society. The search
for this society, said Paul, should be financed on the order of
present funding for armaments and technology (OA 19). His
utopian vision called for "daring and creative innovations"
that include "modern forms of democracy" (OA 42, 47). It
involved the creation of a society in which people are the
"author[s] of [their] own advancement" and the "artisans of
their destiny" (PP 34, 65).

Because Paul mixed elements of orthodox, organic, and

radical economic analyses so thoroughly, an evaluation of his work is difficult. Several contradictions are particularly noteworthy. On the one hand Paul characterizes the problems within capitalism as "abuses." But he also condemned "technocratic capitalism" as a system that had failed at its very root. Paul said that public authorities could reform and regulate domestic and international markets. Yet he also said that their means of doing this, financial aid and technical assistance, for example, are cloaks for further domination. He said that global corporations, the chief actors in economies, are beyond the control of these very authorities. Paul called for justice between superiors and subordinates while at the same time acknowledging that justice only happens within a situation of relative equality of social power. Finally, Paul said that what goes on in a social economy is dependent on who has the political power. But he condemned the various modes of struggle against abusive power, and thereby refused to encourage people who resist and challenge that power. Trade unions were not to be involved in politics, nor was there to be revolutionary uprising or collaboration with Marxist groups. And, as noted above, he recognized that the chief actors in economies, the corporations, are beyond political control. The writings of Paul VI on economic justice are confusing because he analyzed the socioeconomic arena from incompatible perspectives.

Nevertheless, Paul's teaching continued the shift begun by John away from a primary emphasis on premodern organic and modern orthodox theoretical assumptions. Paul criticized these theories when he supported a model of just social organization that is a product of discernment at the local or regional level. This model perceived the "disregarded possibility" hidden within the present through the use of utopian imagination (*OA* 37). Paul shifted Catholic social teaching from a concern with the past as a model for public policy, particularly the feudal past with its emphasis on hierarchy and cooperation, to a concern for "a fresh future."[43] In doing so, Paul shifted from a concern with a "top-down" model of social change to concern with a "bottom-up" model. Paul rejected the orthodox mainstream when he endorsed a pluralism of political options in the search for justice, and it is here that he moved furthest away from the right.[44] In affirming both a model of justice that emanates locally, and the necessity of utopian imagination, Paul rejected an identification of the unconditional obligations of justice with historically conditioned social arrangements. He moved away from the organic and orthodox social models when he said that human understanding of just social arrangements, and implicitly also the Church's traditional understanding of these, is limited by the "relative character" of whatever "model of society" is currently operative (*OA* 40).[45] Paul VI's advocacy for a new society, forged by the imaginative struggle of the people who would be most affected by it, is perhaps the clearest evidence of his alignment with the radical perspective.[46]

Justice in the World

Justice in the World (1971), also issued during Paul's papacy, was written by the World Synod of Bishops. It emphasized the need for an analysis of global economic and political structures, and it continued Paul's condemnation of the way advanced global capitalism functions. The present economic order it said, creates "unjust systems and structures" that inspire "a network of domination" in which "decisions concerning three quarters of income, investment and trade [are] in the hands of one third of the human race." This "new industrial and technological order favors the concentration of wealth, power and decision-making in the hands of a small public or private controlling group" (*JW* 5, 9, 12).[47] Its social analysis identified the arms race as a source of wealth for the rich and impoverishment for the poor. It identified the ideological corruption of education and the communications media by the wealthy minority (*JW* 9, 50). But even more forcefully than Paul, it gave verbal support to indigenous liberation movements, including a liberation model of education in which theory is not divorced from social action (*JW* 18, 51–53, 77). It affirmed democratic participation in economic as well as political spheres that must be obtained by "social and political action" (*JW* 9). At times it seemed to move beyond a traditional understanding of the role of the Church when it said that the Church was to take on "new functions and new duties in every sector of human activity." Authentic proclamation of the gospel included activities that built up a just social order. The Church was to scrutinize injustice in every sector of society, even within its own institution, especially with regard to the economic privilege of the Church (*JW* 20, 41–48).[48] Perhaps the most significant acknowledgment of this document was that earthly liberation, and action on its behalf, is a "constitutive dimension" of the Church's message of salvation (*JW* 6, 34–36).[49]

Despite the presence of elements of a radical social analysis, this document utilized a liberal orthodox model of social change. The primary agents of justice were still the public authorities, international agencies, and individual Christians (*JW* 68, 70). The "unjust systems and structures" that the document identified did not include a class system of economic privilege and economic exploitation. There was no acknowledgment that the laity included not only the impoverished masses but also the one-third who controlled economic decisions and the oppressive structures they had generated.[50] The document believed that the cooperation of rich and poor Christians, and their individual, nonviolent action, could bring about economic justice (*JW* 39, 49, 59).

Despite its constant juxtaposition with an orthodox analysis, the increasing use of perspectives approaching a radical analysis during the papacy of Paul VI cannot be denied. There was a movement toward a more complex structural analysis of capitalism, and increasing support of grassroots movements for social change. This was especially evident in *Octogesima adveniens* and *Justice in the World*, both of which were written in 1971, and both of which were in some sense responses to the documents issued by the 130 Latin American bishops who met in Medellin in 1968.

Medellin and Puebla

The purpose of the Medellin Conference (1968) was to examine, in light of Vatican II and from the perspective of the masses, Latin America's deteriorating socioeconomic reality.[51] Of the sixteen Medellin documents, the ones on Justice and Peace were especially noteworthy. This is so not only for their structural analysis of capitalism, but perhaps most importantly for their support of grassroots movements of poor people who are working for social change.

Despite the efforts of those who had opposed Medellin, the above positions on the part of the Latin American Church were reaffirmed and extended in the Puebla document, issued in 1979, during the early papacy of John Paul II.[52] Like the papal and synodical documents, an analysis of the socioeconomic teachings of these Latin American documents reveals a confusing mixture of orthodox and radical modes of analysis. This reflected the dual perspectives of the bishops who issued them, or viewed from a radical perspective, the class conflict within the body of bishops themselves.

Indicative of an analysis that can be aligned at points with the radical paradigm was the evaluation the documents made of capitalist economic and class structures, the structure of the national security state, sexism, and the social agency of the Church.

Contrary to the orthodox analysis of "underdevelopment," these documents declared that poverty was not a result of misfortune or of a late start in industrialization. Rather, underdevelopment was a result of capitalist development. Capitalist development created economic, social, and political structural injustice that could be called "institutionalized violence." This violence was perpetrated by elites within poor countries and the affluent nations (*Med-Peace* 1, 9, 16, 19, 32; *P* 30). The structural injustice created by the development of "capitalist liberalism" gave rise to "illegitimate privileges," "scandalous contrasts," and "a situation of dependence and oppression on both national and international levels" (*P* 542). Neocolonialism created vertical economies where resources continually flowed out of poor countries. These included not only natural resources, but the financial resources of the elite who invested abroad, the human capital resources of professionals who left the country, and the tax and dividend resources of companies who evaded the system (*Med-Peace* 9). The "mechanisms" of "economic systems" have created "on the international level" a situation of "economic, technological, political and cultural dependence," a growing gap between rich and poor, and the suffering of impoverished propertyless millions (*P* 30, 64, 66, 778). It created a progressive debt that serviced a few but encumbered all (*Med-Peace* 9). This economic neocolonialism was as cruel as political neocolonialism, for the poor who lacked material goods lacked participation in the basic life of the society (*P* 26). A "rigid free market economy" was a "wellspring of injustice" and gave rise to the priority of capital over labor (*P* 437, 47). The resulting economy produced too few jobs and it "totally disregarded people not engaged in production" (*P* 39, 71).

The class analysis contained in the Latin American documents was no less vivid. The Puebla document deplored the "supremacy and domination of some peoples or social strata over other peoples and social strata" (*P* 427). The rigid "free market economy" subsidized a privileged, native upper class that prospered at the expense of the misery of the masses who were left at a "subsistence level" and "exploited harshly," having to endure "humiliating disregard and subjection" (*Med-Peace* 3; P 47, 452, 1208). The Puebla document observed the racial component of class pointing out that indigenous peoples and Afro-Americans are the poorest of the poor (P 34). Meanwhile, said Medellin, the middle classes are vulnerable to increasing marginalization (*Med-Peace* 4). The privileged place of the elites was assured by the legitimating ideology of the media and education (P 61–62, 1069, 1071).

The documents also included a structural analysis of the state. A development model that worked only for the few necessitated a repressive police state. Medellin said that privileged groups "characterize as subversive activities all attempts to change the social system" that favors them. They joined together and obstructed necessary changes, sometimes destroying life and property (*Med-Peace* 5–6, 17). Puebla spoke about the proliferation of political regimes that were "based on force" and "systematic or selective repression," particularly against unions and others who organized for their rights (P 42, 44, 500, 1262). They did this under the "ideology of the national security state" that put people "under tutelage of military and political elites" who "suppress the broad based participation of people" and monopolize the benefits of development (P 547, 549; see also 49, 531, 547). The arms race was linked to poverty, and war was viewed as oppression by the powerful (*Med-Peace* 13; P 67).

The Puebla document noted the exclusion and overburdening of women in all sectors of society. Women were "almost totally absent from political, economic and social life." This was due to the strictures of "male predominance, unequal wages, deficient education, etc.," and the exploitation of women "into an object of consumption" (P 834). For the first time Catholic social teaching recognized women's double day—the dual work of domestic and wage labor (P 837). The

Puebla document said that the perspective of women was "indispensable for the complete representation of the needs and hopes of the people" (*P* 1219).

The Latin American documents were the first to give an analysis of the Church that may be aligned with the radical paradigm. These documents viewed the Church from a radical perspective when they saw the Church as an agent that took seriously the dialectic between social structures and conversion, and that took the side of a struggling poor that challenged the status quo. Puebla acknowledged that social structures of justice (or injustice) conditioned conversion to justice (*P* 438). Medellin said that the work of social justice and the work of salvation were not to be separated (*Med-Justice* 5).

In the Puebla document this came to be called evangelization for an "integral liberation," or evangelization for the "growth of people in all life's dimensions" including "the social, the political, the economic, the cultural, and all their interrelationships" (*P* 193, 480, 483). The Church was responsible for promoting the earthly as well as the transcendent welfare of human beings. The Church did this with a vision that was accompanied by effective institutional action (*P* 1226, 1283). Puebla rejected "various forms of dualism and false antithesis between a catechesis of sacraments and a catechesis of real life" (*P* 988). This holistic evangelization required the Latin American Church to support grassroots movements of poor people who were working for their own liberation. Since dependence was a form of bondage that violated human rights, "the crux of liberative evangelization," said Puebla, "is to transform human beings into active subjects of their own individual and communitarian development" (*P* 485; see also *Med-Peace* 27). This meant that the Church had to take sides, the side of the "preferential option for the poor" (*P* 733, 1134, 1136, 1142, 1145, 1217). But the poor for whom the framers of these documents had a preferential option were not paralyzed victims. They were people involved in the struggle for their own liberation. They were people who heeded the mandate of the Gospel to "rise up and walk."[53]

When the Latin American Church took the side of the poor, this meant the Church changed sides. It acknowledged its participation in the evil ramifications of the social, political, and economic structures around it. The Church acknowledged its "acts of complicity with earthly powers" (P 10, 84). It disassociated itself from supporting those who had economic and political power, divested itself of its privileges, and became a converted Church.[54] In order to be the "voice of the voiceless" it joined the voiceless and named society from their perspective (P 24, 1094, 1268). Thus the Church defended the rights of the poor and denounced injustice. It supported the struggle of the proliferating basic Christian communities, causes for "joy and hope," which functioned as a balance to the minority group in power (Med-Justice 20; P 96). The Latin American Church did this even at the risk of making groups with economic power feel "abandoned" by the Church; it did this even at the risk of loss of privileges, persecution, and death (P 79, 83, 623, 1160).[55]

This struggle for a just order was necessary in a society full of "institutionalized injustice," in a society that was full of conflict (P 46; Med-Peace 16). It was to be waged by the imaginative exploration of new possibilities. The Church must "encourage experiments." The hierarchy served the laity "by nurturing their creativity so that they can explore options that are increasingly in line with . . . the needs of the weakest" (P 525; see also 806, 1046, 1054). Puebla supported nonhierarchical relationships between bishops, priests, and the laity (P 626, 633, 784). The framers of these documents envisioned the active participation of all people in the running of businesses, in reform of agrarian structures and policies, and in worker representation at every level of society (Med-Justice 11, 12, 14; P 136, 1263). It supported intermediate structures, such as local citizens' action groups (on education, land reform, sanitation, etc.), between the person and the state that are governed by the lower classes (*Med-Justice* 7, 15). Because multinationals are beyond the authority of nations and even international organizations, and the international abuse of power was "ubiquitous," a new international economic order must be created by these movements for social change (*P* 1264, 501, 502, 1279, 1280).

While it was clear that this liberating Church supported "non-violent tactics" to establish justice, it was sympathetic to the temptations to violence "by people whose patience had been abused by intolerable socioeconomic situations" (*P* 533; *Med-Peace* 16). It laid the blame for "explosive revolutions of despair" on the power elites who were responsible for provoking them (*Med-Peace* 17).

Finally, the Puebla document contained a more radical analysis of Marxism than had so far been rendered in Catholic social teaching. It acknowledged that Marxism "arose as a positive criticism of commodity fetishism and of the disregard of the value of human labor" (*P* 543). Puebla said that "fear of Marxism keeps many from facing up to the oppressive reality of liberal capitalism" (*P* 92).

Simultaneous with this radical analysis is one that is more in harmony with orthodox theory and demonstrates the deep ideological divisions within the Latin American hierarchy. For example, the Puebla document was also extremely critical of Marxism, particularly for its sacrifice of human values, "use of force," and "utopian forms of unrealism" (*P* 48). It said that all historical experimentation with Marxism has led to totalitarianism, and it even rejected a Christian praxis that utilized Marxist analysis (*P* 544, 545). Puebla laid down the specific criteria for Christian involvement with movements rooted in false philosophical theories, and they all had to do with supervision by and commitment to the institutional Church (*P* 554–557). Puebla said that the only institution that was independent of any ideology and had a "global" perspective on the human situation was the Catholic Church (P 538–540, 558).[56] The framers of the documents said the Latin American Church opposed both liberal capitalism and Marxist collectivism and opted for a "third way"; it "opt[ed] solely for the human being" (P 495, 497, 542–543, 551).[57]

Also in contradiction to the radical analysis in the same documents was the notion that the agents of social change were to be those who already held the power. The laity created the third way by "building up the community" in a process that seemingly had no room for conflict (P 489). They would work through political channels and in communion with their pastors to Christianize the current structures and the people who govern them (P 154, 473, 474, 524, 777, 785, 787, 789, 790–793). These included businesspeople, public authorities, "heads of national and international development programs," and all those "who have a greater share of wealth, culture and power" and who will "radically modify" the economy (Med-Justice 18; Med-Peace 17).[58] It included rich nations who would curb their "consumptionist tendencies" (P 496). In harmony with this view, which rejected a class analysis, was the statement that the glaring rift in religious unity between elites and the masses was due to a lack of pastoral concern by the Church (P 455).

While the Medellin documents are almost totally silent on women's oppression, Puebla includes a traditional assessment of women's role: Women suffer inferiority only "in some cultural groups" (P 57); the Church has "sometimes" undervalued women (P 839); and women have increasing pastoral responsibilities and yearn to improve their situation in line with their "dignity and distinctiveness" and "in line with their specific identity and femininity" (P 419, 443). Like the papal encyclicals, Puebla viewed women as inherently different from men. They may have increasing access to a male world of pastoral responsibility, but their "distinctiveness" rendered a role for them apart from men and in the home, however much they wish advancement. Education, for example, should "accord" with one's sex (*P* 1034).

In other areas of the Puebla document, in the discussion of the family and the consecrated life, for example, women go unnamed. Yet from the ways these areas are discussed, the "distinctive" presence of women can be detected. In the section on the pastoral care of the family, the family is characterized as a "domestic Church," and it is carefully spelled out that the mode of governance in the Church is hierarchical (*P* 639, 645). Women, and the children they raise alone, are referred to by the document as "incomplete families" (*P* 594, 608). In the section on the consecrated life, it was stated that religious, many of whom are women, have their "specific form of membership in the diocesan family" (*P* 765). It was those (women) in religious life who most share with and live alongside the poor (*P* 734). Tensions between women and clerics are noted when the document laments religious who "thoughtlessly abandon" traditional apostolates or lose sight of "the pastoral mission of the bishop" (*P* 737). Even the section that denounces the dependence of women and their double burden in public and private life ends with an affirmation of women's specific aptitude for "unconditional acceptance" and the servicing of human needs, and her "fundamental role . . . as mother, the defender of life and the home educator" (*P* 846, 845).

Along with a traditional analysis of Marxism, social agency, and women's role, the Latin American documents also included a traditional understanding of the role of the institutional Church. The Church teaches "permanently valid elements" rooted in the Gospel and the traditional social teaching of the Church (*P* 472; see also *Med-Justice* 6). Much of this discussion contained a nondialectical understanding of the relationship between theory and practice, between religion and economics, between the Gospel and the world. Catholic education as "a resource for social change" could "consolidate and fortify" the best values in a culture so as to engender cultural conversion (*P* 388, 395). This conversion "will serve as the basis and guarantee of a transformation in structures and the social milieu" (*P* 388; see also 401, 497, 512).[59]

Because this Church was to be a source of unity among greatly divided social strata, it was to eschew all political entanglements and not take sides (*P* 447, 527, 992). It was to be nonpartisan, excluding no one (*P* 754). Priests were not to be involved in politics and were not to "apply social analysis with strong political connotations to pastoral work" (*P* 91). Quoting John Paul II, Puebla said that religious were to avoid "exaggerated interest in the broad field of temporal problems" (*P* 769). Puebla warned the Christian base communities against becoming "homes for ideological radicals" (*P* 630). The "preferential option for the poor" was not "exclusive" and runs the risk of being misinterpreted (*P* 735). The Church should support "the downtrodden of every social class," and always dialogue with elites concerning the common good (*Med-Justice* 20–21).

Thus, an orthodox interpretation of the role of the Church stands alongside a more radical one. And a dual analysis of capitalist structures, social class, women, and the process of social change reflected the differing allegiances of those who did the interpreting. Puebla and Medellin, like the papal and synodical documents before them, had something for both sides. They simultaneously used aspects of both orthodox and radical interpretive paradigms in their assessment of the situation and the needs of the poor.

What has been most noted in the Latin American documents has to do with the content of their radical analysis. Perhaps the most significant element in their analysis was their insistence that the agents of social change will arise not out of the elite but out of those who are most marginalized by the system. A second significant element was their rejection of the traditional understanding of the Church's role where the Church is seen as effecting social change by teaching the right principles to its individual members. Rather, the Latin American documents give voice to the more radical interpretation where the Church is seen as an active collective agent, either supporting or working against a given social order.

According to the radical analytic stream within these documents, the Church's role within an economic system will become clear when it understands the social order through the eyes of those who cannot participate, and when it supports and nurtures their imaginative experimentation for a new social order. The Church learns the very principles it is to apply through its immersion in the social, economic, and political struggles of these people. The Church sees that its role is to facilitate and support the poor in becoming conscious agents of their own development, since human dignity cannot be realized apart from the exercise of self-empowerment.

The Puebla document extended the Church's language about the nature of the common good, and its own mission in relation to it, to include the phrase "preferential option for the poor." This introduced "a principle of transcendent dimensions beyond revolutionary change" where liberation is always an unfinished process. The Church is committed, even after the revolution, to viewing society through the eyes of the marginalized.[60] According to the radical tendencies within these documents, the struggle against extensive structural injustice, and the preferential option for the challenging, not the passive poor, is the core of Christian witness.[61] That this radical understanding is juxtaposed with another, more orthodox, one that would deny this role for the Church makes it no less significant.

Notes

1. *Mater et magistra* (MM) and *Populorum progressio* (PP) are found in Joseph Gremillion, ed. *The Gospel of Peace and Justice* (Maryknoll, N.Y.: Orbis, 1976).

2. Joseph Gremillion designates the Third World as approximately one hundred nations below the thirty-fifth parallel (*Gospel of Peace and Justice*, p. 60).

Duncan Cameron says that the nations of the Southern Hemisphere, with 75 percent of the world's population, survive on less than 20 percent of the world's income. See Gregory Baum and Duncan Cameron, eds. *Ethics and Economics* (Toronto: Lorimer, 1984), p. 131.

3. *Octogesima adveniens* (*OA*), in *Gospel of Peace and Justice*, ed. Gremillion.

4. *Pacem in terris* (*PT*), in *Gospel of Peace and Justice*, ed. Gremillion.

5. *Rerum novarum* (*RN*) and *Quadragesimo anno* (*QA*) are found in *Seven Great Encyclicals* (Glen Rock, N.J.: Paulist Press, 1963).

6. Christine E. Gudorf, *Catholic Social Teaching on Liberation Themes*. (Washington, D.C.: University Press of America, 1981), p. 119.

7. Later John said that not only scientific competence and technological capacity are needed to promote genuine progress but also the implementation of spiritual values (*PT* 150).

8. Gudorf points out that the translation "reduce" is not accurate. The verb *deduco*, correctly translated reduce, is the one used by Pius XI and Pius XII when they spoke of the reduction of principles into social action. John XXIII, however, uses the verb *adduco* (*MM* 236, 238; *PT* 160), which is more correctly translated "bring into effect." Gudorf calls this a "significant shift," unnoticed by most translations (Gremillion, *Gospel of Peace and Justice*, translates only *MM* 238 as reduce), which shows a "subtle lessening of the hold of the idealist philosophical position [ideas change reality] on the papacy." See *Catholic Social Teaching on Liberation Themes*, p. 90.

9. This contrasts with Leo XIII's admonition not to look for temporal solutions to human problems (as the socialists do), but to "suffer and endure" life's ills and look for a remedy to God (*RN* 14).

10. Pius XI spoke of the owner as the only one who was entitled to a "proportionate share of the increased public riches" (*QA* 136). The just wage until John (and sometimes after him) was considered an adequate but modest "living" wage. The wage is not viewed in relation to profit.

11. See *QA* 79 and Pius XII's radio address *La solennita* (1941), quoted in Gudorf, *Catholic Social Teaching on Liberation Themes*, p. 33.

12. See also Gudorf, *Catholic Social Teaching on Liberation Themes*,

p. 126. It is important to note, however, that John is always careful to say that this should never be done if it restricts individual freedom (*MM* 55; *PT* 65).

13. Gudorf, *Catholic Social Teaching on Liberation Themes*, pp. 223–24.

14. Ibid., pp. 302–12.

15. Donal Dorr, *Option for the Poor: A Hundred Years of Vatican Social Teaching* (Maryknoll, N.Y.: Orbis, 1983), p. 263.

16. I argue that John's recommendations for economic rights move out of the orthodox paradigm because, even though some liberal orthodox thinkers have espoused economic rights, they have not restricted capitalist interests so as to achieve universal economic rights (as opposed to a minimalist welfare system) in many capitalist societies.

17. Ibid., p. 256; and Gregory Baum, *Catholics and Canadian Socialism* (Toronto: Lorimer, 1980), p. 90.

18. Baum and Cameron, eds. *Ethics and Economics.* p. 91.

19. Joseph Joblin, "The Papal Encyclical *Pacem in Terris*," *International Labor Review* 84, no. 3 (September 1961): 1–14.

20. This was no small move at a time when most Catholics thought that the major enemy of the day was communism. See David J. O'Brien and Thomas J. Shannon, eds., *Renewing the Earth: Catholic Documents on Peace, Justice and Liberation* (New York: Image Books, 1977), p. 171.

21. Joblin, "The Papal Encyclical *Pacem in Terris*," p. 10.

22. Dorr, *Option for the Poor*, p. 107. Dorr notes that this was not so much a shift to the left as "a decisive move away from the right" (p. 114).

23. For a discussion about the classification of papal documents see Gudorf, *Catholic Social Teaching on Liberation Themes*, pp. xv–xviii.

24. *Gaudium et spes* (*GS*) is found in *Gospel of Peace and Justice*, ed. Gremillion.

25. *GS* 29 marks the first time Catholic teaching denounced socioeconomic hierarchies.

26. Expropriation of land that is kept idle modifies the statement of Pius XI that "the non-use of ownership" does not destroy the right to own private property (*QA* 47).

27. See my discussion in Chapter Two.

28. The other two condemnations made by *Gaudium et spes* were against abortion (*GS* 51) and against the indiscriminate destruction of modern warfare (*GS* 79–80).

29. For example, Gudorf, *Catholic Social Teaching on Liberation Themes*, p. 224.

30. Gudorf argues that while the popes may have denied complete equality, they were offended by the gross inequalities of the twentieth century. Increasingly, "the possibility of socially created inequality—injustice—" became evident (*Catholic Social Teaching on Liberation Themes*, pp. 44–45).

31. Dorr, *Option for the Poor.* p. 138. The Second Vatical Council, however, refused to address a methodology of resistance or the possibility of the social agency of the marginalized. It considered these issues "too sensitive" to be discussed (ibid., p. 132).

32. The development programs of the 1960s engendered a growth in the GNP of Latin American countries "that was actually lower than that of the previous decade, and the gap between rich and poor continued to widen." Penny Lernoux, "The Long Path to Puebla," in *Puebla and Beyond* ed. John Eagleson and Philip Scharper (Maryknoll, N.Y.: Orbis, 1979), p. 9.

33. Like John XXIII (*MM* 123, 127), Paul VI understands that tenant farmers "abandon" the land due to the unavoidable advance of the industrial process. The view that these social problems are the natural outgrowth of the transition from an agrarian to an industrial society is in accord with capitalist theories of development. A structural analysis of the situation would have revealed that peasants were driven off the land by the mechanized farming of the wealthy who could afford such methods. See L. S. Stavrianos, *Global Rift: The Third World Comes of Age* (New York: William Morrow, 1981), p. 442.

For a study that cites countless examples of how "industrial progress" diverted land, labor, and capital from domestic control and from producing food for domestic consumption in order to serve the interests of high-technology farming that produces luxury crops for the Third World elite and the First World, see Frances Moore Lappe and Joseph Collins, *Food First: Beyond the Myth of Scarcity* (Boston: Houghton Mifflin, 1977).

34. Gudorf contends that since the modern popes can no longer deny equality between the sexes, they must make a distinction between "true" and "false" equality. In denouncing a "false equality" that ignores woman's "nature," Paul VI uses the same argument against sexual equality that previous popes had used to oppose socioeconomic equality. Gudorf says, "we are left little option but to assume that in the woman question, there is something more deeply

rooted than in the other areas [of race and class oppression]" (*Catholic Social Teaching on Liberation Themes*, pp. 42, 271, 345).

35. Popes usually quote each other because they like to be seen, not as innovators, but as builders upon the tradition. While *Populorum Progressio* 39 rejects Marxist movements, it accepts a pluralism of organizations or unions as long as they do not share a materialist and atheistic philosophy.

36. See Gudorf, *Catholic Social Teaching on Liberation Themes*, p. 230.

37. *OA* 26–36 can be read as a repudiation of *PT* 159.

38. The history of papal teaching on revolution includes that of Leo XIII who saw all revolution as worse than any possible injustice, and that of Pius XII, who in his apostolic letter, *Firmissimam constantiam* (1937), gave permission for citizens to unite in an uprising against a revolutionary left-wing government. This is the first time papal teaching supports a movement against a constituted order, and it is a politically left order. See Gudorf, *Catholic Social Teaching on Liberation Themes*, pp. 187–89; and Dorr, *Option for the Poor*, pp. 70–75.

39. Gremillion, ed. *Gospel of Peace and Justice*, p. 77.

40. *PP* 81 is modified by *OA* 48. Paul VI, writing *Octogesima adveniens* after the Medellin documents were issued (see below), modifies the work of the hierarchy to include the French worker priest movement. But this was an experiment severely restricted by Pius XII and John XXIII. Reinstated by Paul VI, it continues today as an "experiment" because such movements are not generally accepted by the western hierarchy. See Gudorf, *Catholic Social Teaching on Liberation Themes*, pp. 80–81.

41. Gudorf notes, however, that while the grassroots community determines methods of agency, they still are supposed to apply principles that are not themselves influenced by the situation (*Catholic Social Teaching on Liberation Themes*, pp. 96–97).

42. *OA* 37 is an advance from *QA* 14, which views the concept of utopia as unrealistic.

43. See Gregory Baum, *The Social Imperative* (New York: Paulist Press, 1979), p. 226.

44. Dorr, *Option for the Poor*, p. 168.

45. See David Hollenbach, S.J., "Modern Catholic Teaching Concerning Justice," in *The Faith That Does Justice*, ed. John C. Haughey (New York: Paulist Press, 1977), p. 218.

46. In varying degrees, most scholars acknowledge the passages

OA 31 and 50 as Paul's "opening to the left" in which he accepts Christian involvement with some forms of Marxism. See Gregory Baum, *The Priority of Labor* (New York: Paulist Press, 1982), p. 5; Arthur McGovern, *Marxism: An American Christian Perspective* (Maryknoll, N.Y.: Orbis, 1981), p. 119; Gudorf, *Catholic Social Teaching on Liberation Themes,* pp. 227–30.

In view of Paul's work as a whole, however, I agree with Donal Dorr that Paul's opening to the left was his refusal to lay down a universal solution (*Option for the Poor,* p. 168). I would add that a second component of Paul's opening to the left was his focus on the work and vision of the grassroots population as the basis for a new social order.

47. *Justice in the World* (*JW*) is found in *Gospel of Peace and Justice,* ed. Gremillion.

48. The document says that the Church teaches social justice principles, gospel precepts, and the unity of the human family (*JW* 36–38, 55–56).

49. This reverses the traditional organic view that held that material needs were subordinate to spiritual needs. Dorr documents how those who were opposed to the equalization of the material with the spiritual tried to substitute the word "integral" for "constitutive" since the former would mean that social justice is not absolutely essential to the life of the Church, but rather pertains to its fullness (*Option for the Poor,* p. 188).

50. Ibid., pp. 183–84.

51. Lernoux, "The Long Path to Puebla," in *Puebla and Beyond,* ed. Eagleson and Scharper, p. 11.

52. A preliminary document for the Puebla Conference tried to halt the radicalization begun by Medellin; it defended a hierarchical Church and orthodox arguments for development. This document was rejected by a majority of Puebla's bishops, who faced a political and economic situation even worse than at the time of Medellin. See ibid., pp. 23–25. See also Puebla (*P*) 487 and 1259.

The Puebla document (*P*) and the Medellin documents (*Med-Justice, Med-Peace*) are found in *Gospel of Peace and Justice,* ed. Gremillion.

53. Acts 3: 6 quoted in the introduction to the Puebla document, "Message to the Peoples of Latin America" (*P* 3). See also *P* 1137, 1162, 1163, 1220, 1235, 1244, 1245.

54. See Medellin document, Poverty of the Church in *Gospel of Peace and Justice,* ed. Gremillion. See also *P* 1140, 1221.

55. Penny Lernoux observes that in Latin America the Church has become "a surrogate for democracy, providing a protective umbrella for popular organizations, such as labor unions and peasant federations, which otherwise would succumb to repression." She notes that in the decade between Medellin and Puebla "over 850 religious, clergy and bishops were arrested, tortured, expelled or murdered," and "thousands of lay people were similarly tortured and murdered." See "The Long Path to Puebla," in *Puebla and Beyond,* ed. Eagleson and Scharper, p. 3, 17–18.

Jon Sobrino, S.J., argues that the martyrdom of the Latin American Church, while not explicitly acknowledged in the Puebla document, kept the spirit of Medellin from being silenced by the 360 members of the Puebla Conference, most of whom were known as centrist or conservative. See "The Significance of Puebla for the Catholic Church in Latin America," in *Puebla and Beyond,* ed. Eagleson and Scharper, pp. 296, 299.

56. To demonstrate how divided the bishops were at Puebla, Jon Sobrino, S.J., points out that the only round of applause at the Conference (which was forbidden by the rules of procedure), occurred during the discussion of Marxism, when Peruvian Bishop Schmitz said, "Let him who is without an ideology cast the first stone." See "The Significance of Puebla for the Catholic Church in Latin America," in *Puebla and Beyond,* ed. Eagleson and Scharper, p. 297.

57. The Latin American documents hold out for a "third way," even though the Christian Democracy movement, which had supported a third way in Latin America for decades, had been a failure. See Lernoux, "The Long Path to Puebla," in *Puebla and Beyond,* ed. Eagleson and Scharper, p. 12.

Ivo Lesbaupin says that the bishops who have opted for socialism in Latin America criticize the documents for choosing a "third way," which they see as maintaining the status quo. See "The Latin American Bishops and Socialism," in *Christianity and Socialism,* ed. Johan Baptist Metz and Jean Pierre Jossua (New York: Seabury Press, 1977), p. 120.

58. See also *P* 1227–1228, 1238–1243, 1246–1248; *Med-Justice* 10. The documents make this affirmation of the social justice potential of Christian elites even though Puebla also notes that there is "a poor presence of laity in the area of 'constructing society' (workers, peasants, business people, technical people, politicians)" and "an almost total absence of lay people in the area of cultural creation" (*P* 823, 125).

59. This affirmation is made within a document that also says that education in religion has not fostered social change, or been strong enough to affect the socioeconomic organization of society (*P* 1019, 437).

60. Baum and Cameron, eds. *Ethics and Economics* p. 44. See also Baum, *Priority of Labor*, p. 39; and Rosemary Radford Ruether, *Disputed Questions: On Being a Christian* (Nashville: Abingdon Press, 1982), p. 107.

61. Gregory Baum states that this redefinition of the Church's mission is a result of the religious experience of the Latin American Church, which has a history of religious, social, and political struggle with the poor. The "option for the poor" is a religious conversion and a political commitment (*Ethics and Economics*, ed. Baum and Cameron, pp. 57–58).

Chapter Four. The Social Encyclicals of John Paul II: 1981 and 1987

JOHN PAUL II HAS ISSUED two encyclicals on the topic of economic justice, *Laborem exercens* (1981) and *Sollicitudo rei socialis* (1987). Observing the phenomena of rising poverty and increasing economic suffering in the industrialized nations, papal and episcopal teaching in the 1980s modified the preoccupation with Third World poverty that had been characteristic of Catholic social teaching during the papacies of John XXIII and Paul VI. John Paul II's encyclicals also modified the use of perspectives that could be aligned with a radical paradigm. While *Laborem exercens* contained diminishing progressive elements, this is not the case for John Paul II's second social encyclical, *Sollicitudo rei socialis* or *On Social Concern*. The latter document is especially noteworthy because, for the first time in the history of Catholic social teaching, a letter has been issued that is completely lacking in perspectives that may be aligned with the radical model.

Laborem exercens

Laborem exercens, or *On the Priority of Labor*, was issued to commemorate the ninetieth anniversary of *Rerum novarum*. This encyclical reflected the sensibilities of a Polish pope aware of the struggle of the Polish Solidarity union movement. It focused primarily on the industrialized economies of the First and Second Worlds, and only tangentially on the Third World. While it condemned any economic system that gave priority to capital over labor, it was more critical of the Soviet collectivism of the Second World than of the advanced capitalism in the First.

The most important argument of *Laborem exercens* was that economic justice can be realized if capital serves labor, or if capital and labor are in a relationship of copartnership in a democratically organized and centrally planned economy (*LE* 14, 18).[1] However, this affirmation did not emerge out of radical theory. Since he held that the structure of ownership was morally arbitrary, John Paul II also argued that the priority of labor over capital could be achieved in any economic system. John Paul II advocated a society in which each [male] person "is fully entitled to consider himself a part owner of the great workbench at which he is working with everyone else" (*LE* 14). He argued that since collectivism and "rigid" capitalism have been unable to achieve this, "various adaptations in the sphere of the right to ownership of the means of production" were necessary, because "ownership has never been understood in a way that could constitute grounds for social conflict in labor" (*LE* 14).

An examination of this encyclical reveals that, despite his use of some radical categories, John Paul II basically rejected the perspective of the radical paradigm. Further, John Paul II was more comfortable with an organic social model and selected orthodox economic assumptions as the basis for justice than were John XXIII and Paul VI. What is also very striking about *Laborem exercens* is its methodology, which argued primarily from abstract philosophical principles. This is a method not as strongly utilized in Catholic social teaching since John XXIII, who called the Church to be attentive to the "signs of the times." John Paul II did not subscribe to the view of Paul VI that just social organization was the product of local discernment and the utopian imagination, nor the view of the Latin American documents that truth emanates from our insertion in the process of world building. Rather, this document reflected a return to a more deductive rather than an inductive approach to social ethics.

John Paul II declared that social change could be derived from the application of traditional "first principles" to historical situations. These are: the principle of personalism, or the primacy of persons over things (*LE* 13); the principle of the common use of goods, or the right of all persons to have access to the goods of nature and manufactured goods (*LE* 14); the principle of the priority of labor over capital, or the secondary, instrumental nature of capital, which is the "historical heritage of human labor" (*LE* 12); and the principle of use over ownership, or the subordination of the right to private property to the "right common to all to use the goods of all creation" (*LE* 14).

Gregory Baum has hailed *Laborem exercens* as initiating "a critical and creative dialogue with Marxism."[2] I argue, however, that an analysis of the document in light of radical theory requires recognition that its conviction regarding the potential of ideas or principles to change reality, as well as its bias toward private ownership of the means of production, overpowers any movement toward a dialogue with radical analysis. John Paul II's emphasis on the power of principles or right ideas to effect historical change is inherent to the organic perspective. His predisposition toward the private ownership of the means of production, he even asserts that Thomas Aquinas advocated it (*LE* 15), showed the Church's continued failure to distinguish between the ownership of the means of production in capitalist society and the individual ownership of goods. Like Catholic social teaching before him, John Paul II collapsed all historical forms of ownership into one, reified, ahistorical reality.

Abstract idealism and a predisposition toward private ownership of production is related to the encyclical's explicit rejection of a structural analysis of economics. "Opposition between labor and capital does not spring from the structure of the production process," said John Paul II, "or from the structure of the economic process" (*LE* 13). The encyclical argued that a structural analysis of the economic systems in the East and West has nothing to do with understanding the problems between capital and labor. It insisted that the structure of ownership, which it described as either "collectivist" or "capitalist," was morally irrelevant. Specifically, John Paul claimed that "satisfactory socialization," or the just use of the means of production, will not be achieved by "an apriori elimination of private ownership" or by taking production out of the hands of individual owners (*LE* 14). Rather, a just economic order can exist in *any* economic system in which people are willing to apply correct principles and renounce false "economic premises" (*LE* 15). A just economic order could occur within any economic system in which "the subject character of society is ensured" (*LE* 14).

An idealistic moral methodology was also clearly at work in John Paul II's view that economic injustice in capitalism was the result of immoral choices by individual capitalists who accepted false economic premises. It was not the internal dynamics of the system of capitalism that was the issue, but the "error" of the early capitalists who "did not pay sufficient attention to the rights of workers" (*LE* 7, 8). Depicting an understanding of the system of wage labor that is voluntaristic, John Paul II said that this error of the early capitalists "originated in the fact that the workers put their powers at the disposal of the entrepreneurs" (*LE* 11). Then the capitalists, "following the [incorrect] principle of maximum profit tried to establish the lowest possible wages for the work done by the employees" (*LE* 11).[3] The implication was that if certain individual choices had not been made, capitalism could have developed differently. Specifically, the abuses suffered by labor could have been avoided if capitalists, as individuals, had employed different moral norms.

Capitalism could also have developed differently if workers had not been so ready—and supposedly free—to "put their powers at the disposal of the entrepreneurs" (*LE* 11). Most importantly, capitalism might have developed differently if capitalists had not fallen subject to the wrong values that give priority to the material over the spiritual and the personal. These wrong notions are labeled "the error of economism" or "the error of materialism" (*LE* 13).[4] Thus, opposition between capital and labor has occurred because of immoral personal choices on the part of capitalists who have exploited labor. This exploitation comes from accepting false "economic premises" (*LE* 15).

Laborem exercens explicitly rejected the radical view that the capitalist structure of production produces conflict between capital and labor because this system requires that capital appropriate the wealth created by labor. In John Paul's view it is possible to make the capitalist labor system moral by exchanging the principle of maximum profit for the principle of the priority of labor, or the principle of the primacy of the person over things (*LE* 13). To make the system of ownership moral, capitalists are to apply the normative principles of organic society: the right use of property and the common use of goods (*LE* 14, 19). The structure of the economic system is irrelevant, as is the ownership of land, labor, or resources.

Laborem exercens argued that the error of economism on the part of the capitalists had been countered by another error promulgated by Marxist ideology. John Paul II assumed that Marxism is a theory of state collectivism—and a program for it—that is also the product of false ideas (*LE* 14).[5] Like the capitalist error of economism, John Paul II equated his understanding of the dialectical materialism of Marxism with the error of giving primacy to the material over the spiritual and the personal (*LE* 13).[6] For John Paul II, the systems of private or state collectivist ownership are not the cause of labor's plight, but the incorrect attitudes and values of owners or authorities who do not recognize their moral duties.

This assumption, that the moral quality of economic systems themselves is irrelevant because they can be altered by individual moral choice, is in clear contradiction to Paul VI's analysis that held that the "concrete systems" of liberalism and collectivism, which he described as "technocratic capitalism" and "bureaucratic socialism," were incapable of achieving economic justice (*OA* 35, 37).[7] It is also at odds with John Paul II's own analysis in an earlier encyclical, *Redemptor hominis*, in which he argued that economic systems have a logic and momentum built into them that function autonomously from individual choice.[8]

The rejection of any structural analysis of the two systems did not, however, keep *Laborem exercens* from demonstrating a preference for the capitalist system. John Paul II recognizes that the capitalists' errors have perpetrated abuses, but accuses the Marxist error of creating more extensive problems. He charges Marxist thinking with the promotion of class struggle and revolution, and he condemns the communist system of state collectivism that seeks a monopoly of power throughout the world (*LE* 11).[9] Thus, *Laborem exercens* contended that while capitalism needs "various adaptations," "revision," and "reform" in the sphere of the ownership and management of the means of production, the collectivist system showed that these "reforms cannot be achieved by an apriori elimination of private ownership of the means of production" (*LE* 14). State collectivism demonstrated that socializing property did not guarantee that justice can be achieved by eliminating capitalists (*LE* 14). In harmony with orthodox social theory, *Laborem exercens* argued that personal values are more readily protected under the system of private ownership of the means of production than under the system of collectivism or "excessive bureaucratic centralization." It argued for publicly owned enterprises only as "exceptions . . . to the principle of private ownership" (*LE* 15).[10] John Paul II equated alternatives to capitalism with state collectivism.

John Paul II seemed to move toward a radical perspective when he argued that economic justice can be realized if capital serves labor, or if capital and labor are in a relationship of copartnership in a democratically organized and centrally planned economy (*LE* 12, 14, 15, 18). The partnership of capital and labor made sense, said the encyclical, if one understood the nature of capital. In harmony with a radical perspective, *Laborem exercens* defined capital as the heritage of human labor (plus natural resources) (*LE* 12, 13). John Paul II said that "everything that is at the service of work . . . is the result of work" (*LE* 12). Capital is the "product of the work of generations" (*LE* 14). In the radical mode he advocated the coownership and copartnership of all workers (*LE* 14).

The document, however, again showed a predisposition for private ownership when it juxtaposed advocacy for coownership and copartnership of workers with the affirmation that the structure of ownership is morally arbitrary. "Various adaptations in the sphere of right ownership of the means of production" are demanded because "deeply desired reforms cannot be achieved by an apriori elimination of the private ownership of the means of production" (*LE* 14). Because *Laborem exercens* perceived the structure of ownership to be morally irrelevant, and hoped for the benevolent use of property by private owners, it would seem that John Paul II's advocacy of worker partnership emanated from an earlier organic analysis, which takes the existence of hierarchy and cooperation for granted, rather than a radical one. Radical theory also begins by affirming that, because wealth is to serve the whole community, democracy in production is essential. Radical theorists would hold, however, that because political power, including power in the workplace, cannot be divorced from economic power, democracy in production cannot be divorced from issues of ownership.

In addition to the issue of arbitrary ownership, another qualification to the exercise of democracy in production is the document's view that "the key problem of social ethics . . . is that of just remuneration for work done" (*LE* 19). Just remuneration usually had to do with the distribution process in the economic system. In excluding the productive process from the "key problem of social ethics," John Paul II embraced a view that is in harmony with liberal orthodox analysis.

The document's methodology of moral idealism and its preference for elements in orthodox analysis was further demonstrated by its lack of a structural analysis of the dynamics of class. This has ramifications for both the discussion of human work and the discussion of the appropriate agents of social change.

The encyclical's treatment of the reality of human work seemed at first glance to appropriate a Marxist understanding. As for Marx, work for John Paul II is important because it is a way for people to experience joy in creativity and solidarity in collaboration with others (*LE* 8). Work is a way for people to express their human dignity and to increase it (*LE* 9). *Laborem exercens* contended, in words reminiscent of the young Marx, that work is truly human only insofar as it proceeds from "a conscious and free subject . . . who decides about himself [*sic*]" (*LE* 6).[11] Work that emanates from a free, self-initiating subject is required to maintain and develop one's humanity (*LE* 16). Therefore, a welfare society in which some people participate in consumption but do not participate in work (production) is not a fully human society. But as further analysis of this document shows, the free, self-initiating worker who expresses his or her human dignity in solidarity with others is restricted by class and gender boundaries.

Because the organic model accepts the naturalness of relationships of social inequality, there is no sense in *Laborem exercens* that human work participates in sin by being segregated according to a worker's social class. All people are defined as those who labor, whether or not their labor is sold for a wage. Consequently, coal miners and executives, assembly-line workers and professionals, the unemployed and the owners of capital, remain undifferentiated.[12] All work is affirmed, even "the most monotonous" or "the most alienating" work that puts workers "in danger of injury or death." John Paul II did this by appealing to the principle of personalism, and the "subjective dimension of work," especially the spiritual nature of the person who does it (*LE* 6, 7, 9, 11). The encyclical also affirmed that the character of all work is "creative, educational and meritorious" (*LE* 11). At the same time John Paul II did not differentiate the various kinds of drudgery and dangers of work that he said are "familiar to everyone" since "all work . . . is . . . linked to toil" (*LE* 9, 27). This document reintroduced the theme of enduring the suffering of human work as one's participation in the cross of Christ, a theme happily absent from Catholic economic teaching since Leo XIII.[13]

By describing all work as full of both suffering and the joy of creativity, the encyclical ignored the segmentation of work that creates social class. By ignoring the class segregation of work and by affirming all of work without differentiation, it implicitly endorsed this existing segregation. Thus it remained in harmony with orthodox economic theory that treats all persons as equally "free" to participate in economic activity.

While *Laborem exercens* did not acknowledge the segregation of work by class, it was explicit in its support of the segregation of work according to gender. It spoke of "women's work" as a category set apart (*LE* 26). Opposing his understanding about the primacy of the freedom of the human subject, John Paul II claims that women's labor is determined by their sex. In more radical fashion, the document advocated financial remuneration to mothers and a reorganization of the labor process to take into account the needs of families (*LE* 19). But within the context of the document as a whole, this amounted to support for paying women to keep them in their "proper place": in the home. As in previous teaching, women have special tasks, and a sphere of work that is "natural" to women "in accordance with their own nature" (*LE* 19). Mothers belong in the home engaging in "the mission of a mother." They should not "abandon what is specific to them" and, in what is perhaps the strongest statement to date in the papal teaching about gender segregation, John Paul said that to "take up paid work outside the home is wrong" when it keeps women from doing child-care work that they alone can do (*LE* 19).

This document contended that all work—no matter how class- or gender-segregated, no matter how full of danger, drudgery, or suffering—is good and enables people to "achieve fulfillment" as human beings. Surely it is difficult to reconcile this support of a class- and sex-based division of labor with the document's radical affirmation that truly human work emanates from a free, self-initiating subject (*cf. LE* 6, 7 and *LE* 9, 19).

Similarly, its conception of social agency seemed at first glance to be aligned with a radical perspective. The document declared that there had been a general struggle going on between workers in all sectors of society and the owners of the means of production (*LE* 20). It stressed the "need for ever new movements of solidarity of workers and with workers" (*LE* 8). But like the discussion of human work, the discussion of social agency was constrained by the document's failure to make a structural analysis of class. The struggle of workers envisioned here was for the purpose of redressing "growing areas of poverty and even hunger" (*LE* 8). Workers' struggles, and the union movements they engendered, were not to aim at change in the basic power structure, including the class structures of society. In keeping with organic theory, John Paul II believed that the common good always required the stability of the society. Unions—and strikes—were not to have a political purpose but only a specifically economic one. They may seek economic reform but not reallocation of power and control. Like the union movement in the nineteenth century, which John Paul claimed created "a great burst of solidarity," unions were to "stimulate unity" not conflict (*LE* 8). *Laborem exercens* argued that, whatever the problems, the systems of labor and capital are not to be changed, for they "are indispensable components of the process of production in any social system" (*LE* 20). Since "capital" here means "private ownership of the means of production," a more absolute endorsement of capitalism could hardly be imagined.

Consequently, the agents of social change may reasonably include, not only those who suffer from injustice, but also those who gain great privilege from capital ownership. These latter should make a moral choice to join in solidarity with the former, but they need not relinquish social power. The encyclical seemed at first to support a view from the radical perspective that encouraged the building of a broad-based movement for economic justice that united various coalitions from different sectors of society. However, the encyclical actually encouraged a widespread struggle "of the workers and with the workers" that was to be highly nuanced (*LE* 8).[14] *Laborem exercens* stated:

> There is a need for ever new movements of solidarity of the workers and with the workers . . . a solidarity that must never mean being closed to dialogue and collaboration with others. . . . This solidarity must be present whenever it is called for by the social degrading of the subject of work, by exploitation of the workers and by growing areas of poverty and even hunger. . . . However, this struggle must be seen as a normal endeavor "for" the just good . . . but it is not a struggle "against" others. . . . Even if in controversial questions the struggle takes on a character of opposition toward others this is because it aims at the good of social justice, not for the sake of "struggle" or in

order to eliminate the opponent. . . . Unions . . . aim at
correcting . . . everything defective in the system of ownership of the means of production. . . . Unions do not have
the character of political parties struggling for power; they
should not be subjected to the decisions of political parties
or have too close links with them. (*LE* 8, 20)

Hence, this struggle for justice must be multiclass, nonpolitical, against injustice, but must never oppose other persons or groups and never seek a redistribution of social power.
John Paul II counseled that this ethical achievement must take
place in the absence of all social conflict. Thus, *Laborem exercens*
has an organic understanding of social change, that is, regardless of the power alignments in society, change can occur only
in a cooperative and concessional mode.

John Paul II did not address what kind of relationship
those who own capital and have political power are to have
with those who are waging this struggle for economic justice. Further, the goal of the struggle, coparticipation at the
local level and democratically organized centralized planning,
seems doomed in light of the document's simultaneous acknowledgment that extremely powerful market forces have
"created" and "allowed flagrant injustices to persist" in the
international economy to the detriment of many (*LE* 8, 16–18).
Indeed, at the same time that *Laborem exercens* made individual
ethical choice the primary factor in determining the justice
of an economic system, it also did sufficient passing analysis of advanced global capitalism to observe that the complex
structures of the "indirect employer" "exercise a determining influence on the just or unjust relationships in the field
of human labor" (*LE* 16, 17). According to the encyclical, the
indirect employers include the multinational corporations as
well as all agents at the national and international levels responsible for labor policy (*LE* 17). The indirect employers, it
was acknowledged, conditioned the relationship between the

direct employer and the worker and created a situation that led John Paul II to remark that "something is wrong with the organization of work and employment" (*LE* 18).

Finally, John Paul II's antipathy to Marxism, which he identified with the program of state collectivism (*LE* 14), is evident in *Laborem exercens*. Contrary to the more nuanced statements made by John XXIII and Paul VI regarding the status of Marxist movements (*PT* 159; *OA* 32–34) [15] John Paul II differentiated a Church-endorsed "solidarity" from a Marxist one, which he claimed "diverges radically" from the social teaching of the Church (*LE* 8, 11, 14). John Paul II claimed that Marxist movements created the class struggle by the erroneous principles they developed to counter the error of the early capitalists (*LE* 11).

Like previous Catholic social teaching, *Laborem exercens* is difficult to analyze because it drew upon incompatible analytic perspectives. As we have seen, there are several points at which it drew from the radical analytic stream. In harmony with a radical perspective it gave clear priority to labor over capital and interpreted capital primarily as stored labor. It recognized that capital organized against workers is *the*, if not *a*, major source of injustice in society. [16] At times, the document moved beyond issues of a just wage when it advocated co-responsibility in determining the use of capital and its profits as the central demand of labor (*LE* 14). While John Paul II argued for centralized economic planning, at all times this was to be accountable to "the initiative of individuals, free groups and local work centers and complexes" (*LE* 18). The imperative to balance the need for socialization with the need for subsidiarity—"big whenever necessary, but small is better"—has been a central tenet in Catholic social teaching since John XXIII and is clearly articulated by John Paul II. In harmony with the contemporary radical perspective, the thrust of Catholic economic teaching has been the decentralization, not the nationalization of ownership. [17] In giving support to the need for workers' struggle for justice, *Laborem exercens* conceded that ideas alone do not have power apart from their connection with active historical agents. And it took passing note of international structures of oppression that "exercise a determining influence" on all socioeconomic relationships (*LE* 16).

Perspectives emanating from organic and orthodox social models predominated in *Laborem excercens* because of the document's idealistic methodology, its embrace of the naturalness of social hierarchies, and its insistence that change can only come through personal moral persuasion (*LE* 13, 20). These set the stage for *Laborem exercens* to reject the moral evaluation of economic structures, to exclude control of the productive process from the key problem of social ethics, to explicitly support a gender-based division of labor and implicitly support a class-based one, and to insist on nonconflictual change without consideration of the morality of existing power relations. These perspectives situate the document comfortably within the liberal orthodox mainstream.

Laborem exercens marked a retreat from the more radical concerns found in some Catholic social teaching during the papacies of John XXIII and Paul VI. These included concern for structural analyses of economic and class systems, support for mobilizing grassroots, utopian imagination to determine the direction of social change, growing openness to solidarity with Marxist movements, and recognition of the need for reform within the Church.

Sollicitudo rei socialis

John Paul II's retreat from previous teaching, especially from the more progressive aspects of Paul VI, is made more explicit in his 1987 encyclical *Sollicitudo rei socialis*, or *On Social Concern*.[18] Issued to commemorate the twentieth anniversary of *Populorum progressio*, and impelled by a world in which economic suffering had increased, not diminished, in the ensuing twenty years, John Paul II said he wished to "bring . . . to bear on the present historical moment" the teaching of Paul VI. Because Third World conditions of poverty and underemployment were manifested "even in the rich countries," John Paul II wished to "extend the impact" of Paul's teaching on development by applying it in "a fuller and more nuanced" way (*OSC* 4, 17).[19] John Paul II, however, does not enunciate Paul's teaching more fully. Rather, *On Social Concern* departs significantly from Paul's teaching by failing to appropriate, or even acknowledge, important liberation dimensions of Paul's analysis of capitalism and Paul's understanding of the process of social change. This encyclical also marked a significant retreat from some of the more radical elements in John Paul II's earlier encyclical, *Laborem exercens*.

A first major difference in the social analysis of this encyclical as compared with *Populorum progressio* can be seen in the ways these two documents account for the existence of poverty. In analyzing the economic crisis in Third World countries, Paul distinguished between political independence and economic dependence. Paul said that poverty in the Third World was due to the legacy of colonialism, especially the establishment of one-product economies. Despite political independence, nations were still kept in economic dependence through such neocolonial practices (*PP* 7, 52).[20] He observed that poverty in the Third World was a result of the wide disparity between prices for Third World raw materials and prices for First World manufactured goods. This situation rendered the promotion of "free trade" as a means to equity impossible (*PP* 58, 57). Paul identified "glaring inequities . . . in the exercise of power" and said that trade is only free when "the parties involved are not affected by any excessive inequalities of economic power" (*PP* 9, 58). What was called for, argued Paul, was the emancipation of political structures from the economic interests of the wealthy. He advocated self-directed economic liberation at the local level or "a fitting autonomous growth" (*PP* 6). According to Paul VI, then, one of the chief causes of poverty was the unequal distribution of global economic power and the control of that power by First World governments and business elites.

In the encyclical *On Social Concern* John Paul II had a very different assessment concerning the roots of economic suffering, which he recognized had escalated dramatically since the time Paul wrote. John Paul II claimed that poverty was due to three factors: (1) the immoral economic decisions of individuals that, multiplied enough times, create "structures of sin" or "misguided mechanisms"; (2) the ideological or political conflict between the East and the West; and (3) the cultural value systems peculiar to the Third World (*OSC* 35–37, 20–22, 14). In warning against an analysis that was "too narrow[ly] . . . economic," and in enumerating what he believed to be the threefold nature of the problem, John Paul II showed his allegiance to the capitalist assumption that economic, political, and cultural social spheres function autonomously (*OSC* 15).

When John Paul II located the origins of poverty in individual decisions, he effectively denied that socioeconomic systems are systems of social relations that specify certain relations between persons and groups and preclude others. *On Social Concern* saw the relations in an economic system as entirely voluntary.

> Therefore, political leaders and citizens of rich countries *considered as individuals* . . . have the moral obligation, according to the *degree of each one's responsibility*, to take into consideration in *personal decisions* and decisions of government this relationship of universality, this interdependence which exists between *their conduct* and the poverty and underdevelopment of so many millions of people. (*OSC* 9; emphasis added)

On Social Concern acknowledged the existence of "economic, financial and social mechanisms" that "function almost automatically" on behalf of the richer countries. These mechanisms, however, are not thought to be inherent to the economic systems themselves, but are "manipulated" by individuals and "favor the interests of the people manipulating them" (*OSC* 16). These "misguided mechanisms" fall under the moral category of "structures of sin" that

> are *rooted in personal sin* and thus always linked to the *concrete acts of individuals* who introduce these structures, consolidate them and make them difficult to remove. . . . One can speak of "selfishness" and of "shortsightedness," of "mistaken political calculations," and "imprudent economic decisions." . . . [These structures are a result of] the concrete acts of individuals. (*OSC* 36; emphasis added)

Congruent with capitalist theory, John Paul II assumed that if individual human error, either through accident, prejudice, or ignorance, could be removed, then a capitalist economic system would be capable of eradicating poverty.

On Social Concern stated that a second root of "underdevelopment" or poverty in Third World countries is the existence of "two opposing blocs, commonly known as East and West" that promote "antithetical forms of the organization of labor and the structures of ownership." These blocs pull other countries into their "spheres of influence" and in this process "help to widen the gap already existing on the economic level between the North and the South." The document gave two examples of how economic stagnation in the Southern hemisphere is presumably due to East–West conflict. The first one reduced internal strife in Third World countries to the East–West struggle over capitalism and Soviet communism. The document said that revolutionary uprising is due to the situation of countries "find[ing] themselves in and sometimes over-whelmed by ideological conflicts which inevitably create internal divisions to the extent in some cases of provoking full civil war" (*OSC* 21, 20). A second example of how ideological conflict creates economic stagnation is John Paul II's view that First World countries would be doing more to help the situation of poor nations if they did not have to defend themselves against communism. He said, "Nations which historically, economically and politically have the possibility of playing a leadership role are prevented by this fundamentally flawed distortion from adequately fulfilling their duty of solidarity for the benefit of peoples which aspire to full development" (*OSC* 23).

By blaming communism and a lack of political stability for Third World revolutionary uprising and for First World failures to deal with economic stagnation, this document fell comfortably within capitalist assumptions. It also illustrated a point made by the liberation view. Liberationists argue that in the Bretton Woods agreements made after World War II, the United States and other First World elites created the cold war primarily for three reasons. These were: (1) to justify capitalist penetration of countries where significant numbers would protest their ensuing economic marginalization, (2) to have a scapegoat on which to blame the failures of capitalist development, and (3) to justify the extremely lucrative arms race in order to insure the successful future of the capitalist system.[21]

A third reason this document gave for the origins and persistence of poverty is the particular culture and value systems of Third World countries. John Paul II said that when these cultural values "do not always match the degree of economic development . . . [they] help to create distances" between richer and poorer nations (*OSC* 14). This reading accords with the capitalist view that people in traditional societies are unable to make the individual choices that will insure their economic advancement.[22]

On Social Concern analyzed poverty solely from a stance that claims that economic, political, and cultural institutions function autonomously, and thereby departed not only from the earlier tradition including Paul VI, but in a more limited sense departed from John Paul II's 1981 encyclical, *Laborem exercens*. While this earlier encyclical also rejected an analysis of the interlocking structures of political economy and claimed that social injustice "does not spring from the structure of the production process or from the structure of the economic process" (*LE* 13), it nevertheless acknowledged the activity of international structures of oppression that "exercise a determinative influence" on all socioeconomic relationships (*LE* 16, 17). It argued that the major cause of poverty and injustice in societies was due to the fact that capital was organized against labor (*LE* 12, 14). The social vision of *Laborem exercens* was not out of harmony with Paul VI's advocacy of self-directed economic liberation when it promoted an economy in which capital served labor in a democratically organized and centrally planned economy (*LE* 14, 18). *On Social Concern*, however, refused to locate the origins of poverty in the conflictual nature of any political, social, or economic structures beyond what is created by the selfishness, shortsightedness, mistaken political ideas, or unfortunate cultural values of influential individuals.

In viewing the economic arena as a complex of voluntary associations, John Paul II departed from the social analysis of Paul VI that said that the "concrete systems" of capitalism and collectivism, which he described as "technocratic capitalism" and "bureaucratic socialism," are systems incapable of achieving economic justice (*OA* 37, 35). Further, even though both *On Social Concern* and *Laborem exercens* made individual ethical choice the primary factor in determining the justice of an economic system, they also implied that the internationalization of advanced global capitalism has freed world capitalist leaders from being responsible to domestic political pressures that once worked to mitigate capitalist excesses. Both encyclicals stated that on a global scale "there is something wrong with the organization of international trade, of work, and of employment" (*LE* 16–18; *OSC* 18, 43).

On Social Concern also neglected to address the liberation prescriptions of what might be done about poverty found in *Populorum progressio* (1967) and in *Octogesima adveniens* (1971). Elements aligned with a liberation perspective can be detected in several aspects of Paul VI's teaching about the methods and agents of social change. Paul said that because of the need for "bold transformations," "comprehensive structural changes," "daring and creative innovations," and "modern forms of democracy," the methods of social change would have to be determined by an analysis of the situation done by the local community (*PP* 32; *OA* 42–43, 47). Indeed, Paul noted that the degree of people's participation in shaping the economy was as important as the quantity and variety of goods produced (*OA* 41). Paul called for the creation of a visionary yet historically possible society when he advocated the use of a utopian imagination that would perceive in the present "the disregarded possibility" for justice and direct it "towards a fresh future" (*OA* 37). This new society, then, would be created by the struggles of bold and imaginative people united in "initiating their own strategies" and being "authors of their own advancement" and "artisans of their destiny" (*PP* 34, 65). Paul endorsed a "variety of possible options" in methods and left room for "some degree of commitment" with Marxists in achieving these (*OA* 31, 50).

In contrast to Paul's "bottom up" model of social change through visionary struggle, *On Social Concern* advocates social change from the top down through consensus at the level of ideas. The encyclical implied that what the local situation can reveal in terms of needed reform is not as important as the emergence of ideas of solidarity and interdependence and principles of cooperation and development that need to be implemented at the international level (*OSC* 19, 26, 38). *On Social Concern* showed more confidence than Paul VI in the Church's ability to make an "accurate formulation of the results of a careful reflection on the complex realities of human existence" (*OSC* 41). It championed a solidarity seemingly without struggle that had to do with "gratuity, forgiveness and reconciliation" (*OSC* 40). It assumed that the major initiators of change will be individuals and leaders of nations and international bodies who already have social power and practice individual personal virtue (*OSC* 26, 42–43). As is true of that strain of Catholic social teaching more in harmony with capitalist social analysis, John Paul II assumed that moral conversion and consensus at the level of ideas will mobilize the political will necessary for social change.

But how can those who have produced the inequalities also provide the means for ending them? To expect partners in an unequal relationship to respond to appeals for cooperation and moral responsibility is to ignore the reality acknowledged in the teaching of Paul VI, that since vast differentials in power will decisively affect the outcome of any negotiations, there is no change without social struggle. The position of *On Social Concern* represented only liberal capitalist assumptions regarding the absence of fundamental conflict, the relative equitable distribution of social power, and optimism regarding reform within the present system.

Finally, *On Social Concern* selectively appropriated normative values from a tradition within social teaching that aimed at the reform of economic institutions and reduced them to exercises of individual charity. In *Laborem exercens* John Paul II advocated such ethical norms as the dignified participation of all persons in socioeconomic life, economic democracy or centralized economic planning accountable to worker owner/ managers at the local level, and a "struggle of the workers" and "solidarity of the workers and with the workers" (*LE* 14, 18, 8, 20). These normative values all had to do with changing government, economic, and labor structures. In contrast, *On Social Concern* does not advocate economic democracy and universal dignified social participation. Perhaps they are already presumed to exist or to have the potential to exist in countries with parliamentary democracy (*OSC* 44). This encyclical not only abandoned norms advocated in John Paul's earlier encyclical, but the values it does advocate have to do with individual charitable practices, not reforming structures. For example, in contrast to John Paul's earlier encyclical, which linked solidarity with the struggle of workers, this document developed an individualistic notion of solidarity and said that it had to do with "total gratuity, forgiveness and reconciliation"—regardless of configurations of social power—and that it had "many points of contact [with] charity" (*OSC* 40). Similarly, the preferential option for the poor had little if any resonance with Paul VI's awareness that people struggling for a new society are to be opted for because they are examples of human dignity at work. Rather, this value also became a "primacy in the exercise of Christian charity . . . [for] each Christian" (*OSC* 42). These norms are reinterpreted apolitically so as not to upset present structures since the option for the poor must never endanger the common good (*OSC* 39). Here we see how the meaning of social justice values is contingent upon social theory or the particular way of organizing society that is assumed.

Because *On Social Concern* is devoid of analysis that can be aligned with the liberation model, selective normative values have been abstracted from the liberation model and are radically transfigured into individual charitable acts that support rather than challenge the status quo. John Paul II's rupture with and individualistic understanding of traditional normative values violated a mandate central to the Catholic tradition since Pius XI, who opposed "abandon[ing] to charity alone" the task of addressing economic structures that cause "the open violation of justice" (*QA* 4).[23] Devoid of any analysis that can be aligned with the radical paradigm, this encyclical represented a significant departure not only from the teaching of Paul VI that it claimed to articulate more fully but from the wider Catholic social justice tradition.

Notes

1. *Laborem exercens (LE)* is found in Gregory Baum, *The Priority of Labor: A Commentary on* Laborem exercens (New York: Paulist Press, 1982).

2. Baum, *Priority of Labor*, p. 3.

3. For the first time in Catholic social teaching, the history of how some came to be owners and others did not is addressed. The freedom of the parties who created this situation is not questioned. See Christine E. Gudorf, *Catholic Social Teaching on Liberation Themes* (Washington, D.C.: University Press of America, 1981), p. 30.

4. Gregory Baum says that this encyclical interprets the practice of the early capitalists as being "distorted" because it broke away from the feudal practice of ownership, which was tied to paternalistic responsibility (*Priority of Labor*, p. 27).

5. John Paul II understands "the philosophy of Marx and Engels" not primarily as an evaluation of capitalism but as a blueprint for state collectivism (see *LE* 11).

6. Radical theorists would claim that John Paul II does not understand dialectical materialism, which holds that involvement in the historical process influences roles and values, shapes ideas, and changes reality. They would say that John Paul II equates Marxism with the "crass materialism" that Marx himself criticizes in *Grundrisse* and volume 1 of *Capital*.

7. *Octagesima adveniens (OA)* is found in *The Gospel of Peace and Justice*, ed. Joseph Gremillion (Maryknoll, N.Y.: Orbis, 1976).

8. *Redemptor hominis* 15, *Origins* 8, no. 40 (March 22, 1979). See Baum, *Priority of Labor*, p. 58.

9. For John Paul II, Marxism is equated with the state collectivism of the Soviet East. From a radical perspective, this is comparable to a view that would equate Christianity with Christian fundamentalism.

10. It is important to note that radical theorists differentiate Marxism from Leninistic politics that advocate "the party of the vanguard

of the people" and create a party-controlled system of state collectivism. Neo-Marxian social theory stresses the decentralization, not the nationalization, of ownership.

11. For Marx's understanding of the nature of human work see "Economic and Philosophical Manuscripts," in *Karl Marx: Selected Writings*, ed. David McLellan (New York: Oxford University Press, 1977), esp. pp. 82–85, 90, 94. See also Marx's essay "On James Mill," esp. pp. 115, 122.

12. See Baum, *Priority of Labor*, p. 13. While Baum views the lack of distinction in *Laborem exercens* between productive and nonproductive labor, and between the laboring and leisured, as an expansion of Marx, radical theory would see it as a corruption, a way of ignoring class conflict.

13. *Cf. LE* 27 and *RN* 14. In contrast, John XXIII and Paul VI were more concerned with speaking out against all forms of human suffering. *Rerum Novarum (RN)* is found in *Seven Great Encyclicals* (Glen Rock, N.J.: Paulist Press, 1963).

14. See Baum, *Priority of Labor*, pp. 38–39.

15. *Pacem in terris (PT) is found in Gospel of Peace and Justice*, ed. Gremillion.

16. While this encyclical ignores sexism and racism as equally key elements in worldwide social oppression, its assertion of "the priority of labor over capital" theoretically rejects the capitalist system in which all other components of socioeconomic life must be subordinate to capital accumulation.

17. Gregory Baum and Duncan Cameron, *Ethics and Economics: Canada's Catholic Bishops on the Economic Crisis* (Toronto: Lorimer, 1984), p. 74.

18. The discussion that follows about the encyclical *On Social Concern* was originally part of my larger essay published as "Conflicting Paradigms in Social Analysis," in Gregory Baum and Robert Ellsberg, *The Logic of Solidarity: Commentaries on Pope John Paul II's Encyclical On Social Concern* (Maryknoll, N.Y.: Orbis, 1989). It is reprinted here with permission.

19. *Sollicitudo rei socialis*, or *On Social Concern (OSC)*, is found in *Origins* 17, no. 38 (March 3, 1988).

20. *Populorum progressio (PP)* is found in *Gospel of Peace and Justice*, ed. Gremillion.

21. Lee Cormie, "La Iglesia y la crisis del capitalismo: perspectiva norteamerica," *Opciones* (Chile), no. 11 (May–August 1987): 9–30.

In contrast to John Paul II's line of argument, the U.S. bishops' pastoral letter on the economy says that the tendency to evaluate "North–South problems" in terms of an "East–West assessment" must cease because it is done at the expense of meeting basic human needs in the Third World. See *"Economic Justice for All: Catholic Social Teaching and the U.S. Economy,"* *Origins* 16, no. 24 (November 27, 1986): 262.

22. See Walter W. Rostow, *The Stages of Economic Growth: A Non-Communist Manifesto* (New York: Cambridge University Press, 1960).

23. *Quadragesimo anno* (*QA*) is found in *Seven Great Encyclicals* (Glen Rock, N.J.: Paulist Press, 1963).

Chapter Five. Canadian and U.S. Bishops' Documents: 1983 and 1986

NATIONAL BISHOPS' STATEMENTS on economic questions, encouraged by Vatican II's doctrine of collegiality,[1] first appeared in Latin America with the Medellin documents of 1968 and the Puebla document of 1979. The 1980s have seen increasing problems with unemployment and a rise in the number of working poor in the countries of the First World as corporate capital increasingly shifts to the cheaper labor and resources of the Third World. The bishops of Canada and the United States have responded to this changing reality by issuing pastoral letters. *Ethical Reflections on the Economic Crisis* and its follow-up statement come from the Canadian Catholic bishops; the U.S. bishops have contributed *Economic Justice for All: Catholic Social Teaching and the U.S. Economy* to the discussion.

Canadian Documents

The Canadian economic pastoral letter, *Ethical Reflections on the Economic Crisis* (January 1983), and its follow-up statement, *Ethical Choices and Political Challenges* (December 1983), are built on a series of economic statements made by the Canadian bishops since 1975.[2] Like the Latin American documents and unlike the social encyclicals of John Paul II, these documents reflected a method of doing social ethics by beginning with the experiences of the marginalized. They also offered a structural analysis of the Canadian political economy.

The Canadian bishops focused their attention on people

who have been laid off, or have had their wages cut, or have suffered suspension of collective bargaining rights, and experienced "repressive measures for restraining civil liberties and controlling social unrest" (*EREC*, pp. 5, 9–10). These experiences have contributed to "personal tragedies, emotional strain, loss of human dignity, family breakdown and even suicide" (*EREC*, p. 5). The bishops noted that there has been "increasing alcoholism . . . vandalism, crime, racism and street violence" (*ECPC*, p. 13).[3] It was not just the random bad luck of people that creates poverty and engenders economic suffering. Rather, the bishops offered an analysis that found that such suffering is concentrated among Native peoples, women of all ages, the young, and other men who work for poverty wages (*EREC*, p. 6). Although the bishops did not mention the specific burden of women, they outlined a pastoral methodology for arriving at social change that was to begin and end with the lived experiences and needs of these marginalized people (*ECPC*, p. 2).[4]

Issued during the time when unemployment and underemployment in Canada had reached over two and a half million people, or 20 percent of the work force, the bishops' economic analysis challenged the officially articulated reasons for economic decline and inflation—the orthodox claim that high wages, government spending, and low productivity created these problems (*ECPC*, p. 20, n. 1). They also challenged the economic policies of wage restraint and high interest rates as a remedy for inflation.

The bishops' economic analysis traced the origins of Canada's economic decline to a "structural crisis in the international system of capitalism." The structures of capital and technology have evolved so that "capital has become transnational" and technology and production have "become increasingly capital [and not labor] intensive." Because of the mobility of capital in search of cheap labor and resources, governments have tried to provide a favorable climate for investment by introducing cutbacks in social spending, wage restraint programs, corporate tax reductions, and deregulation of pollution control (*EREC*, pp. 8–9, 11–12; *ECPC*, p. 8).

By contrast, the bishops identified both the increase in capital intensive technology, especially military technology, and the adoption of measures for attracting capital—wage restraints, repression of unions, cutbacks in social spending—as actions that create permanent structural unemployment. Consequently, the bishops argued that western, advanced industrial capitalism was evolving structurally in ways that are unaccountable to society and in opposition to serving basic human needs.

> The current structural changes in the global economy, in turn, reveal a deepening moral crisis. Through these structural changes, "capital" is reasserted as the dominant organizing principle of economic life. . . . By placing greater importance on the accumulation of profits and machines than on the people who work in a given economy, the value, meaning and dignity of human labor is violated. By creating conditions for permanent unemployment an increasingly large segment of the population is threatened with the loss of human dignity. . . . As long as technology and capital are not harnessed by society to serve basic human needs, they are likely to become an enemy rather than an ally in the development of peoples. (*EREC*, p. 10)

The bishops insisted that the Catholic social tradition mandates the moral evaluation of economic structures in the social order (*ECPC*, p. 3).

The bishops then analyzed the dynamics of the class system, both domestically and internationally. The emerging evolution of capital and technology "increase[s] the domination of the weak by the strong, both at home and abroad" (*EREC*, p. 10). The poor nations of the southern hemisphere who survive on less than 20 percent of the world's income are mirrored by Canada's bottom fifth of the population who receive only 4.1 percent of the country's total personal income. Similarly, the rich northern hemisphere that utilizes 80 percent of the world's income is mirrored by the top 20 percent of Canada's population that receives 42.5 percent of the total Canadian income. In between are the middle-income strata that "are the most vulnerable to increasing marginalization due to the new technologies" (*EREC*, p. 11; *ECPC*, p. 10).

The bishops noted that as corporate taxes decrease, differentials between social stratas increase. This occurs because personal income taxes must rise to make up the difference and "lower income Canadians pay a proportionately larger percentage of their income in taxes than wealthier Canadians" (*ECPC*, p. 11). Disparities between regions increase in the same way. The bishops observed that "the highest rates of unemployment and plant closures, plus some of the sharpest cut-backs in social services, are occurring in the poorer regions of the country" (*ECPC*, p. 11). The Canadian bishops acknowledged the basically conflictual nature of the social relations that capitalism creates when they recognized that these "patterns of domination and inequality are likely to further intensify" within the present economic order (*EREC*, p. 11).

After examining the way that advanced monopoly capitalism increases injustice by creating class conflict and reproducing social relations of domination, the bishops then argued that current strategies to address these ills were misplaced. It is not wages and government spending that should be restrained. Rather, it is capital flight, monopoly control of prices, corporate tax reductions, and investments that shift production from labor to capital that should be restrained. These, they argued, are the real sources of economic decline (*EREC*, pp. 11–12). The bishops even contended that profits for corporations have led to higher unemployment since these profits are "reinvested in some labor saving technology, exported to other countries, or spent on market speculation or luxury goods" (*EREC*, pp. 12–13).

Reminiscent of the support of Paul VI for the "utopian imagination," the Canadian bishops mandated the need to "envision and develop alternatives" to the present economic planning of governments and corporations. The bishops argued that corporations' "industrial vision" of a capital intensive, energy intensive, export oriented, and high-tech economy will provide growth and profits for a few, but is injuring most Canadians. Indeed, this kind of planning will increase what the bishops called "such structural problems as high levels of foreign ownership and economic dependency on the United States" (*EREC*, pp. 14–15; *ECPC*, p. 9).

The bishops noted difficulties inherent to the values and goals of capitalist society when they advocated pursuing alternative models. Capitalist culture, they claimed, "stifle[s] the social imagination" by restricting choice either to capitalism or communism. It inhibits imagination with its dominant mode of thought which the bishops designated "technological rationality" whereby more fundamental problems of power and control are reduced to technical issues (*ECPC*, p. 15).

Still, the bishops urged the search for an alternative society that avoids economic dependency and moves toward "integral development" (*ECPC*, p. 4). They advocated a society characterized by the goods of full employment, adequate income, and basic social services. These would be the priorities of social ownership by workers and local communities who manufacture socially useful goods with technology that is in harmony with nature and uses renewable energy resources. This requires an alternative model of economic organization involving "an equitable re-distribution of wealth and power" so that it is based on the fullest possible local participation (*EREC*, pp. 15–16; *ECPC*, p. 5). The bishops said that people need to "acquire communal control over the necessary means of production" in order to "organize their economy to serve their own basic needs" (*ECPC*, p. 6). This involves no less than a "radical inversion" of present economic structures (*ECPC*, p. 14).

To achieve this, the Canadian bishops urged multiple forms of grassroots involvement. They wished to promote "a real public debate" regarding economic models (*EREC*, p. 16; *ECPC*, p. 2). This was to include both "working and non-working people" who have "a creative and dynamic contribution to make" (*EREC*, p. 16). As individual Christians the bishops themselves wished to encourage and become involved in "grassroots events or activities" and "visions and strategies" for economic justice (*EREC*, p. 17). They asked the consensus question contained in radical analysis: How do you nurture a process that will bond individuals in solidarity and radicalism (*ECPC*, pp. 18–19)? In particular, they advocated support of specific struggles of the marginalized and the unemployed in each region (*EREC*, p. 18; *ECPC*, pp. 2, 16). Chief among their goals was "increasing community ownership and control of industries" and the community accountability of national and international business (*EREC*, pp. 15, 18; *ECPC*, p. 18). For "unless communities and working people have effective control over both capital and technology," the bishops said, "the tendency is for them to become 'destructive forces' . . . in economic development" (*ECPC*, p. 13).

In the midst of an analysis that was radical in its structural diagnosis, these documents also included elements of organic social theory, particularly with regard to the function of the institutional Church. The Canadian documents asserted that the primary role of the Church is to teach (*ECPC*, p. 3). They exhibited the organic and orthodox assumptions that politics and culture have an autonomous existence apart from economic organization. They argued that the Church's effectiveness lies in a separate cultural arena—changing human values—because the role of the Church is to remain politically nonpartisan. Presumably, the Church can help wage an effective economic struggle outside the realm of politics (*EREC*, p. 4).[5]

Despite the traditional analysis of the function of the Church, the Canadian documents are highly significant. They come from an advanced industrial capitalist economy—albeit a neocolonized country within the west—but they are about political and economic structural change. They are not about keeping basic economic and political institutions intact. In their radical analysis of the unjust functioning of capitalist economic and class structures, in their call for creative alternatives, for social change from the bottom, for grassroots struggle for local control over production and distribution with global accountability, they encouraged a genuine restructuring of the foundations of the capitalist order. *Ethical Reflections on the Economic Crisis* and *Ethical Choices and Political Challenges* advocated a radical transformation of capitalist economic structures in a way that closely resembles that found in the Latin American documents.

U.S. Bishops' Letter (1986)

Like the Canadian pastoral letter and its follow-up, the U.S. bishops' letter, *Economic Justice for All: Catholic Social Teaching and the U.S. Economy*, was written in response to a situation of rising underemployment and escalating poverty in the United States. This letter reflected upon the economic suffering experienced in a society in which almost 60 percent of the new jobs that were being created paid $7,000 a year or less. The reality of the enormous wealth of the United States, and the simultaneous fact that "since 1973 the poverty rate has increased by nearly a third," impelled the bishops to deplore this "social and moral scandal that we cannot ignore" (*EJA* 16, 171).[6] In light of the financial hardships experienced by increasing numbers of U.S. citizens, the bishops wished to "foster a serious moral analysis" by "propos[ing] an ethical framework that can guide economic life today" (*EJA* 133, 61). In a lengthy document that sought to unite biblical and other ethical norms with selected economic policy issues, this pastoral letter strove to give "constructive guidance" toward the goal of "a new American experiment" in economic democracy (*EJA* 21, 23, 95).

Like their Canadian counterparts, the U.S. bishops begin by describing the situation of economic dislocation and the consequent human suffering that is ongoing across the United States. This was known to the bishops because of their own pastoral engagement.

> As bishops . . . we also manage institutions, balance budgets and meet payrolls. In this we see the human face of our economy. We feel the hurts and hopes of our people. We feel the pain of our sisters and brothers who are poor, unemployed, homeless, living on the edge. The poor and vulnerable are on our doorsteps, in our parishes, our service agencies and our shelters. We see too much hunger and injustice, both in our own country and around the world. (*EJA*, introduction, para. 10)

The bishops spoke about "the struggle of ordinary families to make ends meet" and "the growing economic hardship and insecurity experienced by moderate income Americans" (*EJA*, introduction, para. 11; see also 172). The U.S. bishops documented the reality of people facing the illness of loved ones without access to health care and the rise of alcoholism, child abuse, spouse abuse, and divorce. They spoke of millions of U.S. children "so poorly nourished that their physical and mental development are seriously harmed" (*EJA* 141, 172, 177).

However, in contrast to the Canadian bishops' statements, *Economic Justice for All* strongly maintained basic orthodox economic assumptions regarding the possibility for substantial reform within capitalism. The U.S. bishops assumed the possibility of capitalist reform through liberal social policies even though they sometimes exhibited a radical mode of evaluating capitalist dynamics. The U.S. bishops were able to sustain the incompatibility of radical diagnosis and liberal prescriptions because, like John Paul II, they would not agree that economic systems are also systems of social relations that specify certain relationships between persons and groups and preclude others. "The Church is not bound to any particular economic, political or social system," the bishops said (EJA 130). The bishops observed that "the Church must encourage all reforms" as it "works for improvement in a variety of economic and political contexts" (EJA 129). The economic system itself is not as important as the reforms in social relations of which any given system is presumably capable. Like the idealistic methodology of John Paul II, Economic Justice for All argued that moral norms may be applied to any economic structure, without the need of altering the structure itself (EJA 129–130).

Consequently, the U.S. bishops assumed that their strategies for achieving social justice could be accomplished within the U.S. capitalist economy as it presently exists. The U.S. pastoral letter assumed that production and jobs must be governed by corporate profit (EJA 299). It assumed the wage-contract system is just as long as wages and benefits can "sustain life in dignity" (EJA 103). It held that individualism and social fragmentation are the inevitable by-products of the specialization required by industrialization (EJA 22). The bishops assumed that plant closures may be inevitable for an economy in transition (EJA 303). They assumed that farmers, as "free" operators in the market, should blame themselves in part for the loss of their farms (EJA 224).

Like previous Catholic social teaching, Economic Justice for All draws on analytic perspectives from both social models. In harmony with the orthodox perspective, the U.S. pastoral letter argued that some of the burdens the economic system creates must be borne in light of its greater benefits. It enumerated individual "economic policy issues" facing U.S. society. These include unemployment that is unequally and unfairly distributed, "massive national spending on defense," and poverty. They also include increased foreign competition, capital mobility, discrimination against white women and minorities, plant closings, farm foreclosures, federal deficits, high interest rates, drug traffic, and trade imbalances. The bishops also mentioned the ecological crisis (*EJA* 15, 146–147, 227, 320).[7]

In harmony with a radical model, the bishops acknowledged that these problems are all interrelated, and they called for a more extensive examination and diagnosis of economic institutions and the problems they generate. "None of these issues . . . can be dealt with in isolation . . . [for] they are interconnected," the bishops said, and they called for a "finer discernment" and "a diagnosing [of] those situations" (*EJA* 293, 55, 126). Yet the bishops themselves did not attempt to analyze the connections between these tragic realities because they are "the subject of vigorous debate today" (*EJA* 312). Unlike the Canadian document, which targeted "a structural crisis in the international system of capitalism," including wage restraints, and monopoly control of prices and corporate tax reductions as the most recent causes of economic decline (*EREC*, pp. 8, 11–12), the U.S. bishops made the more general statement that "the structure of the U.S. economy is undergoing a transformation" (*EJA* 144). They did not entertain the thesis that such changes are indicative of the internal logic of the system, as did the Canadian document. Rather than develop the more fundamental issues that would connect the "selected policy issues" as the Canadian bishops did, the U.S. bishops preferred to understand these problems as due to "external" forces. An example of such would be the absence of political will at work on a system that could be directed otherwise (*EJA*

294). The U.S. bishops asserted that "the economy is not a machine that operates according to its own inexorable laws" (*EJA* 96). As much as this championed the possibility of change in a humanly developed system, it also precluded the possibility of taking seriously the dynamics of capitalism as a single political and economic system.

Gregory Baum has observed that the Canadian bishops were able to do a structural analysis of capitalism in ways the U.S. bishops were not because of the historic dependency patterns in the Canadian economy. The Canadians were also at ease with a more radical analysis because Canada contains a wider ideological spectrum, including not only liberal theory but the organic theory of the Tory tradition and the legacy of British socialism. To remain within their national debate, however, the U.S. bishops for the most part had to stay within the neoclassical tradition. The bishops also had to contend with the organized voice of neoconservative American Catholics. In light of this volatile ideological atmosphere, the U.S. bishops were more comfortable, not only with neoclassical economic assumptions, but with a traditional idealist methodology in which universal norms are applied to the historical context without taking into consideration specific power configurations and conflicts.[8]

Since the U.S. bishops assumed that reforms that will effectively implement their moral norms are possible within capitalism without altering the basic dynamics of the capitalist system itself, most of their policy prescriptions remained well within the liberal orthodox mainstream. However, in their description of individual "economic policy issues," as well as in their descriptive analysis surrounding the discussion of their strategies for change, the U.S. bishops have appropriated elements that can be aligned with the critical analysis of radical theory.

Economic Justice for All took the perspective of radical theory when it commended that "the allocation of income, wealth and power in society be evaluated in light of its effects on persons whose basic material needs are unmet" (*EJA* 70; see also 87). Radical theory's perspective and policy bias seek to be informed by the experience of those who are marginalized by the capitalist system. By advocating that Catholic social teaching "bear directly on the larger questions concerning the economic system itself," the U.S. bishops invited systemic—and therefore structural—analysis of the dynamics of capitalism and a "continuing exploration of these systemic questions" (*EJA* 132). They envisioned the need for "major adjustments and creative strategies that go beyond the limits of existing policies and institutions" in order to meet the needs of those who are presently marginalized (*EJA* 150).

This radical perspective was also reflected in the radical evaluation of the capitalist system that this document sometimes incorporated in its description of economic policy issues. However, these elements of the radical perspective did not keep the bishops from maintaining orthodox economic assumptions and policy prescriptions. This appropriation of incompatible social models is seen in the discourse regarding the relationship of capital and labor, the function of economic elites, the factors of political economy, and the analysis of income distribution.

Like John Paul II, the U.S. bishops assumed that existing structures of labor and capital—or the reality of many selling their labor power for a wage, and a few owning and controlling the means of production—can be made beneficial to workers. Quoting *Rerum novarum*, the bishops stated that "each needs the other completely: capital cannot do without labor, nor labor without capital" (*EJA* 299). Yet the bishops also argued that the majority of workers should not be wage earners, but should be at least partial owners of the means of production.

In our 1919 Program of Social Reconstruction we observed "the full possibilities of increased production will not be realized so long as the majority of workers remain mere

wage earners. The majority must somehow become own-
ers, at least in part, of the instruments of production."
We believe this judgment remains generally valid today.
(*EJA* 300)

While assuming that labor and capital are structures that
can be beneficial to workers, an assumption in harmony with
orthodox theory, the bishops also called for more democratic ownership of the means of production. Quoting *Laborem exercens*, the bishops also called for "overall [economic]
planning" with democratic accountability to "individuals, free
groups and local work centers and complexes" (*EJA* 315–
316)—which are central policy goals of radical theory. Also in
harmony with a radical perspective, the bishops recognized
that the structural inequality that exists in capitalism has precluded democratic partnership. "Partnerships between labor
and management," they said, "are possible only when both
groups possess real freedom and power to influence decisions (*EJA* 302). Elsewhere the bishops recognized that "the
poor are, by definition, not powerful" (*EJA* 260). They also
acknowledged that "the way power is distributed in a free
market economy frequently gives employers greater bargaining power than employees possess in the negotiation of labor
contracts" (*EJA* 103). It would seem that, by the bishops' own
descriptive analysis, democratic ownership and control of the
means of production—authentic partnership—is not likely to
happen within the structures of capital and labor consider-
ing "the way power is distributed in a free market economy"
(*EJA* 103). Yet the bishops also believe that this partnership
is possible within the present system and they characterized
the relationship between capital and labor as one of "mutual
partnership" (*EJA* 299).

The document also employed incompatible modes of
analysis in its description of the function of economic elites.
The document's radical perspective portrays elites as perpe-

trators of the economic crisis; the liberal orthodox perspective sees them as agents of reform. The bishops argued that U.S. and other First World leaders can increase the participation of the marginalized within and between their countries.

> Building a just world economic order . . . demands that national governments promote public policies that increase the ability of poor nations and marginalized people to participate in the global economy. Because no other nation's economic power yet matches ours, we believe that this responsibility pertains especially to the United States. (*EJA* 261)

At the same time the bishops acknowledged that U.S. policy operates in the Third World not in a way that "increase[s] the ability of poor nations and marginalized people to participate in the global economy" but in a way of "selective assistance based on East-West assessment of North-South problems" (*EJA* 262). This leads to relationships marked, not by partnership, but by domination and dependence. The bishops observed that

> rising global awareness calls for greater attention to the stark inequities across countries in standards of living and control of resources. . . . Nor may we overlook the disparities of power in the relationships between this nation and developing countries. . . . What Americans see as a growing interdependence is regarded by many in the less developed countries as a pattern of domination and dependence. (*EJA* 13)[9]

Yet because the relationships between economic elites and the majority are seen as affected by voluntary attitudes, not systemic patterns, the bishops assumed that the traditional methods of aid, trade, finance, and investment can still be made to serve as "transfer channels" to correct these imbalances (*EJA* 281).[10] They ignored their own radical perception that aid from elites simply does not function this way. They also ignored the protests of Third World people, including Third World bishops, that economic development must be "from below."

Another example of the use of incompatible modes of analysis at the level of policy issues is found in the bishops description of the components of the capitalist political economy. In orthodox fashion, the bishops assumed that the realms of politics and culture are autonomous from the economy. They stated that, "we see an opportunity for the United States to launch a worldwide campaign for justice and economic rights to match the still incomplete, but encouraging, political democracy we have achieved in the United States with so much pain and sacrifice (*EJA* 290). The assumption that the political sphere in the United States is democratic in a way that the economic sphere is not undergirded the document's advocacy for the creation of an economic democracy to parallel the U.S. political democracy.

> The economic challenge of today has many parallels with the political challenge that confronted the founders of our nation. . . . *We believe the time has come for a similar experiment in securing economic rights: the creation of an order that guarantees the minimum conditions of human dignity in the economic sphere for every person.* (*EJA* 95)

However, at the same time that the bishops argued for the autonomy of the political and economic arenas, they also argued in radical fashion for their basic interconnection. They acknowledged that "political democracy and a commitment to secure economic rights are mutually reinforcing" (*EJA* 83). They observed that lending policies and exchange rates, the causes of such great inequity, are "not only economic questions, but are thoroughly and intensely political" (*EJA* 276).

This use of incompatible modes of social analysis is problematic because one is left with the question: If the bishops are correct in their radical assumption that the economic and political spheres are and have been one political economy, then on what basis will the current political arena allow the development of an economic democracy?

Incompatible social perspectives are also present in the bishops' analysis of income distribution. *Economic Justice for All* does a breakdown of income distribution showing the deteriorating status of the lower and middle strata of U.S. society (*EJA* 183, 184, 170–173).[11] They acknowledged that "hundreds of thousands of women" suffer economic misery while holding full-time jobs (*EJA* 174, 179, 199). In radical fashion they observed that poverty, unemployment, and underemployment are not located randomly in the population but are concentrated among racial minorities and other women and the children of these groups (*EJA* 140, 175, 182, 199). But what radical theory analyzes as the structural subordination of these groups within a labor market that must be segmented for purposes of private capital accumulation, the bishops described simply as a situation in which "women and minorities are locked into jobs with low pay, poor working conditions, and little opportunity for career advancement." The bishops assumed that low wages and the racism and sexism that legitimate the secondary labor market are voluntaristic—the result only of individual sin—not also systemic (*EJA* 199).[12] They recommended "job training, affirmative action and other means" in order to move the poor into "more lucrative jobs" (*EJA* 199). The bishops were reluctant to face what radical theorists would call the fundamental clash of interests that shapes the labor market and other capitalist structures. Yet perhaps they sensed the possibility of real conflict when they warned that people should not become "polarized" and "pit one group or class against another" (*EJA* 88, 360).

Although at times it reflected the radical perspective in its description of the policy issues emanating from the current economic crisis, *Economic Justice for All* by and large remained solidly in the liberal orthodox tradition. While at one point this document implied that it did not matter whether Catholic social teaching supports capitalism or socialism, since the structure of economic systems is presumably irrelevant (*EJA* 129–130), elsewhere the document clearly indicated a preference for capitalism. The U.S. bishops claimed that "the Catholic tradition has long defended the right to private ownership of productive property" (*EJA* 114). The bishops based this claim on Leo XIII's letter, *Rerum novarum*. As discussed in Chapter Two, an analysis of this encyclical, however, clearly shows that Leo's primary intent was to affirm the right of individual ownership of cultivatable land (*RN* 7, 35).[13] The U.S. bishops, like Catholic social teaching before them, have used this agrarian tradition to support not only goods, land, and home ownership but the private ownership of the means of production in capitalist society (*EJA* 114). The bishops continued the traditional concern in Catholic ethics that all have the possibility to own private property. When advocating private ownership as an "incentive for diligence" in the economy, the U.S. bishops were speaking about the ownership of moderate-sized family farms (*EJA* 233). It is important to see that Catholic social teaching has not yet differentiated individual ownership of land and goods from the private ownership of the means of production. Consequently, it continues to ignore the distinctive issues that encompass the private ownership of the means of producing social wealth, and it continues to puzzle over why fewer and fewer people own any land at all.

This misconception about the nature of ownership is applied not only to capitalist economies but to all possible noncapitalist alternatives as well. Catholic social teaching still warns against "universal dispossession" (*EJA* 51). The U.S. bishops have this concern even though most secular socialists of the nineteenth century and virtually no socialists of the twentieth century advocate that private property must be abolished along with private ownership of the means of production.[14] In addition to equating socialist forms of ownership with the propertyless goals of primarily religious socialists of the eighteenth and early nineteenth centuries,[15] U.S. Catholic social teaching continues to equate all of socialism with the "collectivist and statist economic approaches" presumably of the Soviet East (which also have not advocated universal dispossession) (*EJA* 115). *Economic Justice for All* caricatured radical theory and misrepresented the political Left when it claimed that those who "argue that the capitalist system is inherently inequitable and therefore contradictory to the demands of Christian morality," support "a radically different system that abolishes private property, the profit motive, and the free market" (*EJA* 128).

Indicative of their preference for capitalism, the U.S. bishops adopted contemporary liberal orthodox goals and means of reform. But just as their description of the factors surrounding economic policy issues drew from both orthodox and radical perspectives, so did their arguments for actual policy prescriptions. The bishops argued that the necessary reforms could be achieved through strengthening the regulatory and welfare aspects of government as presently organized. But they were also aware of ways that the political economy functioned to resist these reforms, and their overall analysis sometimes implied that their proposed methods would not work. However, since they presumed the voluntaristic nature of social relations in the capitalist economy, it was easy to discount what they observed *actually* to be the case in light of their normative preferences about what *ought* to be the case.

In proposing reforms, the bishops aimed to correct "extreme inequalities in income and consumption" (*EJA* 74). They did not wish "absolute equality" for, in orthodox and organic fashion, they argued that some inequality is needed for the purpose of providing incentives and rewarding risks (*EJA* 185). But the situation in the United States, where the bottom 40 percent of all families receive only 15.7 percent of the total income in the nation while the top 20 percent receive almost half the nation's income, was "unacceptable" (*EJA* 183–185). While the poor, and increasingly even the middle strata, are falling "victim to a downward cycle of poverty generated by economic forces they are powerless to influence," the bishops advocated "minimum material resources" and "minimum levels of participation" for all in the society (*EJA* 70, 77).[16]

In order for U.S. citizens to become at least minimally participatory and less unequal, the bishops proposed reforms in such areas as investment policy, job creation, education, the government and business alliance, and agency for social change. Their arguments for these liberal policy reforms, however, often draw upon elements of a radical analysis.

Without acknowledging the role that radical theorists claim military spending and education play in maintaining the stability of late capitalism, the document urged a switch in investment priorities from luxury goods and military technology to education, health care, the basic social infrastructure, and other urgently needed goods and services (*EJA* 92). Yet the bishops also agreed that the primary responsibility of management is to exercise prudent business judgment in the interest of a profitable return on investment (*EJA* 305). Even investors of funds belonging to the Church have "a moral and legal fiduciary responsibility" to guarantee "adequate returns" (*EJA* 354). The document did not clarify how the higher profitability of luxury goods and military technology as compared to education and low-income housing was to be addressed. The bishops simply noted that: "One of the most vexing problems is that of reconciling the transnational corporations' profit orientation with the common good that they, along with governments and their multilateral agencies, are supposed to serve" (*EJA* 256).

Since over an eighth of the population is affected by joblessness, the bishops made job creation at a just wage the greatest moral priority. The bishops said that "full employment is the foundation of a just economy" (*EJA* 136). In harmony with their proposed reforms for investment, they advocated job creation in the areas of low-income housing construction, education, day care, creation of senior citizen and other community programs, and bridge, road, and park repair (*EJA* 165). However, the bishops made two observations that seem to contradict the implementation of this reform. The first was their acknowledgment, in keeping with orthodox theory, that unemployment is "becoming a more widespread and deep seated problem." However, from a radical perspective, they also acknowledged that "even in good times" unemployment in the United States has kept rising (*EJA* 138–139). They observed that the jobs now being created, the ones profitable for investors, are the "lowpaying, high turn-over jobs" in the service sector that keep people in poverty (*EJA* 145). The bishops were not able to address ways in which this trend might be reversed in order to achieve their goal of full employment at a wage adequate to sustain a dignified life.

A third area in which the document's liberal proposal for reform failed to address the difficulties it raised is in education. *Economic Justice for All* endorsed greater access to education because "lack of education . . . prevents many poor people from escaping poverty." Education is also required to retrain workers, helping them keep abreast of the rapid pace of technological change (*EJA* 203, 160). In harmony with radical analysis, however, the bishops said that education serves the privileged and often abandons the poor (*EJA* 85). They did not clarify how additional education would raise human dignity, or why people would seek education for the unskilled jobs that the bishops themselves acknowledged are becoming increasingly characteristic in the labor market (*EJA* 145).

A fourth area in which the bishops' policy proposal failed to address the difficulties raised in their discussion was the area of the government and business alliance. The bishops advocated a form of democratically controlled national planning that would seek "effective new forms of partnership" between government and business interests as a means of achieving the common good (*EJA* 318). Earlier the document acknowledged what the bishops called military "defense Department expenditures" (*EJA* 20) and described how government and business are "already closely intertwined" in an alliance that "often depart[s] from the competitive model of free-market capitalism" (*EJA* 320). The cost of this alliance to the taxpayers is $300 billion, and the bishops said it has been "disastrous for the poor and vulnerable members of our own and other nations" (*EJA* 20, 320).[17] How the United States will be emancipated from this disastrous form of government-business alliance and initiated into a more beneficial form of alliance was not addressed. Without a moral evaluation of the structure of the military industrial complex it could not be addressed. The most the document could say is that what is needed is a "greater coordination" of the two (*EJA* 318).

The gap between the document's liberal policy proposals and the radical perceptions contained in the arguments for these proposals is evident again in the bishops' discussion of agency for social change. In harmony with orthodox theory, the bishops named the primary agents of change to be government and business. But in addition to the example given above, their other perceptions about the way government and business actually function would seem to preclude the possibility of these institutions being able to implement reform.

For example, at the prescriptive level, the bishops stated that justice is to be achieved through the leadership of "property owners, managers and investors or financial capital," especially when they collaborate with governments "that serve their citizens justly" (*EJA* 110, 116). Governments can initiate fair labor practices and job creation programs (*EJA* 123). The corporate sector can create national and global solidarity (*EJA* 116). At the descriptive level, however, the bishops' analysis seemed to preclude this. The bishops acknowledged the unjust ramifications of the government-military alliance, the successful corporate assault on unions, and the fact that private enterprise "increase[s] inequality and decrease[s] stability . . . by paying low wages for resources and labor in order to maximize profits" (*EJA* 104, 116, 320). They acknowledged that "the global system of finance development and trade," like the International Monetary Fund and the World Bank, often lends for "specific projects rather than for general economic health." These projects often mean that the poorest people will suffer the most (*EJA* 273–274).

True to the tradition of Catholic social teaching, the U.S. bishops endorsed unions as important agents in social change. They may prevent capital flight and keep workers employable through their education and training programs (*EJA* 303, 304). Presumably, they may accomplish this despite the bishops' simultaneous observation that unions are plagued by rapid decline in existing membership, by cheaper labor in the Third World, by automation, and by widespread organized efforts to break them (*EJA* 104, 108). Despite the radical perspective that is evident in their descriptive analysis, there was no acknowledgment by the bishops that the prescriptions they advocated as the solution to U.S. economic problems—full employment and strong unions—have always been and still are opposed by corporate America.[18]

The document also acknowledged a role for the poor in the process of social change, and it reflected both liberal and radical social models in its analysis of this role. The bishops spoke of the need to "avoid paternalistic programs," and to encourage small-scale, locally based "self-help efforts" that would "empower the poor to take charge of their own futures" (*EJA* 188, 200, 201, 357). They spoke of the need to "evaluate socioeconomic activity from the viewpoint of the poor," the need particularly to learn from "our fellow Catholics in developing countries," and the need for all Catholics to evaluate society "in light of its effects on persons whose basic material needs are unmet" (*EJA* 87, 59, 70). The bishops also spoke of the poor as "agents of God's transforming power" (*EJA* 49).

But another model was also used to describe the role of the poor, one that was in harmony with the liberal orthodox and organic perspectives. In this view, which the bishops based on their interpretation of the Bible, the poor are recipients, not active agents. The poor are "often alone and have no protector or advocate" (*EJA* 38). Because the poor are "beneficiaries of God's mercy and justice" and "objects of God's special love" they are the "weak and powerless" whom others are to "support and sustain" (*EJA* 50–51). "A constant biblical refrain," said the bishops, "is that the poor must be cared for and protected" (*EJA* 49). "Such perspectives," the bishops said, "provide a basis for what today is called the "preferential option for the poor" (*EJA* 52). In this interpretation, those in the mainstream are not called to support those who wish to speak for themselves. Rather the emphasis is on "speak[ing] for those who have no one to speak for them" (*EJA* 52).

The radical emphasis on the empowerment of a struggling, militant poor, so pervasive in the Latin American documents, was not the only model of the poor in the U.S. document, which also stressed that the primary agents of social change were national and business elites. Consequently, the U.S. bishops' interpretation of the phrase "option for the poor," is essentially different from that of the Medellin and Puebla documents because it draws from a different social model. However much they stressed the importance of participation, the bishops did not see their task as that of analyzing problems and developing the strategies for social change in conjunction with those who are poor and needy, a quarter of the U.S. population, according to the document's statistics. *Economic Justice for All* was not primarily concerned with encouraging the marginalized to be central actors in the process of social change, nor did it express the views of the marginalized themselves in analyzing the sources of existing problems. From a more radical perspective, the U.S. document presumed to give voice to what the poor needed and thereby indulged in "the indignity of speaking for other people." [19]

Finally, the document conceived the role of the Church as an agent of social change in a traditional way. Consistent with the teaching of John Paul II, the method of engagement in social change described in this document presupposes philosophical idealism. The Church can foster social change by teaching the right principles, particularly the principles of human dignity (*EJA* 61), social solidarity (*EJA* 187, 258), participation and the preferential option for the poor (*EJA* 188, 87, 260, 291), subsidiarity (*EJA* 297, 308, 323), and wide distribution of ownership (*EJA* 114, 233). The goal of such teaching is for the Church to "foster a serious moral analysis" that will "encourage and support a renewed sense of vocation in the business community" (*EJA* 133, 117). The bishops asserted that by achieving a consensus on these values, social change will occur. Theoretical consensus will be able to mobilize political will (*EJA* 153).

While the bishops quote the mandate in the *Justice in the World* document, that the Church is called to "action on behalf of justice and participation in the transformation of the world," the document's notion of "the Church as economic actor" is limited (*EJA* 328). Neither the U.S. bishops nor the Canadian bishops assess the economic function and responsibility of the institutional Church within national and world capitalism. The Church as a collective body has no responsibility to exert political or economic pressure in order to implement its economic ethics. Rather, its responsibilities are limited to what its individual members and agencies can do. The discussion focuses on sustaining existing Church agencies, advocacy of just wages, and "ethical," but adequately remunerative, investment by Church institutions and agencies (*EJA*

347, 351, 353–358). Despite the Church's stated wish to apply the right principles—of dignity, solidarity, preferential option for the poor, subsidiarity—to its own internal affairs, the discussion assumes current hierarchical arrangements and does not prescribe change for the (mostly) white, clerical males who monopolize power and decision making in the Church.

Economic Justice for All is provocative at the level of its discussion and argument that reflects elements of radical analysis to challenge what most people in the United States have been taught to assume—the justice of current economic arrangements. At the descriptive level it highlighted the millions who suffer economic misery because of these arrangements, and it sought to place them at the center of the discussion. In defining injustice as marginalization, and justice as participation with dignity, it was strongly at odds with a business-as-usual approach. Yet at the prescriptive level, it endorsed and commended more capitalism as the solution to the suffering it dramatically described.

Like the encyclicals of John Paul II, *Economic Justice for All* demonstrated the legacy of the organic and orthodox economic perspectives in its idealistic moral methodology that shapes a model of social change that, at the prescriptive level, ignores power analysis. The document's prescriptive embrace of U.S. capitalism while simultaneously showing in its descriptive analysis the increasing numbers of people marginalized by capitalism, makes its portrayal of social reality one that is full of contradictions. The U.S. bishops paint a confusing picture of harmony and conflict, of progress toward equality and growing gaps in income, of prosperity for poor and working people and of their increasing marginality. Depending on moral choice and political will, it seems that the same capitalist system is able to produce either outcome.

Because it is assumed that the present capitalist order is open to significant modification and reform, and because there is no moral evaluation of economic structures within this order, *Economic Justice for All* remained well within a liberal orthodox analysis. In this it is more in harmony with the teachings of John Paul II than with the statements of the Canadian bishops.

Notes

1. *Lumen gentium* 22–23 in Walter M. Abbott, S.J., *The Documents of Vatican II* (New York: American Press, 1966), pp. 42–46.

2. The complete texts of these earlier statements, as well as the January 1983 statement, *Ethical Reflections on the Economic Crisis* (*EREC*), are found in Gregory Baum and Duncan Cameron, *Ethics and Economics: Canada's Catholic Bishops and the Economic Crisis* (Toronto: Lorimer, 1984).

3. The Canadian Conference of Catholic Bishops, *Ethical Choices and Political Challenges* (*ECPC*) (Ottawa, Ontario: CCCB, 1983).

4. Pamela Brubaker observes that the oppression of women with regard to domestic labor, including their unpaid agricultural labor and their reproductive labor is never named. She makes the point that Catholic social teaching never regards domestic labor as economically valuable, ignoring current debates about this in both radical and neoclassical economic theory. See "Rendering the Invisible Visible: Methodological Constraints in Economic Ethics in Relation to Women's Impoverishment" (Ph.D. diss., Union Theological Seminary, 1989), chap. 2, pp. 28, 51, 54.

5. The Canadian letter in particular illustrates an important point made by Christine E. Gudorf that applies to all the documents studied here. She argues that the hierarchy can accommodate to elements in a radical social theory at the level of applied theology or social teaching. But as a result of the institutional Church's traditional theological method, the findings of social theory and social science have nothing to do with fundamental theology, including the understanding the Church has of itself as the teacher of eternal spiritual truths. This split between social teaching and theology is at the heart of the hierarchy's dispute with liberation theology. See *Catholic Social Teaching on Liberation Themes* (Washington, D.C.: University Press of America, 1981), pp. 59–68.

6. National Conference of Catholic Bishops, "*Economic Justice for*

All: Catholic Social Teaching and the U.S. Economy" (*EJA*), *Origins* 16, no. 24 (November 27, 1986).

Barry Bluestone and Bennett Harrison document the economic restructuring of U.S. society at this time. They show that almost 60 percent of the jobs created between 1979 and 1984 paid $7,000 per year or less. They further show that since 1979 nearly 97 percent of net employment gains among white men have been in this low-wage stratum. See "The Great American Job Machine: The Proliferation of Low Wage Employment in the U.S. Economy," study prepared for the Joint Economic Committee (December 1986), pp. 6, 43.

7. The bishops do not move beyond an understanding of ecology that considers only a responsible *use* of the environment. Their understanding of justice in this regard remains incomplete because it stops at requiring what is necessary for the well-being of humanity, not what is required for the fullest possible flourishing of *all* creation. From a feminist perspective, this is a problem that is indigenous to patriarchy. See Larry Rasmussen, "On Creation, on Growth," *Christianity and Crisis* 45 (November 25, 1985): 473–76; and Rosemary R. Ruether, *Sexism and God-Talk* (Boston: Beacon Press, 1983), pp. 85–92.

8. See Gregory Baum, "A Canadian Perspective on the U.S. Pastoral," *Christianity and Crisis* 44 (January 21, 1985): 517. For the conservative Catholic voice see the Lay Commission on Catholic Social Teaching and U.S. Economy, *Toward the Future: Catholic Social Thought and the U.S. Economy* (New York: The American Catholic Committee, 1984) and the Commission's *Liberty and Justice for All* (New York: The American Catholic Committee, 1986).

9. As an example, the bishops cite how dependence is indicative of the debtor relationship of Third World countries, some of which have to pay 100 percent of their export earnings on interest, thus never touching the principle of their debt (*EJA* 268).

10. In a recent study of the system of international aid, Graham Hancock claims that foreign aid enriches those who administer it, the corporations that provide shoddy goods at inflated prices, and the ruling classes who misuse the aid or steal it. Hancock offers considerable evidence that the poor of the Third World have not benefited from international aid at all. See *Lords of Poverty: The Power, Prestige and Corruption of the International Aid Business* (New York: Atlantic Monthly Press, 1989).

11. "Social strata" is used for the orthodox understanding of levels of income, or how one is attached to the distribution pro-

cess in the economy. It is differentiated from the word "class" used in radical theory to mean a group that shares objective conditions of social privilege or social exploitation according to their relationship to the process of production. See James Stolzman and Herbert Gamberg, "Marxist Class Analysis Versus Stratification Analysis as General Approaches to Social Inequality," *Berkeley Journal of Sociology* (1973–1974): 105–25.

12. Racism, is defined here, as in an earlier pastoral letter, as a sin, which is the result of "prejudice and discrimination" as well as "the effects of past discrimination" (*EJA* 182). This document is the first to specifically designate the oppression of women as "sexism" and to call it immoral, although it recognizes sexism only as discrimination in the public arena (*EJA* 179).

13. *Rerum novarum* (*RN*) in *Seven Great Encyclicals* (Glen Rock, N.J.: Paulist Press, 1963).

14. Beverly W. Harrison, "Theology, Economics and the Church," Kellogg Lecture, Episcopal Divinity School, Cambridge, Mass., May 5, 1986, p. 8.

15. Ibid., p. 9.

16. On the declining middle strata see *EJA* 17, 85, 172.

17. What the document calls "defense expenditures" is more accurately defined as "the militarization of the economy" in that, by 1971, the managers of the U.S. military system had superseded private firms in control over capital. One ethicist has said that "none of the current problems in the economy can be understood apart from this dynamic." See Lee Cormie, "The U.S. Bishops on Capitalism," from the working papers of the *American Academy of Religion* (1985), pp. 14–16.

18. Unions are not only opposed by corporate America, they are also opposed by Catholic institutions. Since the U.S. bishops' pastoral letter was released, the press continues to report incidences of antiunion activity by Catholic institutions. A recent example is an article by John Russo, director of labor studies at Youngstown State University, about the antiunion campaign by Archbishop Roger Mahony against the Catholic Cemetery Workers of Los Angeles. According to Russo, in 1989 Archbishop Mahoney hired Carlos Restrepo, a well-known antiunion consultant, to keep the Catholic Cemetery Workers of Los Angeles, who were losing benefits, from voting to be represented by the Amalgamated Clothing and Textile Workers Union. A similar situation developed at St. Elizabeth's Hospital, Youngstown, Ohio, where the administration hired anti-

union consultants and were not opposed by Bishop James Malone, who was largely responsible for the U.S. bishops' pastoral. See John Russo, "Tensions Run High Again Between Unions," *In These Times* 14, no. 23 (May 2–8, 1990): 17.

19. Sharon D. Welch, *Communities of Resistance and Solidarity: A Feminist Theology of Liberation* (Maryknoll, N.Y.: Orbis, 1985), p. 43.

Chapter Six. *Paradigms in Conflict: The Need for Coherence and Commitment*

FOR A CENTURY Roman Catholic teaching on economic justice has attempted to address and evaluate the social structures that keep people in socioeconomic marginalization. The institutional Church has promoted social justice norms such as universal, dignified social participation, economic democracy, and a preferential option for the poor. It has also developed a body of social analysis concerning the functioning of capitalist societies and the continuing economic suffering of persons who live in them.

Since the nineteenth century and even to the present time, Catholic social teaching has presented a tripartite analysis of capitalist economic structures, reflecting organic, orthodox, and radical paradigms of social theory. The institutional Church's incorporation of the organic social model, appropriated from feudal social relations, has predisposed it to elements in orthodox analysis that support a stratified society. However, its organic communitarian sensibilities, as well as its history of pastoral engagement in the concrete struggles of marginalized people, have predisposed it toward elements of a radical analysis as well. While the major social change strategies of Catholic teaching have remained consistent with a liberal orthodox paradigm, the juxtaposition of these strategies with a diagnosis that sometimes reflects a radical mode of analysis fails to frame a coherent agenda for social change. Analysis that uses incompatible social models—particularly the radical model at the descriptive level of social analysis and the orthodox model at the prescriptive level—leads to confusion about what must be done to solve our economic problems.

In this chapter I argue that if the institutional Church's radical analysis of political economy is correct, its advocacy of liberal policy prescriptions will not rectify injustice within a capitalist mode of production. I further argue that the moral imperatives of Catholic economic teaching would in fact be best served by a more consistent analysis and policy commitment informed by radical theory. Moral values must finally decide the debate concerning which model of social analysis best interprets capitalist dynamics, and which model of social organization might best serve the social justice priorities of the Catholic tradition.

Finally, I offer reasons why the use of incompatible social models has been sustained within Catholic social teaching. I attempt to shed some light on the Church's ambivalence with regard to the sort of embodied commitment—that is, the taking sides in concrete social struggle with all its risks—that is demanded by the radical model.[1]

Conflicting Analyses

The assumptions of orthodox economic theory, particularly those congenial with premodern, organic conceptions of social organization, are found at the origins of modern Catholic social teaching, in *Rerum novarum* of Leo XIII and *Quadragesimo anno* of Pius XI (see Chapter Two). Contrary to earlier Church tradition, these encyclicals held that the right to private ownership was more fundamental than the duty to use property in a socially responsible way (*RN* 7, 12, 35; *QA* 47).[2] While this right to private property was not identical with the right to private ownership of the means of producing social wealth, it served chiefly to affirm the morality of the capitalist system. These encyclicals insisted that there was an existing harmony of interests between capital and labor (*RN* 15; *QA* 110). They assumed that the wage-contract system could be made just (*RN* 31, 35; *QA* 53, 58), and they assumed the patriarchal family as a model for all just social relations (*RN* 33; *QA* 28, 71). These encyclicals condemned socialism in all its forms (*RN* 11, 12, 14; *QA* 117, 119, 120, 139).

However, in conflict with the assumptions from the orthodox model that were grafted onto the organic one, Leo XIII and Pius XI also offered structural analyses of the capitalist system that reflected elements of the radical social model.[3] Their analyses described the interstructuring in capitalism of wealth, social power, and government. They acknowledged the relationship between economic power and political control, and the existence of a class society in which the interests of capital and of labor are significantly opposed. Pius XI went further and made a connection between class struggle and wars between states (*QA* 108). He assumed that the structural exploitation within capitalism was not to be remedied by charity, but by a just change in the structures themselves (*QA* 137). This might even necessitate the social ownership of the means of production and worker "ownership or management" (*QA* 65, 114).

Leo XIII and Pius XI offered social change strategies, however, that were at odds with their radical analyses. They located the agents of social change within the very structures they had taught were not only at the origin of the economic conflict but were benefiting from it—the state and the wealthy who controlled the state (*RN* 26; *QA* 110, 88). The organic assumptions of these popes led them to believe that moral ideals could change practice apart from social struggle, and that dutiful subordination could elicit paternalistic benevolence. Hence, their commitment to premodern social theory allowed them to ignore their own analyses and to assume that Church teaching and the industriousness of a nonmilitant labor movement would be able to convince elites and the state to abandon social injustice and to serve the commonweal.

An almost identical dualism can be found in the economic analyses of official Church teaching during the papacies of John XXIII and Paul VI. The analyses of these popes exhibited orthodox assumptions about the basic justice of the private ownership of capital and the potential for justice in the wage-contract system. To varying degrees, John more than Paul, they were confident that a capitalist mode of economic development was the best way to create wealth and, therefore, to eradicate poverty. Their writings continued to embrace the inevitability of a class-based, and the naturalness of a sex-based, division of labor.[4]

Like the previous popes, however, John XXIII and Paul VI utilized elements of the radical perspective in ways that were strikingly at odds with some of the assumptions of orthodox economic theory. There was a noticeable shift from concern about private property, which dominated the economic teachings of Leo XIII and Pius XI, to concern about the increases in poverty, especially in the Third World. The Church's pastoral engagement with the struggles of poor people was reflected in this analysis.

The teaching of Thomas Aquinas was reinstated as John XXIII and Paul VI argued that the universal purpose of the earth's resources and the adequate sustenance of all human beings was prior to the rights of private ownership (*MM* 43; *PT* 22; *GS* 69). Their observations of peasant flight from the land and massive poverty coexisting with elite wealth caused these popes to have some doubt about the justice potential of the capitalist project. During their papacies, the Vatican Council noticed, for example, the escalation of "militaristic thinking" within capitalist development (*GS* 85). Paul VI continued Pius XI's interpretation of the economic causes of war by linking peace with economic justice (*PP* 49, 55, 76, 83, 87).[5] These popes became less preoccupied with socialist "collectivism" than their predecessors and more concerned with strengthening democratic political structures that can serve the commonweal.

This led John to modify the principle of subsidiarity in order to restrict the powers of private interests and to affirm economic rights for all people (*MM* 53–54, 117; *PT* 56, 64). Like Leo XIII and Pius XI, John XXIII and Paul VI observed that present political structures needed emancipation from the interests of the wealthy; for without this, financial aid and technological assistance were cloaks for further domination (*PT* 65; *MM* 36; *PP* 52, 70). John XXIII specifically acknowledged the widespread reality of legalized violence, a violence enforced by the state. He therefore moved beyond the traditional organic view of commutative justice that assumed that the status quo necessarily contained the potential for justice (*PT* 51, 61; see also *GS* 74). Finally, the social encyclicals issued during the papacies of John XXIII and Paul VI took hesitant steps toward the possibility of Christian-Marxist collaboration. The encyclicals also addressed the notion that resistance to concrete suffering, not philosophical agreement, could be a basis for social solidarity (*PT* 159; *OA* 31, 50).[6] Paul encouraged grassroots movements for social change and the imaginative struggle of protesting people (*PP* 34, 64–65).

As a result of such social analysis, Paul VI and the Second Vatican Council made proposals for more fundamental social change that may be aligned with the radical paradigm. For example, they advocated self-directed liberation and economic democracy, or a "fitting autonomous growth" (*GS* 86; *PP* 6). This included not only worker ownership and control of enterprise, but a move toward democratic control of production with worker representation at every level of society (*GS* 68; see also *PP* 34, 65 and *OA* 47). It included the possible expropriation of land owned by the wealthy, and the renunciation of economic and political privileges by the Church (*GS* 71, 76). This economic liberation and democracy could be achieved by grassroots movements for social change at the local level, led by protesting people with the courage to imagine and to actualize the lost possibilities for justice inherent in the present order (*PP* 34, 65; *OA* 4, 37, 42, 47; *JW* 18, 51–53, 77).[7]

Like Leo XIII and Pius XI, however, the most often repeated social change strategies offered by John XXIII and Paul VI were in conflict with radical prescriptions. The papal documents consistently incorporated the organic notion that governments, international agencies, and power elites were capable of voluntary responsibility for the domestic and global commonweal (*MM* 54; *PT* 98, 141; *PP* 23, 61, 48–49; *OA* 18, 23; *JW* 68, 70; *GS* 65, 70, 71, 74, 83). Again, echoing Leo and Pius, these documents are filled with confidence that Church teaching and nonpolitical trade unions would reform economic and political structures and influence the individuals who controlled them to use their power to implement social justice (*MM* 218–221; *PT* 37–38; *GS* 10–12, 40–42; *PP* 81).

Issued in response to the economic crisis of the 1980s, *Laborem exercens* and *Sollicitudo rei socialis* (*On Social Concern*) by John Paul II and *Economic Justice for All* by the U.S. Catholic bishops offered descriptive analyses that acknowledged widespread economic injustice in the Second and even the First Worlds. In contrast to earlier Catholic social teaching, these documents proposed social change strategies that reflected the orthodox paradigm exclusively or almost exclusively.

The teachings of the 1980s offer a more modest analysis drawn from the radical model and represent strategic regressions from earlier gains. They agreed with the orthodox paradigm that extending the capitalist system is the best way to eradicate poverty. John Paul II asserted that freedom and personalism are more readily protected under capitalism than under any other system (*LE* 14, 15).[8] I argue that *Laborem exercens* co-opts radical language about work, social agency, and economic organization in the service of an affirmation of capitalist modes of political and economic organization. John

Paul II's encyclical *On Social Concern* marks a major departure from the Catholic tradition in that this document, which consistently assumes the justice potential of the status quo, is completely lacking in any analysis that can be aligned with the radical model (see Chapter Four).

In a similar embrace of capitalism, the U.S. bishops held that because production and jobs must be governed by corporate profit, the primary responsibility of management is to achieve a profitable return on investment (*EJA* 305, 354).[9] Both *Laborem exercens* and *Economic Justice for All* affirmed the existing structures of capital and of labor, and the potential justice of the existing wage-contract system (*LE* 20; *EJA* 299). In fact, John Paul II reaffirmed a class-based division of labor and more strongly embraced a gender-based division of labor than his predecessors (*LE* 6, 7, 9, 11, 14, 26–27). The U.S. bishops insisted that capitalist development is capable of eradicating poverty, and they argued for liberal methods of social change (*EJA* 196–215). They wished to strengthen the regulatory and welfare aspects of the present system so that government and business would increase jobs, job training, affirmative action, education, and changes in investment policy (*EJA* 92, 110, 163–166, 199). John Paul II's encyclicals and the U.S. bishops' letter supported nonpolitical union movements and a belief that consensus at the level of moral principles would be able to mobilize the political will needed for reform (*LE* 13–14; *EJA* 153). All three documents rejected Marxism and equated it with Soviet state collectivism (*LE* 11, 14; *EJA* 115, 128; *OSC* 41).[10]

But even in *Laborem exercens* and *Economic Justice for All* analysis reflective of the radical social model is not altogether absent and stands in contradiction to the above affirmations. Both documents describe justice as a dignified participation in socioeconomic life and injustice as marginalization from it. Therefore, both aspired to a strategy in which the majority of workers may be owners and/or managers of the instruments of production (*LE* 14; *EJA* 300). Both documents also advocate centralized economic planning that is accountable to democratic structures at the local level (*LE* 18; *EJA* 315). John Paul II supported a broad-based struggle "of the workers and with the workers." And the U.S. bishops, much as their own policy prescriptions made this impossible, called for economic policies that place the marginalized at their center in order to achieve the goal of economic democracy (*LE* 8; *EJA* 87, 90, 291).

The strongest reflections of the radical social model are found in the regional Latin American and Canadian documents. The analysis of economic and class structures contained in Medellin and Puebla is similar to that made by the Canadian bishops. Both sets of episcopal documents stated that capitalist development, by its very nature, creates economic structures that marginalize the majority in Latin America and increasing numbers in Canada. Growing populations have no access to the market and thus no participation in the economic life of society. Because this development enriches only a small elite, claimed these documents, it necessitates repressive police states in Latin America and increased patterns of domination and inequality in Canada.

Additionally, the Latin American documents included elements of a radical analysis of the institutional Church. Drawing on liberation theology, which more fully incorporates radical modes of analysis, the Latin American bishops argued that it was historically impossible to be neutral or to transcend economic conflict. Consequently, they viewed the Church as an agent that, necessarily, either impedes or champions the struggle for justice. The task of the Church was to nurture the liberation of the whole person and to use its institutional power on behalf of that total liberation. The Church would learn its local role, the Latin American bishops maintained, as it struggled to enable the marginalized to assume their own power and to create their own society. While the Canadian documents applied this task to individual Christians, the Latin American documents applied the work of liberation to the Church as an institution, challenging it to change sides and to leave economic and political privilege behind (see Chapters Three and Five).

The Latin American documents, however, juxtaposed an orthodox analysis with this radical one. Unlike the Canadian documents, they included the incompatible argument that present capitalist structures need only be reformed. This could be done through conversion of the society to the universal principles taught by the Church, principles which, when accepted, had the power to transform social structures (P 388).[11] The Church should transcend economic conflict and remain nonpartisan. The agents of social change were the laity who would work to Christianize social structures as they convert the people and nations already in power (P 154; 524). All experiments with Marxism, this stream in the Puebla document concluded, led to totalitarianism (P 48, 544–545).

Because the Canadian documents do not contain a simultaneous orthodox analysis of capitalism, they are the most coherent statements to date that incorporate an analysis that many be aligned with the radical paradigm. On the other hand, John Paul II's encyclical *On Social Concern* is the most coherent to date that incorporates an analysis that may be aligned only with the orthodox paradigm.

Thus, other than the Canadian statements and *On Social Concern*, every major document on economic teaching since 1891 has drawn its analysis from two incompatible social models. At the same time, these documents have contained primarily, if not exclusively, liberal strategies for social reform that are based on the orthodox social model. These liberal strategies, however, have not addressed the structural injustices revealed by the elements of radical analysis contained in the documents themselves. For example, the prescribed social change agents are those very governments, international agencies, and business elites that the documents' own analysis has already located as a source and beneficiary of the existing economic system and the crisis it generates. Or they have proposed such policy changes as job creation, job training, affirmative action, and increased education that do not touch the structural dynamics they have explicitly identified.

For a century, Catholic social teaching has documented the way in which the capitalist system, through the interstructuring of wealth, social power, and government, has marginalized people from social participation, first in the newly industrialized West, then in the Third World, and now increasingly again in the First World. From Leo XIII to the U.S. bishops' letter, a radical stream in this social teaching has cited evidence that challenges the basic tenet of the orthodox paradigm—that formal political democracy and liberal reform can control capitalist economic power. However, Catholic social teaching has consistently ignored its own historical analysis of the effects of capitalist dynamics when it formulates strategies to respond to the consequences described.

Instead, Catholic social teaching has simply embraced a social agenda consistent with its own traditional normative standards of social harmony and moral–philosophical idealism that appeal to the moral potential of the individual and the state.[12] In violation of its own historical–structural diagnosis, the last word in most circumstances for mainstream Catholic social teaching has been the defense of the private ownership of the means of production. Official Catholic social ethics locates the economic problem not in production but in distribution. Through government intervention and appeals to those who control production, society's wealth presumably can be redistributed in a minimally equitable way.

The Church continues to sanction the private wealth necessary for capitalist production and to teach that it is possible to reform distribution within capitalism because it remains attached to the traditional organic assumptions that (1) socioeconomic privilege is necessary for the effective ordering of society; (2) those who enjoy economic privilege are capable of benevolence through individual conversion; (3) the state is capable of representing the common good regardless of the concentration of economic power; and (4) mobilizing a consensus at the level of biblical and other moral principles through Church teaching will compel those elites who enjoy economic privilege, as well as their governments, to abandon unjust practices and to work for the commonweal. These assumptions, although they stand in fundamental contradiction to one analysis of capitalist dynamics within the documents studied here, are extremely important to the Catholic hierarchy. They are held onto tenaciously because they sanction the Church's own hierarchical organization and the privileges inherent to that hierarchy.

Why Liberal Strategies Are Not Feasible

Why are capitalist governments and other business elites unable to be agents of genuine social change? Why will so-called remedies such as job creation, affirmative action, and increased education either not occur or not be effective in achieving the goal of Catholic economic teaching; namely, the inclusion of ever larger numbers of people into the socioeconomic life of capitalist societies?

If the radical paradigm (see Chapter One) accurately reflects existing economic reality and correctly diagnoses the way capitalist socioeconomic structures interact, then business elites cannot initiate long-term structural change even if they want to. Indeed, capitalists have often "reformed" themselves in order to avoid change that rectifies injustice. Capitalists cannot initiate structural change because of the dynamics of the system of which they are apart. This system mandates that businesses must work continuously to increase their capital by driving competitors out in order to gain control of markets and prices. Consequently, business elites must decrease their costs, at least in the long run. Because wages are one of the largest components of cost, owners of capital are dependent on the segmented labor market, the patterns of racism and sexism that help to keep it segmented, and an underclass of structurally unemployed that together keep wages down. Wage differentials between people of color and whites and between men and women, and the accommodation to low wages of those who fear unemployment, save those who own capital billions of dollars a year and are essential to the profits of these businesses. One businessman, in responding to the U.S. bishops' letter on the economy, alluded to this situation when he observed that the general stance of Catholic social teaching implies "that the actions of businessmen [sic] are arbitrary. But the businessman cannot be arbitrary. If he pays above the market . . . he is expelled. He is captain not pilot." [13]

This requirement to enhance capital accumulation and decrease cost is a continuous incentive for business to achieve monopoly control of markets wherever possible. [14] Monopoly, which often cuts production and raises prices, reduces business risk and insures necessary capital formation. But monopoly also contributes to inflation and increases unemployment and low-wage jobs. Radical theorists insist that the accelerating reality of monopoly in advanced industrial capitalism reveals the fallacy in orthodox theory's claim that labor can achieve priority only if capital does well. As the Canadian bishops observe, to equate business profits with economic well-being is misguided because profits increase unemployment as capital invests in corporate mergers, laborsaving technology, or the export of capital. [15]

Nor can the military–industrial state be the agent of effective change. When the economy is dependent on the well-being of the system of private accumulation of capital, the capitalist state promotes the interests of business, and economic arrangements that serve business, at the expense of the marginalization of many of its citizens. Militarism is one such economic arrangement. Through the militarization of the economy, the state has sustained sufficient aggregate demand to keep corporations profitable and to keep the world "safe" for expanding global capitalism.

Thus, if business elites were to pay higher wages, or were to create new jobs sufficient for full employment or effective affirmative action, they would preclude the possibility of monopoly. If governments were to engage in socially useful spending such as education, housing, day care, and the creation of public service jobs, there would be less money to subsidize the private accumulation of capital and the well-being of global business would be jeopardized. The shadow side of this process for the capitalist system, of course, is a decline in aggregate demand from citizens who are jobless or without much income. Hence, the ever-increasing militarization of the economy.

If radical theory is correct about the dynamics of global capitalism, then implementation of the liberal reform options of Catholic social teaching would in fact destabilize the capitalist system. If the structural logic of capitalism requires increasing polarization between the accumulators of capital and those without capital, and between the capitalist-dominated state and its average citizens, on what basis can there be effective reform that simultaneously guarantees the well-being of the capitalist system? To urge class collaboration and cooperation in order to achieve a just economy is to urge the impossible in a system that both requires and produces continuous, privately controlled capital accumulation and the social injustices necessary to sustain this process. Contrary to the view in Catholic social teaching that the problem is distribution rather than the organization of production, radical analysis demonstrates that the process of generating wealth cannot be separated from the process of generating the maldistribution of wealth. Although there may be temporary alliances, genuine, long-term cooperation between capitalists and the rest of society is ruled out by the very dynamics of the system.

A historical study of the relationship between capital and organized labor in the United States, for example, concludes that there has never been a cooperative agreement between capital and labor.[16] Rather, after a long and bloody struggle, capital achieved only a temporary truce in which labor was willing to abandon all other demands in return for high wages in the most profitable industries for workers who were primarily white and male. Such wages, thought to come from the superiority of the "free-market system," could be paid to U.S. workers only as long as capital was successfully exploiting resources and markets in the Third World. This truce ended in the 1970s when U.S. capital, due to a revived European and Japanese corporate sector, could no longer maintain accustomed profits while continuing the social contract that included a relatively powerful labor organization and provision for social and community services. Since the late 1960s, the trend is for capital to pay low wages to Third World labor while white male laborers and others lose better paying jobs altogether—between 450,000 and 650,000 U.S. industrial jobs were lost in the 1970s alone. When the effects of plant, store, and office shutdowns are included, 32 million to 38 million jobs disappeared during this time.[17] Most of these jobs have been replaced with much lower paying ones.

It is crucial to radical theory to illuminate the role that international capital plays in opposing domestic and international workers and in pitting the elite-dominated states against the majority of their citizens. If radical analysis is correct, political movements for socioeconomic democracy in all countries—not merely formal, parliamentary democracy—are necessary for the security of workers anywhere.[18] The broad sources of these movements for socioeconomic democracy will break the system of privately accumulated capital; this explains why political repression is so widespread in the nations of Africa, Asia, and Latin America that have high levels of international capital penetration.[19]

As I suggest in Chapter One, other signs of polarizing tendencies within the capitalist system that point to the impossibility for liberal, cooperative reform include the fact that blacks, white women, and other racial and ethnic men and women have lost economic ground in the United States over the past twenty years. This has occurred despite the post–World War II economic boom, the civil rights movement, and the feminist movement. As one economist has asked, since capital could not afford to do without racism and sexism during a time of economic prosperity, is it realistic to expect that capital can do without them in a time of slow economic growth?[20] Is it not rather true, as current movements generated by the religious and political right demonstrate, that during economically difficult times racism and sexism increase as do the ideological justifications for them?

Historical evidence does not support the belief that the U.S. capitalist state is capable of reforms that genuinely challenge racism, sexism, or the power of class to shape our lives. For purposes of social welfare spending, including Social Security, the United States has never debated publicly about more than 1 to 4 percent of the gross national product. The basic income distributional patterns in U.S. society have not yielded to reform measures of either Democratic or Republican administrations.[21] Indeed, when reform efforts are serious capital flight occurs.

The internationalization of advanced monopoly capitalism has freed world capitalist leaders from having to be responsive to domestic political pressures that once may have worked to mitigate capitalist excesses. The normal workings of capitalist economic institutions and the capitalist state reproduce and, because of greater global competition, even intensify hierarchies of sex, race, and class that are indispensable to the func-

tioning of the capitalist economy.[22] Capitalism operates structurally according to a preferential option for the rich. Contrary
to the assumptions of liberal reform proposals, the small inner
circle of people who manage both corporate structures and the
state[23] will not sacrifice their power, any more than the marginalized will receive power as a gift from them. The power
of privileged elites can only be limited by organized, imaginative counterpower. This will surely involve conflict as the now
unaccountable power of capital is constrained. The achieving
of human dignity and genuine social justice will not be the
result of gifts bestowed by business elites and the states they
control. Rather, social justice will occur when the marginalized mobilize to exercise their own self-empowerment. Some
of the analysis of Paul VI and the Latin American and Canadian bishops suggests that official teachers of Catholic social
ethics have recognized this reality.

Despite its own radical analysis, Catholic social teaching
currently insists that adequate social change occurs by opening up reform possibilities within the capitalist system under
the leadership of corporations. Social policy that has the orthodox paradigm at its base, however, cannot address what is
actually going on within capitalism. Joe Holland has reflected
on some of the consequences for the Church of its past mis-
reading of economic reality.

> Because Western European Catholicism of the late nine-
> teenth century did not understand the new socio-eco-
> nomic forces emerging in industrial capitalism, it was
> not able to design creative pastoral strategies for its own
> people. The result was the loss to the Church of much
> of the Western European working classes. Pius XI later
> called this the greatest religious tragedy of the nineteenth
> century.[24]

Although there is more at issue here than lack of understanding, insofar as the Church does not sufficiently compre-

hend the forces shaping postindustrial global capitalism, and the dynamics of capitalist economy that daily shape the lives of people, it will not do any better at designing pastoral strategies for the late twentieth century and the twenty-first century than it did for the nineteenth. The U.S. bishops, even though they recommend traditional, liberal, social change strategies, insist that accurate analysis of the socioeconomic arena is an indispensable requirement to responsible theological reflection and social ethics. "The soundness of our prudential judgements," they observe, "depends not only on the moral force of our principles, but also on the accuracy of our information and the validity of our assumptions" (*EJA* 134).

I believe that as long as the orthodox model prevails, both in the Church's ethical analysis and particularly in its social change strategies, the kind of democratic social participation that Catholic teaching advocates as fundamental to minimal levels of economic justice cannot be adequately reflected in its social ethics. As long as Catholic social teaching continues to employ tripartite models of social analysis, and continues to formulate its social change strategies primarily within the orthodox model, its social analysis will be internally incoherent. And if its radical analysis is correct, the moral imperatives it advocates will remain at variance with what is economically feasible within the current capitalist system.

Embracing a coherent economic analysis will be difficult for the leadership of the Roman Catholic Church because it will necessitate addressing why the Church has remained committed to an organic social theory that justifies hierarchy and enables it to ignore the radical implications of its own analysis when it comes to social policy prescriptions. The institutional Church has always objected to the individualism sustained by liberal capitalism. Indeed, the suspicion of capitalism and its affirmation of the autonomous, nonrelated individual was already built in by the organic paradigm. The communitarian sensibilities of the Church have always made it uncomfortable with the liberal rejection of concrete shared goods that are necessary for the commonweal. But Church leadership is even more fearful of the egalitarianism of the radical paradigm and its commitment to the transformation of the hierarchies of Church, civil powers, and the patriarchal family that alone presume to speak for God. This is so, even as popes and bishops cannot help but use elements of radical analysis when, as a result of their pastoral engagement, they adopt the perspective of the marginalized and interpret what is going on in capitalism from their point of view. Indeed, the Church's continued immersion in concrete struggle with the poor in various parts of the globe insures the persistence of radical analysis in its social ethics.

When compared to the democratic social model endorsed by the radical paradigm, however, the hierarchies sustained by capitalism, both in the market and in the family, have in fact been more congenial to the traditional organic bias of the institutional Church and its ruling elites. Thus, the orthodox social model has prevailed, especially as the Church has almost exclusively advocated liberal social policy prescriptions. Insofar as capitalist society "at the center," or in the First World, appeared to be minimizing inequality—though at the unacknowledged cost of exploiting the periphery to foot the bill at the center—liberal reform strategies issuing from the First World seemed rational. Now, however, with the evolution of global capitalism, which is reproducing Third World or peripheral patterns of rising poverty, structural unemployment, and underemployment even in the First World, such moderate reform strategies will seem increasingly beside the point.

More and more Catholics live in the Third World and are informed by radical analysis that, however ambiguously, has always been present in the Church's teaching. This radical analysis will move ever-more swiftly to center stage for Catholic Christians, especially as even First World bishops are now employing elements of its perspective. But as we have seen,

John Paul II and the U.S. bishops have yet to move the major thrust of official teaching into a more discerning direction so that its policy prescriptions may touch the reality of present political and economic dynamics.

The Common Values of Radical Theory and Catholic Social Teaching

Every social ethic is shaped by social theory or sets of explanations as to how the dynamics of political economy function within a society.[25] The social theory in turn is based on underlying normative assumptions regarding how social relations and institutions ought to be. Because the meaning of ethical norms and values is determined by the social theory out of which they operate, ethical norms that are not consciously related to a specific social theory are not adequate. They fail to specify an understanding of what constitutes moral social relations and how the dynamics of political economy affect the realization of these relations. Norms that are not purposefully related to social theory, or norms based on an inconsistent use of social theory, mystify both the social relations we ought to have and the nature of the socioeconomic arena in which they are to be realized. A viable social ethic needs to clarify how its moral norms—of justice, mutuality, and interdependence, for example—relate to its assumed model of social relations, and how the dynamics of the political economy either inhibit or promote the actualization of these norms.

For example, what kind of justice, mutuality, or interdependence is possible in a political economy that depends on classism, sexism, and racism to maintain the social hierarchies necessary to a system based on the private accumulation and control of capital? What concrete meaning can justice, mutuality, and interdependence have within a political and socioeconomic system that has this particular internal dynamic?

Such ethical norms cannot be embodied in the same way in an economy that demands market autonomy and perpetuates labor and familial hierarchies as they would in a society where democratic organization took precedence in market, labor, and family relations. Unless justice values are related to the dynamics of the socioeconomic situation in which they are to function, they clarify little about the quality of ethical life that is realized or even possible.[26]

When an ethic uses social theory inconsistently, as I have argued is the case in modern Catholic social teaching, it is critical in the interests of both coherency and credibility to examine the implications of the theoretical paradigms at issue, and to ask which social model best serves Catholic teaching's ethical concerns. I propose that it is within the radical social model that the questions put by the U.S. Catholic bishops in *Economic Justice for All* can best be answered. The bishops ask: "What does the economy do *for* people? What does it do *to* people? And how do people *participate* in it?" Radical analysis is essential to understand how the social relations of advanced capitalist production and other structures it generates (the military industrial complex, debtor nations, the gendered and racially segmented labor market, and the class-structured education and welfare systems) are decisive in determining how people actually participate in late twentieth-century capitalism. Efforts to adjust maldistribution and less than equitable participatory patterns without restructuring the relations of production are clearly limited in their effect. One cannot fundamentally alter social structures that marginalize people through the use of nonstructural social change strategies that are based on the orthodox economic model. Indeed, if radical analysis provides the more accurate picture of capitalist dynamics, then the moral norms in Catholic social teaching, such as universal dignified social participation, including authentic partnership in the workplace and a preferential option for the poor, cannot be achieved in a society organized around the private ownership and control of wealth.

Radical theory is also more compatible with the normative social justice claims of the Roman Catholic tradition, particularly its preferential option for the poor. Orthodox theory places an ahistorical and unrelated "economic man" at the center of its analysis, and it supports a social ethic based on the individual pursuit of self-interest. The orthodox model assumes that in their economic lives people are nonmutual, that their basic sustenance needs may be assumed, and that their primary motivation is individual maximum consumption. The orthodox paradigm assumes that the maximization of social wealth is best effected by the private ownership and control of the means of production, which has as its goal the creation of maximum profit for individual investors. It assumes that within the capitalist system the creation and distribution of socially useful wealth will, in essence, take care of itself. Because the capitalist market is benevolent in long-term outcomes if not in input, the isolated individual or financial group need not value the commonweal or embody active commitment to it.

Orthodox theory thus literally grounds the common good in an ethic that is shaped by the preferential option for those few who have capital, and its analysis of economic rationality is constructed to support this conclusion. If the normative assumptions of orthodox theory determine the way a society makes its choices, social policies like taxation, welfare, and government spending will be shaped to sustain an option for the rich. If the normative assumptions of orthodox theory are drawn upon, however unconsciously, in the construction of a social ethic, this ethic will reflect, even if subtly, this option.

Radical theory places those who are marginalized in the society, and their concrete historical situation, at the center of its social analysis and concern. The radical model promotes a social ethic based not on the presumed benevolence of the privately controlled market but on the democratically achieved plans of men and women. Radical theory offers an alternative interpretation of what is basic to the economic well-being of people and of how economic and political life should be structured. It reflects the experiences of those without capital, of those on the margin who are excluded from full social participation and from the benefits of the ownership of capital. The analysis of the radical paradigm is congenial to the concerns of Catholic social teaching and its preferential option for the poor in at least the following ways:[27]

1. Radical theory gives attention to concrete human suffering and its reproduction in society. Radical theory seeks to illuminate the dynamics of marginalization and exploitation in society. Its normative concern is to clarify and address human suffering and to develop effective social change strategies based on a critical, rather than a self-justifying, theory of capitalist dynamics. The radical paradigm demonstrates the historical and structural relationship between the evolution of the capitalist system and the socioeconomic problems that have preoccupied Catholic social teaching for a century, including poverty, unemployment, underemployment, and lack of dignified social participation for increasing numbers of people everywhere on the globe. This emphasis on attention to the suffering caused by economic marginalization has been a major reason for the construction of modern Catholic social ethics since its inception. Beyond this, we have also seen key moments when Catholic social teaching has demonstrated a focus on concrete human suffering, as when John XXIII overturned tradition to make resistance to suffering, rather than philosophical agreement, the basis for human solidarity movements. The U.S. bishops make economic suffering their central ethical concern when they ask: What is the impact of an economic system on people, especially the ones at the bottom (PT 159; EJA 130, 319)?

2. The radical paradigm claims that the question of justice must be related to the question of ownership and control of the means of production in society, not merely to the question of income distribution. Ownership and control of production is a primary issue of social justice because this concerns

who controls and uses human and other resources. It concerns who decides what is to be done with society's wealth, including its natural and technological assets, and what new forms of wealth are to be produced. It concerns who decides how most people in the society are going to spend most of their lives. Radical theory argues that unequal power and participation in social life as a whole is dialectically related to unequal control over the means of production and unequal control over the structure of work.[28] The structure of work is just when the entire process of work, including the nature and use of the wealth created by it, is shared democratically and in a way that is responsible to the larger society in which the work is done.[29] Radical analysis holds that to be just the arena of work must be subject to democratic participation and control. Those who work must have a voice in determining what their labor produces and how what they produce is used.[30] Catholic social teaching shares this value also. From Pius XI (1931) to the U.S. bishops (1986), the Church has spoken consistently about employment as a human right and about the need for democracy in the workplace (QA 65; *EJA* 298–303).

3. Radical analysis claims that social theory must be accountable to human experience just as solidarity movements must be accountable to the marginalized. Radical theory seeks to present "human society" in a way that demystifies social relations so that human subjects may effectively act to reproduce a social world amenable to their welfare. Informed by feminist theory, radical theorists have challenged the prevailing definitions of human nature, gender, and the family. Radical theory strives to illuminate what is actually going on in people's lives, especially the lives of women and other marginalized groups. The choice of problems it regards as important and the areas of human life to which it directs its attention are congruent with what majorities of people actually experience.

Thus, radical theory aims constantly to test its theory by the actual experience and practice of human agents, especially those who challenge injustice. The goal of collective resistance to injustice, or solidarity, is to create social space within which people can begin to locate the ways in which so many of their "private" troubles are in fact the result of public structures. The goal of solidarity is to nurture an environment wherein those struggling against injustice can be empowered to act together to challenge those structures that keep them marginalized. The truth of social theory and the integrity of solidarity are measured by how they contribute to the creation of life patterns that support mutuality in human relationships.

Commitment to such values is represented particularly in some of the teaching of Paul VI and in those Latin American documents that give a preferential option to a militant poor who seek to become active agents in their own lives, people who do not simply live out a script they have been given by others. These people are "opted for" because, in their struggle to be artisans of their own destiny, they exemplify human dignity at work. These values are also reflected in the Canadian bishops' statement, *Ethical Choices and Political Challenges*, which outlines a social change strategy that should begin and end with the lived experiences of the excluded.[31]

4. Radical theory believes that economic systems originate in history and therefore are capable of being transformed by human action in history. Radical theory relativizes the capitalist order by insisting that the capitalist era can be historically transcended by a more just and inclusive political economy. Its analysis assumes that the economic system is responsive to collective human agents through their search for unrealized possibilities in the present order. Catholic social teaching also reflects this awareness especially in the encyclicals of Paul VI, the perspectives of the Latin American and Canadian bishops, and in some aspects of the U.S. bishops' letter, all of which have called for greater utopian imagination and have supported the experimentation of those who struggle for a new and more just social order.

Official Catholic social teaching has yet to acknowledge the existence of conflicting social theories in its analysis, nor has it addressed the question of which social theory would best support its ethical sensibilities and moral imperatives. The orthodox paradigm gives primacy to the nonmutual individual and fails to integrate historical processes and political or economic structures into its analysis. Because its value assumptions give a preferential option to the few who are capitalists, this social model will not serve the articulation and implementation of the Church's moral norms.

Radical social theory, on the other hand, begins and ends its analysis with a consideration of concrete human suffering, seeks accountability to the marginalized, is centrally concerned with the structure of human work, and is committed to the creation of new democratic socioeconomic institutions. In these crucial ways, it converges with the ethical sensibilities that have informed Catholic social teaching for the last century. The values that radical analysis uses to critique capitalist structures and the values that this social model seeks to embody in a new economic order are those it shares with the tradition of Catholic social teaching.

Attention to these values is essential in resolving the social theory debate. Consequently, the Catholic social justice tradition needs to make a more informed choice between these two opposing interpretations of capitalist society and must acknowledge the greater compatibility of radical analysis with its own value assumptions.

Why Does the Church Use Conflicting Social Paradigms?

Gar Alperovitz has observed that most of the teachings of the U.S. bishops' letter on the economy "are likely to be seen historically as transitional . . . away from capitalism, towards . . .

something new. They depart from traditional reform ideas and approach far more radical conclusions—yet in a confused way, pull back from the implications at the last moment."[32] While this reading of the bishops' letter is perhaps more hopeful than mine, there is a valid point here. For the argument can be made not only for the U.S. bishops' letter but for almost the entire tradition of Catholic social justice theory reviewed here that it avoids conclusions to which its own radical analysis might lead by opting for the safety of reform measures consistent with the orthodox paradigm. Document after document fails to follow through on its own perceptive analysis. Why does the Church use conflicting paradigms and avoid radical conclusions?

A radical approach suggests that to understand why, we look at the ongoing practice of the Church itself. Lee Cormie has asked, To what extent do the practices and priorities of the Church reflect or fail to reflect its own teaching?[33] Gregory Baum has observed that "the option for the people at the base and in the margin draws a dividing line right through the Church with hierarchy and laity on both sides."[34] William Tabb concurs with this when he observes that the Roman Catholic Church is "riddled with internal dissension."[35] The mainstream Church seeks economic security, and racial and patriarchal privilege, and is more comfortable with the orthodox social model that supports its own interests. This is true not only in terms of its analysis of capitalist society but of its analysis of its own institutional life within that society. The Catholic churches on the periphery, which live close to and include marginated men and women of color, white women, poor white men, and all the children of these groups, seek to be faithful to the values in the more prophetic teachings of Scripture and tradition. These churches, in contrast, are drawn to the radical social model that has a reading of history and political economy more faithful to their experiences.

Thus, as the Church itself is riddled with internal dissension and class division so are the documents it has produced. In the search for justice, these propose two incompatible models for structuring community life and organizing economic and political relationships. Consequently, it does not clarify much to say that justice is an integral part of Catholic social teaching if the Church is caught in a "pluralism of interpretations of justice."[36] If, as David Hollenbach argues, there is in Catholic social teaching "an urgent need to clarify the meaning of justice," then I would also argue that there is an urgent need to clarify the social model upon which the conception of justice is based.[37] Otherwise, as is evidenced in the body of Catholic social teaching studied here, one is left with "radically different conclusions about the concrete actions demanded by justice."[38]

Therefore, it is crucial to understand that ethical norms and values have different meanings depending on the social theory that informs them. The value commitment of an option for the poor, for example, has different ethical implications when it emanates from a radical social model than when it emanates from an organic one—as the differences between the Latin American and U.S. bishops' conceptions of this social justice value clearly demonstrate.

The official Church needs to acknowledge its use of social theories and to critically assess them both for their interpretive power of capitalist dynamics and for their compatibility with the Church's own normative moral claims. I have shown that on both these counts Catholic social analysis has, at times, recognized the truth in the radical social model. I think that the Church needs to be in more fundamental and consistent dialogue with the radical position.

For example, the radical paradigm, when evidenced in Catholic teaching, is applied only to selected social relations. While the Church has reflected a radical analysis since 1891 in its illumination of the exploitation of people by class, the analyses of racial and sexual oppressions are almost nonexistent. Nor has the hierarchical Church made serious use of the radical perspective to reflect on itself. It is evident that the commitment to a consistent radical analysis cannot be made without an enormous internal struggle. Directly facing the realities of racial, class, and gender privilege runs counter to the Roman Catholic hierarchy's preference for organic models of social relations and would demand dramatic transformations in the Church's institutional system.

To begin, honesty will be necessary to demonstrate how social location, including class, race, and sex privilege, affects moral sensibility, the conception of moral reason, and the conclusions of moral reasoning itself. The institutional Church cannot weigh the plurality in interpretations of justice, and the incompatible social models that undergird them, or consider their consequences for Catholic ethics in part because Church leaders presume a homogeneity in the Church that does not exist. Popes and bishops tend to universalize a relatively affluent, mostly white, and wholly male clerical perspective that perceives diversity as a threat to the unity of the Church. Their belief in the possibility of a universally agreed upon "rational resolution" of conflict ignores "the messy conflictual and diverse character of historical reality."[39] Viewed from the elegant surroundings of the Church hierarchy, the anger of those who have been excluded not only from power in society but from power in the Church itself seems arrogant.[40] Consequently, Church leaders sometimes skillfully devise methods to co-opt not only the conflictual nature of reality but the very language of the marginalized themselves. At other times, when they offer a more radical analysis, their teaching still is seen as a paper tiger—there is often no institutional commitment behind their social ethical norms with concrete practice to support these norms.

Perhaps a most basic reason the institutional Church does not face the conflict inherent in its analysis of justice is because of the internal socioeconomic ramifications this acknowledgment would entail. Since the Lateran Treaty of 1929, the Church's financial administrators have given priority to making profit through the capitalist system regardless of moral considerations.[41] Even apart from the assets of individual religious communities, the Vatican alone is known to own some $25 billion in real estate, stocks, and bonds including sizable holdings in some of the world's largest multinational corporations.[42] The institutional Church appears unable to face the tremendous financial implications to itself of acknowledging the intrinsic injustice of capitalist institutions. It exhibits a contradictory social analysis and evades the implications of its own teachings because these would require alternative ways of survival and an end to the internal and external privileges associated with supporting patriarchal capitalism. Justice cannot be articulated with a coherent analysis within a Roman Catholic Church that has not faced the socioeconomic dilemmas of its own existence. Given the enormity of the challenge posed by the radical perspective, it is easy to see why official Church teaching has preferred to remain at the level of general moral norms and an inconsistent use of social theory.

The peripheral churches are by far the majority in a Church that is growing disproportionally in the Third World even as Catholicism has been losing membership in the First. At the end of the twentieth century almost 70 percent of the Catholic Church's 907 million members live in the Third World.[43] As many Third World Catholics incorporate the radical perspectives of liberation theology, they believe that conceptual analysis is only as just as the social practice out of which it emerges, and consequently theory cannot have priority over "lived world sensuous experience."[44] These churches believe that it is not theoretical consensus but attention to concrete suffering that will mobilize a political will for social change. As movements in many Third World countries have shown, it is participation in grassroots struggle that refines theoretical insight and confirms awareness that justice and power will not be bestowed freely upon the excluded. They can only be won by them through struggle. Cardinal Flahiff of Winnipeg, Canada, has said, "henceforth our basic principle must be: only knowledge gained through participation is valid in this area of justice." [45]

These peripheral churches call the mainstream Church to face the implications of its own best insights. They call the Church to the awareness that advocacy is not an option but an already established fact. As a historical agent, the institutional Church takes sides whether it wishes to or not. Therefore they call the Church to use its collective weight to help incarnate its own principles, both within the Church and in society at large. They call the Church away from its trust in investment portfolios and away from the patriarchy and racism in its own institutions. [46] They call the Church to offer to the excluded the physical space and the networking systems of an international organization that are crucial in the process of social change. Most of all, they call the Church to be a community where all people, especially women, children, and marginalized men experience a radical inclusiveness within the Church itself, and so can celebrate their common longing for a wider world in which the same radical justice will also exist. They call the Church to nurture people in the experience and the possibility of this kind of world, for it is within communities like these that Christians experience the Divine. The U.S. bishops have said that solidarity with the suffering and confrontation with institutional injustice enables Christians to experience the presence and power of Christ (*EJA* 55).

Unless this kind of embodied commitment, not only demanded *by* a radical analysis but demanded *for* a radical analysis, becomes indicative of the institutional Church, its interpretation of justice and how we must act for it will remain inconsistent. Most importantly, the strategies for social change that the hierarchy recommends will not touch the depth of the problem of human economic suffering that it has diagnosed so well.

Notes

1. I am grateful to Beverly Harrison for the term "embodied commitment." See "Theological Reflection in the Struggle for Liberation," in *Making the Connections: Essays in Feminist Social Ethics*, ed. Carol S. Robb (Boston: Beacon Press, 1985), p. 242.

2. *Quadragesimo anno* (*QA*) and *Rerum novarum* (*RN*) are found in *Seven Great Encyclicals* (Glen Rock, N.J.: Paulist Press, 1963).

3. José Porfirio Miranda notes that as early as 1951, Roman Catholic scholars have recognized that these papal encyclicals utilized Marxist analysis. See Christine E. Gudorf, *Catholic Social Teaching on Liberation Themes* (Washington D.C.: University Press of America, 1981), p. 169.

4. See for example *Mater et magistra* (*MM*), *Pacem in terris* (*PT*), and *Gaudium et spes* (*GS*), which are found in *The Gospel of Peace and Justice*, ed. Joseph Gremillion (Maryknoll, N.Y.: Orbis Books, 1976).

5. *Populorum progressio* (*PP*) is found in *Gospel of Peace and Justice*, ed. Gremillion.

6. *Octogesima adveniens* (*OA*) is found in *Gospel of Peace and Justice*, ed. Gremillion. I have, however, argued that *OA* 26–36 can be read as a repudiation of *PT* 159.

7. *Justice in the World* (*JW*) is found in *Gospel of Peace and Justice*, ed. Gremillion.

8. *Laborem exercens* (*LE*) is found in Gregory Baum, *The Priority of Labor: A Commentary on* Laborem Exercens (New York: Paulist Press, 1982), pp. 95–149.

9. National Conference of Catholic Bishops, "*Economic Justice for All: Catholic Social Teaching and the U.S. Economy*" (*EJA*), *Origins* 16, no. 24 (November 27, 1986).

10. *Sollicitudo rei socialis*, or *On Social Concern* (*OSC*), is found in *Origins* 17, no. 38 (March 3, 1988). All three documents view all forms of Marxism as deterministic, and every alternative to capitalism as Marxist-inspired state collectivism. Offical Catholic social teaching persists in equating Marxism with a theory of state socialism or with communist state politics. From a Marxist perspective, this may be comparable to equating Christianity with Christian fundamentalism.

11. The Puebla (*P*) and Medellin documents are found in John Eagleson and Philip Scharper, eds. *Puebla and Beyond* (Maryknoll, N.Y.: Orbis, 1980).

12. Samuel Bowles and Herbert Gintis argue that a social agenda that "displaces historical concerns and simply develops an ideal structure that meets favored normative standards" is utopian in the worst sense of the term. See *Democracy and Capitalism* (New York: Basic Books, 1986), p. 186.

13. Eugene Kennedy, "America's Activist Bishops: Examining Capitalism," *New York Times Magazine*, August 12, 1984, p. 25. While orthodox theory would say that the consumer is pilot, and radical theory would argue that the capitalist system is pilot, the point is still the same. Capitalism has rules that must be followed if one is to survive.

14. Many assume that the purpose of antitrust laws is to curb the power of monopoly and oligopoly. Radical theorists claim that the purpose of these laws is to give the federal government the power to decide which corporations should be supported in a conflict of interest. As a result, prosecutions have been few and the courts have been lenient. Between 1950 and 1967, for example, almost half of the prosecutions were of small firms of less than $100 million in sales. In addition, the due-process clause of the Fourteenth Amendment (intended to give equal rights to blacks) has been interpreted to prohibit state regulation of corporations, which are considered legal "persons," in order to deny state governments the power to interfere with corporate behavior. See E. K. Hunt and Howard J. Sherman, *Economics: An Introduction to Traditional and Radical Views*, 3d ed. (New York: Harper and Row, 1978), pp. 296–99; and Richard J. Barnet and Ronald E. Müller, *Global Reach: The Power of the Multinational Corporations* (New York: Simon and Schuster, 1974), pp. 230–31.

15. Canadian Conference of Catholic Bishops, *Ethical Reflections on the Economic Crisis* (EREC) in *Ethics and Economics: Canada's Catholic Bishops and the Economic Crisis*, ed. Gregory Baum and Duncan Cameron (Toronto: Lorimer, 1984), pp. 12–13.

16. Noteworthy studies of labor struggles in the United States include: Richard O. Boyer and Herbert M. Morais, *Labor's Untold Story* (New York: Cameron Associates, 1955); Jeremy Brecher, *Strike!* (Boston: South End Press, 1972); David Montgomery, *Workers' Control in America* (New York: Cambridge University Press, 1979); Herbert Gutman, *Work, Culture and Society in Industrializing America* (New York:

Knopf, 1976); James R. Green, *The World of the Worker: Labor in 20th Century America* (New York: Hill and Wang, 1978); James R. Green, ed., *Workers' Struggles, Past and Present* (Philadelphia: Temple University Press, 1983); Sydney Lens, *Radicalism in America* (New York: Crowell, 1966); James Weinstein, *Ambiguous Legacy* (New York: New Viewpoints, 1975).

17. Barry Bluestone and Bennett Harrison, *The Deindustrialization of America* (New York: Basic Books, 1982), p. 9.

18. For a discussion of the common interests and responsibilities of international labor, see John C. Raines and Donna C. Day-Lower, *Modern Work and Human Meaning* (Philadelphia: Westminster Press, 1986), pp. 125–29.

19. As noted in Chapter One, since over 50 percent of the world's population cannot enter the capitalist market, the expansion of capitalist development always requires the use of force. See Lee Cormie, "The U.S. Bishops on Capitalism," from the working papers of the American Academy of Religion (1985), pp. 16–19. Even neoconservative apologist Michael Novak acknowledges that the unaided market has no way of bringing the poorest of the world's population into the capitalist market. See *The Spirit of Democratic Capitalism* (New York: Simon and Schuster, 1982), p. 109.

20. Nancy Bancroft, "Women in the Cutback Economy," in *Women's Consciousness, Women's Conscience*, ed. Barbara H. Andolsen, Christine E. Gudorf, and Mary D. Pellauer (New York: Winston Press, 1985), p. 27.

21. Gar Alperovitz, "The Coming Break in Liberal Consciousness," *Christianity and Crisis* 46 (March 13, 1986): 60. Alperovitz points out that it has not been social spending, but the spending of war and its aftermath that has made some reform in domestic redistribution of wealth.

22. For a historical analysis of specific capitalist economies that suggests that capitalist states may be quite distinct with regard to labor markets and employment, see Goran Therborn, *Why Some People Are More Unemployed Than Others* (London: Schocken Books, 1986). For a review of this book that wonders if the success stories are "skillful adaptations" to capitalism, or only temporary exceptions to it, see William K. Tabb, "Jobs: A Matter of Commitment," *Christianity and Crisis* 47 (May 18, 1987): 194–97.

23. See G. William Domhoff, *Who Rules America Now?* (Englewood Cliffs: Prentice-Hall, 1983).

24. Joe Holland, "Marxist Class Analysis in American Society," in *Theology in the Americas*, ed. Sergio Torres and John Eagleson (Maryknoll, N.Y.: Orbis, 1976), p. 320.

25. This view conflicts with the work in Catholic social ethics of David Hollenbach, S.J. Hollenbach believes that Catholic social teaching distills ahistorical, transcendent norms that are untained by social theories or models. See "Modern Catholic Teachings Concerning Justice," in *The Faith That Does Justice*, ed. John C. Haughey (New York: Paulist Press, 1977), pp. 218–19. I contend that one's theoretical understanding of a norm is conditioned by one's experience of it within a specific historical and cultural situation. While moral norms and principles (like mutuality and interdependence) are vital for a social ethic, they are never untainted or universally understood in the same way. They are always understood through one's experience within a specific social location and within a specific culture. There may exist multiple understandings of mutuality, for example, not only between cultures but within a culture. Hollenbach at times seems to give credence to this, but at other times he does not. He says that "moral norms, including the norm of justice, cannot be determined apart from careful scrutiny of the cultural milieu in which they are affirmed to be normative," but he also opts for the need to "distill ethical norms" from "the undue influence of conditioned social theories and models" (217–19).

26. I am indebted to the work of David Hollenbach, and especially to the work of Gregory Baum. However, in calling for attention to social theory, I differ with Hollenbach, who fails to take seriously the historicity of ethical norms, and from Baum, who reads the use of social theory differently. My analysis follows the lead of ethicists like Christine E. Gudorf, who argues that a radical social model may be slowly appropriated at the level of Catholic social teaching, but not at the level of Catholic theology, and Marvin M. Ellison, who clarifies the use of social models in the global debate on economic development. See Gudorf, *Catholic Social Teaching on Liberation Themes*, esp. chap. 11; and Marvin M. Ellison, *The Center Cannot Hold: The Search for a Global Economy of Justice* (Washington, D.C.: University Press of America, 1983).

This study seeks to contribute to scholarly discussion by calling Catholic social teaching to "come clean" on its theoretical social model, a model that is always operative, consciously or not, when the tradition attempts to clarify norms of social justice. We can no longer avoid the fact that all ethical perspectives are shaped by social theory that conditions the quality of the moral activity with which ethics is most centrally concerned.

27. The following discussion is indebted to Beverly Harrison's analysis of the theological and moral viability of radical political economy in "The Role of Social Theory in Religious Social Ethics," in *Making the Connections: Essays in Feminist Social Ethics*, ed. Carol S. Robb (Boston: Beacon Press, 1985), pp. 74–80.

28. Raines and Day-Lower, *Modern Work and Human Meaning*, p. 111.

29. For a discussion of meaningful work that engages some of the assumptions of the radical paradigm, see Raines and Day-Lower, *Modern Work and Human Meaning*, esp. chaps. 6–9.

30. Beverly Harrison observes that, however diverse the various socialisms have been in accounting for the problems of capitalism, the origin of radical theory lay in their common perception of the alienating results that occurred when work was divorced from ownership and communal responsibility. See "The Role of Social Theory in Religious Social Ethics," p. 55.

31. See especially *PP* 34, 65; *P* 3, 1137, 1162, 1163, 1220, 1235, 1244, 1245; and *Ethical Choices and Political Challenges* (*ECPC*) (Ottowa, Ontario: Canadian Conference of Catholic Bishops, 1983), p. 2.

32. Gar Alperovitz, "The Coming Break in Liberal Consciousness," p. 59.

33. Lee Cormie, "The U.S. Bishops on Capitalism," pp. 29–30.

34. Baum and Cameron, *Ethics and Economics*, p. 83.

35. William K. Tabb, "The Shoulds and the Excluded Whys: The U.S. Catholic Bishops Look at the Economy," in *Churches in Struggle: Liberation Theologies and Social Change in North America*, ed. William K. Tabb (New York: Monthly Review Press, 1986), p. 286.

36. David Hollenbach, S.J., "Modern Catholic Teaching Concerning Justice," pp. 208–9.

37. Despite Hollenbach's desire to clarify interpretations of justice, since he holds the meaningfulness of ahistorical, transcendent norms, he ultimately rejects a focus on social theory. He says that "sociological and political analysis . . . cannot provide a model of society which will in some way fully embody the norm of justice in a definitive way" (ibid., p. 217). In his rejection of social analysis, Hollenbach minimizes the historicity of ethical norms, and refuses a consideration of the degrees of concrete justice that are possible within a specific structure. If I understand him correctly, he assumes that all social models are equally flawed. The point, I think, is to use

social analysis in an effort to clarify in what circumstances a greater *relative* degree of embodied justice (and of mutuality and interdependence) is possible.

38. Ibid., p. 215.

39. Susan B. Thistlethwaite, "Narrative and Connection," *Christianity and Crisis* 47 (March 2, 1987): 71.

40. Richard W. Gillett, "The Church Acts for Economic Justice," in *Churches in Struggle*, ed. Tabb, p. 275.

41. See Penny Lernoux, *In Banks We Trust* (New York: Penguin Books, 1986), pp. 169–74, 209. See also Nino LoBello, *The Vatican Empire* (New York: Trident Press, 1968).

42. Penny Lernoux, *Cry of the People: The Struggle for Human Rights in Latin America* (New York: Penguin Books, 1982), pp. 454–55.

43. Penny Lernoux, "Shadow Darkening Church of the Poor," *National Catholic Reporter* 24 (June 17, 1988): 8.

44. Beverly W. Harrison, "Theological Reflection in the Struggle for Liberation," in *Making the Connections*, ed. Robb, p. 242.

45. Quoted in Baum and Cameron, *Ethics and Economics*, p. 26.

46. Phillip Berryman, "How Christians Become Socialists," in *Churches in Struggle*, ed. Tabb, p. 161.

Selected Bibliography

Sources in Economic and Feminist Theories

Alperovitz, Gar, and Jeff Faux. *Rebuilding America*. New York: Pantheon, 1984.

Bancroft, Nancy. "Women in the Cutback Economy." In *Women's Consciousness, Women's Conscience*, edited by Barbara H. Andolsen, Christine E. Gudorf, and Mary D. Pellauer. New York: Winston Press, 1985.

Banfield, Edward C. *The Unheavenly City Revisited*. Boston: Little, Brown, 1974.

Barnet, Richard J., and Ronald E. Müller. *Global Reach: The Power of the Multinational Corporations*. New York: Simon and Schuster, 1974.

Barrett, Nancy S. "How the Study of Women Has Reconstructed the Discipline of Economics." In *A Feminist Perspective in the Academy: The Difference It Makes*, edited by Elizabeth Langland and Walter Gove. Chicago: University of Chicago Press, 1981.

Berger, Peter L. *The Capitalist Revolution*. New York: Basic Books, 1986.

Blau, Francis D., and Wallace D. Henricks. "Occupational Segregation by Sex." *Journal of Human Resources* 14 (Spring 1979): 197–210.

Bluestone, Barry, and Bennett Harrison. *The Deindustrialization of America*. New York: Basic Books, 1982.

Boston, Thomas D. "Racial Inequality and Class Stratification." *Review of Radical Political Economics* 17 (1985): 46–71.

Bowles, Samuel, and Herbert Gintis. *Democracy and Capitalism*. New York: Basic Books, 1986.

————. *Schooling in Capitalist America: Educational Reform and the Contradictions of Economic Life*. New York: Basic Books, 1976.

Canterbery, E. Ray *The Making of Economics*. 2d ed. Belmont, Calif.: Wadsworth, 1980.

Darvasy, Wendy, and Judith Van Allen. "Fighting the Feminization of Poverty." *Review of Radical Political Economics* 16, no. 4 (Winter 1984): 92–102.

Deane, Phyllis. *The Evolution of Economic Ideas*. New York: Cambridge University Press, 1978.

Donovan, Josephine. *Feminist Theory: The Intellectual Traditions of American Feminism*. New York: Frederick Ungar, 1985.

Edwards, Richard C., Michael Reich, and Thomas E. Weisskopf. *The Capitalist System.* 2d ed. Englewood Cliffs, N.J.: Prentice-Hall, 1978.

Eisenstein, Zillah R., ed. *Capitalist Patriarchy and the Case for Socialist Feminism.* New York: Monthly Review Press, 1979.

Ferguson, C. E. *The Neoclassical Theory of Production and Distribution.* London: Cambridge University Press, 1969.

Folbre, Nancy. "The Pauperization of Motherhood: Patriarchy and Public Policy in the United States." *Review of Radical Political Economics* 16, no. 4 (Winter 1984): 68–83.

Friedman, Milton. *Capitalism and Freedom.* Chicago: University of Chicago Press, 1962.

Gordon, David M. *Theories of Poverty and Underemployment.* Lexington, Mass.: Lexington Books, 1972.

Gordon, David M., ed. *Problems in Political Economy.* Lexington, Mass.: D. C. Heath, 1977.

Gordon, David M., Richard Edwards, and Michael Reich. *Segmented Work, Divided Workers: The Historical Transformation of Labor in the United States.* New York: Cambridge University Press, 1982.

Gordon, Donald F. "The Role of the History of Economic Thought in the Understanding of Modern Economic Theory." *American Economic Review,* May 1965, pp. 122–34.

Goulet, Denis. "Sufficiency for All: The Basic Mandate of Development and Social Economics." *Review of Social Economy* 36, no. 3 (December 1978): 243–61.

Gurley, John G. "The State of Political Economics." *American Economic Review* 61 (May 1971): 51–60.

Harrington, Michael. *Taking Sides: The Education of a Militant Mind.* New York: Holt, Rinehart, and Winston, 1985.

Hayter, Teresa, and Catharine Watson. *Aid: Rhetoric and Reality.* London: Pluto Press, 1985.

Hunt, E. K., and Howard Sherman. *Economics: An Introduction to Traditional and Radical Views.* 3d ed. New York: Harper and Row, 1978.

Hunt-Landsberg, Martin, and Jerry Lembcke. "Class Struggle and Economic Transformation." *Review of Radical Political Economics* 16, no. 4 (Winter 1984): 98–105.

Institute for New Communications. *Women in the Global Factory.* Pamphlet No. 2. 853 Broadway, Room 905, New York, N.Y. 10003.

Jessop, Bob. *The Capitalist State: Marxist Theories and Methods.* New York: New York University Press, 1982.

Joblin, Joseph. "The Papal Encyclical *Pacem in Terris.*" *International Labor Review* 84, no. 3 (September 1961): 1–14.

Kaysen, Carl. "The Social Significance of the Modern Corporation." *American Economic Review* 47 (May 1957): 311–19.

Keohane, Nannerl O., Michelle Z. Rosaldo, and Barbara C. Gelpi, eds. *Feminist Theory: A Critique of Ideology.* Chicago: University of Chicago Press, 1982.

Lernoux, Penny. *In Banks We Trust.* New York: Penguin Books, 1986.

Lindblom, Charles E. *Politics and Markets.* New York: Basic Books, 1977.

Marx, Karl. *Karl Marx: Selected Writings.* Edited by David McLellan. New York: Oxford University Press, 1977.

Max, Steve. "New Alliance Between the Middle Class and the Poor." *Democratic Left* 17 (May–August 1987): 3–4.

Meek, Ronald L. *Economics and Ideology and Other Essays.* London: Chapman and Hall, 1967.

Myrdal, Gunnar. *The Political Element in the Development of Economic Theory.* London: Routledge and K. Paul, 1953.

———. *Value in Social Theory.* Edited by Paul Streeten. London: Routledge and K. Paul, 1958.

Nickerson, Gary W. "Introduction." *Review of Radical Political Economics* 16, no. 4 (Winter 1984): i–viii.

Novak, Michael. *The American Vision: An Essay on the Future of Democratic Capitalism.* Washington, D.C.: American Enterprise Institute, 1979.

———. *The Spirit of Democratic Capitalism.* New York: Simon and Schuster, 1982.

Okun, Arthur M. "Equality and Efficiency: The Big Tradeoff." *New York Times Magazine,* July 4, 1976.

Peabody, Gerald E. "Scientific Paradigms and Economics: An Introduction." *Radical Review of Economics* 3, no. 2 (July 1971): 6–9.

Rosenberg, Randall. "The Neoliberal Club." *Esquire,* February 1982, pp. 37–46.

Rostow, Walter W. *The Stages of Economic Growth: A Non-Communist Manifesto.* New York: Cambridge University Press, 1960.

Samuelson, Paul. *Economics.* 9th ed. New York: McGraw Hill, 1973.

———. "Wages and Interests: A Modern Dissection of Marxian Economics." *American Economic Review* 47 (1957): 891–905.

Sargent, Lydia, ed. *Women and Revolution.* Boston: South End Press, 1981.

Shulman, Steven. "Competition and Racial Discrimination: The Employment Effects of Reagan's Labor Market Policies." *Review of Radical Political Economics* 16, no. 4 (Winter 1984): 120–31.

Sidel, Ruth. *Women and Children Last: The Plight of Poor Women in Affluent America.* New York: Penguin Books, 1986.

Smith, Adam. *An Inquiry into the Nature and Causes of the Wealth of Nations.* Edited by Edward Canaan. New York: Modern Library, 1937.

Spitz, Ruth. "Women and Labor: Unfinished Revolution." *Democratic Left* 14 (September–October 1986): 15–17.

Stavrianos, L. S. *Global Rift: The Third World Comes of Age.* New York: William Morrow, 1981.

Steindl, Josef. "Reflections on the Present State of Economics." *Montly Review* 36 (February 1985): 35–48.

Stigler, George. "The Politics of Political Economists." *Quarterly Journal of Economics* 73 (November 1959): 522–532.

Thomas, Eloise. "Myths and Facts of Women and Work." *Probe* 14 (January–February 1986): 7–10.

Thurow, Lester C. *Investment in Human Capital.* Belmont, Calif.: Wadsworth, 1970.

———. *Poverty and Discrimination.* Washington, D.C.: Brookings Institute, 1969.

———. "Who Stays Up with the Sick Cow?" Review of *The Capitalist Revolution* by Peter L. Berger. *New York Times Book Review*, September 7, 1986, p. 9.

———. *The Zero Sum Society.* New York: Basic Books, 1980.

Weisskopf, Thomas E. "The Current Economic Crisis in Historical Perspective." *Socialist Review* 11 (May–June 1981): 13–20.

Wilson, William Julius. *The Truly Disadvantaged.* Chicago: University of Chicago Press, 1987.

Wolff, Richard D., and Stephen A. Resnick. *Economics: Marxian versus Neoclassical.* Baltimore, Md.: Johns Hopkins University Press, 1987.

Sources in Religious Studies

Abbott, Walter M., S.J., ed. *The Documents of Vatican II.* New York: America Press, 1966.

Baum, Gregory. "A Canadian Perspective on the U.S. Pastoral." *Christianity and Crisis* 44, no. 22 (January 21, 1985): 516–17.

———. *Catholics and Canadian Socialism.* Toronto: Lorimer, 1980.

———. *The Priority of Labor: A Commentary on* Laborem Exercens. New York: Paulist Press, 1982.

———. *The Social Imperative.* New York: Paulist Press, 1979.

Baum, Gregory, and Duncan Cameron, eds. *Ethics and Economics: Canada's Catholic Bishops and the Economics Crisis.* Toronto: Lorimer, 1984.

Camp, Richard L. *The Papal Ideology of Social Reform.* Leiden: E. J. Brille, 1969.

Canadian Conference of Catholic Bishops. *Ethical Choices and Political Challenges.* Ottawa, Ontario: CCCB, 1983.

Cormie, Lee. "The U.S. Bishops on Capitalism." Working papers of the American Academy of Religion (1985).

Dorr, Donal. *Option for the Poor.: A Hundred Years of Vatican Social Teaching.* Maryknoll, N.Y.: Orbis, 1983.

Eagleson, John, and Philip Scharper, eds. *Puebla and Beyond.* Maryknoll, N.Y.: Orbis, 1979.

Ellison, Marvin M. *The Center Cannot Hold: The Search for a Global Economy of Justice.* Washington, D.C.: University Press of America, 1983.

Gremillion, Joseph, ed. *The Gospel of Peace and Justice.* Maryknoll, N.Y.: Orbis, 1976.

Gudorf, Christine E. *Catholic Social Teaching on Liberation Themes.* Washington, D.C.: University Press of America, 1981.

Harrison, Beverly W. "Response to David Hollenbach." Paper presented at the Symposium on Theology, Ethics and the Church, Episcopal Divinity School, Cambridge, Mass., May 5, 1986.

———. "The Role of Social Theory in Religious Social Ethics." In *Making the Connections: Essays in Feminist Social Ethics,* edited by Carol S. Robb. Boston: Beacon Press, 1985.

———. "Social Justice and Economic Orthodoxy." *Christianity and Crisis* 44, no. 22 (January 21, 1985): 513–15.

Hollenbach, David, S.J. *Claims in Conflict: Retrieving and Renewing the Catholic Human Rights Tradition.* New York: Paulist Press, 1979.

———. "Modern Catholic Teaching Concerning Justice." In *The Faith That Does Justice,* edited by John C. Haughey. New York: Paulist Press, 1977.

McGovern, Arthur F. *Marxism: An American Christian Perspective.* Maryknoll, N.Y.: Orbis, 1981.

Maier, Hans. *Revolution and the Church: The Early History of Christian*

Democracy. South Bend, Ind.: University of Notre Dame Press, 1969.

Metz, Johan Baptist, and Jean Pierre Jossua, eds. *Christianity and Socialism*. (Concilium) New York: Seabury Press, 1977.

Moody, Joseph N., ed. *Church and Society: Catholic Social and Political Thought and Movements 1789–1950*. New York: Polyglot Press, 1953.

Murray, John Courtney, S.J. "Leo XIII: Two Concepts of Government, II. Government and the Order of Culture." *Theological Studies* 15 (1954): 1–33.

National Conference of Catholic Bishops. *"Economic Justice for All: Catholic Social Teaching and the U.S. Economy."* Origins 16, no. 24 (November 27, 1986): 409–55.

O'Brien, David J., and Thomas A. Shannon, eds. *Renewing the Earth: Catholic Documents on Peace, Justice and Liberation*. New York: Image Books, 1977.

"On Social Concern." Origins 17, no. 38 (March 3, 1988).

Raines, John C., and Donna C. Day-Lower. *Modern Work and Human Meaning*. Philadelphia: Westminster Press, 1986.

Robb, Carol S. "A Framework for Feminist Ethics." In *Women's Consciousness, Women's Conscience*, edited by Barbara H. Andolsen, Christine E. Gudorf, and Mary D. Pellauer. New York: Winston Press, 1985.

Ruether, Rosemary Radford. "Home and Work: Women's Role and the Transformation of Values." *Theological Studies* 36 (December 1975): 647–59.

Seven Great Encyclicals. Glen Rock, N.J.: Paulist Press, 1963.

Tabb, William K., ed. *Churches in Struggle: Liberation Theologies and Social Change in North America*. New York: Monthly Review Press, 1986.

———. "Competitiveness and Workers." *Christianity and Crisis* 47, no. 15 (October 26, 1987): 364–66.

Torres, Sergio, and John Eagleson. *Theology in the Americas*. Maryknoll, N.Y.: Orbis, 1976.

Viner, Jacob. *Religious Thought and Economic Society*. Edited by Jacques Melitz and Donald Winch. Durham, N.C.: Duke University Press, 1978.

Wogaman, J. Philip. *The Great Economic Debate*. Philadelphia: Westminster Press, 1978.

Index